Managing Outside Pressure

Managing Outside Pressure

Strategies for Preventing Corporate Disasters

Matthias Winter
and
Ulrich Steger
International Institute for Management
Development, (IMD), Switzerland

JOHN WILEY & SONS
Chichester • New York • Weinheim • Brisbane • Singapore • Toronto

National   01243 779777
International   (+44) 1243 779777
e-mail (for orders and customer service enquiries):
cs-books@wiley.co.uk
Visit our Home Page on http://www.wiley.co.uk
or http://www.wiley.com

Other Wiley Editorial Offices

John Wiley & Sons, Inc., 605 Third Avenue,
New York, NY 10158-0012, USA

WILEY-VCH Verlag GmbH, Pappelallee 3,
D-69469 Weinheim, Germany

Jacaranda Wiley Ltd, 33 Park Road, Milton,
Queensland 4064, Australia

John Wiley & Sons (Canada) Ltd, 22 Worcester Road,
Rexdale, Ontario M9W 1L1, Canada

John Wiley & Sons (Asia) Pte Ltd, 2 Clementi Loop #02-01,
Jin Xing Distripark, Singapore 129809

British Library Cataloguing in Publication Data

A catalogue record for this book is available from the British Library

ISBN 0-471-97933-3

Typeset in 11/13pt Times by Dorwyn Ltd, Rowlands Castle, Hants
Printed and bound in Great Britain by Biddles Ltd, Guildford and King's Lynn
This book is printed on acid-free paper responsibly manufactured from sustainable forestry, in which at least two trees are planted for each one used.

Contents

Foreword

Managing Outside Pressure can best be described as a practical guide to issues identification and issues management.

On the basis of the analysis of a large number of examples the authors, Matthias Winter and Ulrich Steger, offer the reader a valuable insight into the techniques applied in issues identification such as checklist-based screening of issues and the use of computer-based early awareness systems.

Having sat through the Brent Spar case I can confirm how important it is to know the facts in order to keep the company out of trouble and yet. . . . I have come to the conclusion that a company should proactively work on its identity and reputation and apply "best practice" all the time. In doing so it should move away from incidents management to the building of relationships, from managing the most threatening outside pressures to establishing – in a proactive way – its corporate identity in an external multi-dimensional environment.

The value of *Managing Outside Pressure* is that not only is it a handbook on issues identification and issues management, but it provokes thoughts about the evolution into reputation management.

C.A.J. Herkströter
Chairman of the Committee of Managing Directors of the Royal Dutch/Shell Group of Companies

Introduction

We were fortunate, in performing our research, to have the opportunity to discuss the issues with many thoughtful colleagues in the business, academic and activist communities. Those exchanges often concerned not only the specifics of our methodology, but the "contextual environment" of the proposed book itself. How would its conclusions be viewed, and used? What unexpected interpretation might be put on our findings themselves? In that context, the executives, journalists, scholars and students who reviewed the drafts of this book tended to express one of two concerns. Some thought our book would help activist groups target companies' Achilles' heels more precisely, and thus campaign more successfully against them. Others worried that, conversely, our purpose was to help corporations get away with their "sins" through more skillful public relations. Neither, of course, was our goal. The purpose of our book is to help managers in pluralistic societies, where different values, interests, perceptions and risk assessments inevitably lead to conflict, to handle those conflicts more professionally.

We suggest that handling these types of conflicts more professionally involves expanding the decision-making process, evaluating and prioritising issues and identifying action plans for dealing with them. This need not be done in a combative or confrontational way; in many cases, cooperative, win–win solutions satisfactory to both the company and activists can be found. We hope, in fact, that the book will encourage companies to behave responsibly, as part of a global community making decisions about the future, and that it will also encourage activists to move away from single-issue, fight-to-win campaigns toward the strategies that will bring the greatest benefit to society as a whole.

We have to thank a number of people who helped us in writing this book in a relatively short time. Among our colleagues at IMD we wish to mention especially Karen Lindquist for her valuable advice and support. Other people who are merit acknowledgment are Christiane Schelling, Carol Michel, Els van Weering, Gordon Adler, John Evans and Peter Killing. Our special thanks goes also to the MBA class of 1997 who contributed empirical material for the case studies.

In our general research on outside pressure issues, we are grateful to a large number of companies and pressure groups who agreed to talk to us throughout our research, and from whom we learned a great deal about these issues. We wish to mention especially Cor Herkströter, the CEO of the Shell Royal Dutch Company, Peter Duncan, CEO of Shell Germany, Thilo Bode, Executive Director of Greenpeace, and Jorge Wernli from Novartis.

1

Caught by Surprise

There can't be a crisis next week. My schedule is already full.
Henry Kissinger

On 21 June 1995 the Royal Dutch Shell Group, one of the largest and most profitable companies in the world, was forced to give up its attempt to sink the abandoned oil storage platform, Brent Spar, in the North Sea. Shell's management was caught by surprise by the impact that an activist group – Greenpeace, in this case – could have on years of careful planning and on the company's reputation. Obviously, the company's handling of the platform issue was seriously flawed in several areas, such as technically-driven crisis management, but for many observers the most important question was: Could Shell have anticipated – and avoided – the Brent Spar crisis? On the basis of our empirical research, we believe that the answer is a clear *yes*.

Despite our assumption in this book – that effective analysis and predicting of controversial issues can prevent a crisis from developing – the fact remains that their impact still comes as a complete surprise to many companies.

One of the reasons companies are so often surprised by controversy is that their existing decision-making processes, including the processes by which they evaluate the ethical (or environmental, or legal) dimensions of their activities, are primarily based on "rational", scientific or technical criteria. Companies that find themselves looking down the barrel of an "issue" pointed at them by an activist group may therefore have forgotten not only that there are usually several different ways of looking at an issue, but that the real danger can lie in the power of strong opinion and emotion.

In addition, if companies were confronted with only a few simple, predictable issues, then dealing with them might be straightforward. Steering clear of obstacles is easy when there are only a few and you know where they are. Instead, the number of demands on companies seems to be increasing rapidly, and they pop up suddenly from the least obvious sources.

Why do managers have so much trouble foreseeing the emergence of these issues? First, the sheer variety is overwhelming. Consider just some of the types of companies in the news at the time of this writing: airlines (for transporting monkeys); credit card companies (for Third World debt); Faroese fish (whaling); mahogany (indigenous peoples); McDonald's (fast food culture); Mitsubishi (deforestation and racial discrimination); Norway (whaling); poultry meat (animal testing); Texaco and Total (indigenous peoples, Burma, etc.); Avis (racial discrimination); Disney (gay-friendly policies); film companies (Tom Cruise's membership in the Church of Scientology; and Madonna's controversial picture of the former Argentinean First Lady Evita Peron). Numerous drug companies are targeted, as are Holiday Inns, Marks & Spencer, Sainsbury and Tesco (employment issues). Procter & Gamble and Gillette (animal testing) and Barbados (more monkeys) are all losing business. The Royal Dutch Shell Company alone has been under attack recently for: oil spills; platform disposal; operations in Nigeria; sales of pornographic literature in its service stations; selling chemicals that cause sterility in men to Third World countries; water pollution in Turkey; membership in the lobby organisations Global Climate Coalition, and more.

Secondly, as companies become more global, the international dimension makes the issues themselves more complicated. Products that are appropriate and acceptable in one social environment may be inappropriate in another. For example, in the Western world, infant formula is a safe and convenient product that can help to make life easier for a large number of women and children. The Swiss food giant Nestlé produced and sold infant formula from 1867 with the clearest possible conscience, until, in 1973, a group of doctors reported negative effects of formula use in Third World countries – that usage of infant formula in these environments was dangerous for babies because of the lack of pure water, refrigeration or sufficient income to purchase enough formula to satisfy daily nutritional needs. Very soon, a Third World organisation called War on Want published a pamphlet titled *The Baby Killer*. In the following years Nestlé was accused of: improper behaviour to the detriment of the health of babies by showing advertisements with white mothers using infant formula that conveyed the message that it was a product for "modern" women; giving away free samples of the product to new mothers in the hospital, which caused the mothers' milk to dry up, forcing them to use infant formula once they left hospital; and continuing these practices despite knowing that many mothers could not continue using the formula properly once leaving the hospital (Kund, Gale and Taucher, 1979).

Another corporation that ran into local problems in its broad international operations was W.R. Grace and Company. Indian farmers have used the seed of the neem tree as a pesticide for centuries, and studies showed it to be an ecologically sound solution. But when Grace decided to produce this pesticide on a commercial basis, some organisations in India protested vehemently that the neem tree is considered sacred by Hindus. Grace was criticised for failing to respect religious beliefs.

Another aspect of this international dimension is that the rapid social transition in some regions like Africa, Eastern Europe and South East Asia, and resulting lack of a clear rule of law, has involved multinationals in behaviours like paying bribes and collaborating with organised crime, practices for which they may be strongly criticised or even prosecuted in their home countries.

Thirdly, companies face the added complexity that the fulfilment of one group's demands may very often be at the expense of those of other groups, so that managers constantly have to balance various conflicting interests. Companies often see a contradiction between the interests of environmentalists aiming at higher environmental standards, and unions demanding that more jobs be provided in a certain country.

Finally, the situation becomes even more confusing when corporations are asked to take sides, to stand up for various principles, on issues in which they may not even be directly involved. As sixties radicals used to say, "If you're not part of the solution, you're part of the problem." In other words, in addition to being taken to task for violating various principles, businesses are sometimes coming under fire for not taking stands on issues deemed important by the public. For example, in the United States, AT&T and IBM were asked to take sides on the abortion issue (regarding donations to Planned Parenthood).[1] Their silence on these issues is viewed as complicity: "*Silence = Death*" is a popular slogan with many AIDS organisations.

In light of all these factors, it is not surprising that companies often fail to spot potential trouble spots.

HISTORICAL DEVELOPMENT

Given the number and complexity of issues today, it is no wonder companies can be caught off guard. But why is this pressure on companies apparently growing now?

Formerly, it was up to the government to set rules for business behaviour and the sole concern of companies was to create wealth without breaking the law:

> In a free society, there is one and only one social responsibility of business – to use its resources and engage in activities designed to increase its profits so long as it stays within the rules of the game, which is to say, engages in open and free competition without deception or fraud (Nobel Laureate economist Friedman, 1962).

This recipe has helped to make corporations the dominating institution in society – transnationals may enjoy turnovers many times higher than national governments' budgets. The largest 500 companies now control 42% of the world's wealth; only 27 countries in the world have a turnover greater than the sales of Shell and Exxon combined.

Although multinationals are perceived as powerful and exciting symbols for progress, a large segment of the public also believes that while companies were busy transforming themselves into the giants they are today and creating wealth (especially for their managers and shareholders), they were also creating many of society's problems. Since governments seem to be less able to cope with these problems, the public therefore sees large corporations increasingly having the power and the responsibility for the solutions. Consequently, they have found ways to put pressure on the companies in order to bring about changes in behaviour.

Increasingly, activist groups – environmental organisations such as Greenpeace, consumer groups such as Public Citizen or social organisations like War on Want – are taking on some of the roles previously filled by unions, politicians and governments. They are becoming a *countervailing power*, a check that activates itself whenever one of society's institutions grows too powerful, against the rising importance of corporations (Galbraith, 1952).

One reason why activist groups are now the countervailing power is that the public has lost confidence in traditional authorities such as political parties. Governments and their influence on corporations are definitely in decline. Other institutions, such as unions, are losing members dramatically, as workers see less reason for them.[2] Another probable factor is the globalisation trend. While governments normally only have jurisdiction over companies within their national borders, companies now operate all over the globe and can easily be seen as getting around local laws. International activist organisations have the advantage that they can affect companies on all fronts. They are the new players in the global village (connected by the global medium Internet) whose mission is to protect present and future generations from the corporate machine.

Of course, activist groups cannot replace governments – they are an additional influence to persuade companies of society's interests. Unlike governments, these groups have no legal authority. They are for the most part applying pressure on issues where the company is not breaking any existing laws, but where the group (and often the general public) feels the company should alter its practices.

From the manager's perspective, this can be a frightening picture. For a number of reasons, companies face an increasingly high risk of suffering severe financial damage by an unprecedented number of activist demands, often triggered through powerful international organisations running sophisticated campaigns. What does all this imply for companies?

PATTERNS OF ACTIVIST ISSUES

To avoid being caught up in a crisis or finding themselves giving in to every demand, managers should learn how to predict potential problems. They must determine effectively to what extent companies can adjust to appropriate activist demands, or resist those that the company considers unjustified. A system of evaluation is necessary to deal with the increased number and power of activist organisations. Is such a system possible?

Controversial issues come in many shapes and sizes, and no two are alike. At first glance it may be tempting to consider these developments as random and irrational attacks, and therefore unpredictable. In our research we challenged the "random" assumption and tried to identify patterns in typical crises. We analysed a great number of issues in depth and tried to understand their impact on companies.

Our analysis included interviews with executives from concerned companies and with managers from organisations such as Friends of the Earth and Greenpeace, and unions. Another source for our research was a survey and interviews among 200 senior managers who participated in courses at IMD, the International Institute for Management Development, one of the world's leading business schools in Lausanne, Switzerland. Additionally, we reviewed more than 100 cases from all parts of the world, the most interesting of which will be referred to throughout the book.

Although we could find no patterns that predict the kind of pressures companies might be confronted with, we did find clear correlations in characteristics of issues that did come up and which of them would be strong enough to challenge the survival of a company. Knowing what those correlations are can be a powerful aid in analysing problems and working out solutions where needed. With the help of our proposed "toolkit", managers can analyse the characteristics of an upcoming issue and create a consistent interpretation. The tools provide a basis for analysis of activist issues to spot the most important ones and analyse their possible consequences to the firm.

The general question of how to avoid these types of crises can be split into several subtopics that will be examined throughout the book:

- *Where does the pressure come from, and how can it damage companies?* In Chapter 2 we introduce the stakeholder concept and explain how stakeholders can influence companies.

- *How do these relatively small groups get to the jugular vein of powerful corporations?* Chapter 2 goes on to show the difference between a company's transactional and contextual environments and explains the application of pressure on companies through transmission belts.
- *What models are helpful in evaluating issues?* We have come up with a new model for analysis, introduced in Chapter 3.
- *Which activist demands need to be dealt with strategically and which can be resisted?* Chapters 4 and 5 introduce two systematic checklists as a practical tool for managers to replace guesswork.
- *What systems can act as early warning systems?* We present in Chapter 6 some suggestions and examples as to how best-practice companies implemented computerised strategic awareness systems to trace and evaluate potential controversies.
- *How do we know this checklist model works?* The best proof is in specific examples. Chapter 7 is made up entirely of applied case studies that we have analysed according to our checklists.
- *What can managers do when faced with a potential crisis?* The final chapter examines some possible strategies for responding to activist demands.

The concepts outlined in this book are ground-breaking, because to date no such practical application for activist demands on companies exists. We have combined elements of existing management theory, especially stakeholder theory, issue management and public relations (PR), to form a totally new concept to provide managers with hands-on recommendations that can help them to avoid steering a company head-on into a crisis. The reader who is well-versed in stakeholder theory will notice that we have taken the transactional/contextual environment idea and left behind other aspects of the theory. In issue management theory, we look only at issue recognition and not at related tasks such as litigation, negotiating, mediation, arbitration, etc. From PR theory, we have taken some findings to support our arguments on public and media perception of issues. So, here the manager has, for the first time, an effective tool to detect, appraise and deal strategically with emerging activist concerns.

Notes

1. The abortion issue also shows country-specific differences in outside press-
    ure. While in the United States some Americans believe abortion is ethically
    permissible, others believe it is wrong. On the other hand, in countries like
    the former Soviet Union, abortion was the most common form of artificial
    birth control (De George, 1990), and in China the government even tries to
    force pregnant women who already have one child to get an abortion.
2. The percentage of all employees who are members of a union fell in the
    United Kingdom from more than 50% in 1980 to 30% in 1996, in Germany
    from 38% to 30%, in the United States from 25% to 18% and in France
    from 20% to less than 5%.

2
Activist Groups and the Stakeholder Concept

THE STAKEHOLDER CONCEPT

Where do the issues and demands described in the first chapter come from? Who are the groups who are able to force the management of a profitable company to change its way of doing business? How could Greenpeace succeed in stopping Shell from disposing of the Brent Spar platform at sea?

Consumer groups, customers and competitors, employees, environmental organisations, local communities, suppliers, special interest groups, owners, the media, judiciary and lawmakers, the public and public authorities, as well as scientists and researchers, all make demands on corporate management. These groups are often referred to as *stakeholders* since they each have a "stake" in the success and actions of the company. A list of typical stakeholders of a company might be seen as in Figure 2.1.[1]

The kinds of demands stakeholders may make vary from group to group, but they have one common characteristic: stakeholders can affect significantly and are affected significantly by an organisation's activities, whether it is in a positive or negative way (Freeman, 1984). Unfortunately, different stakeholder demands pull companies in different directions, making the manager's job even more difficult, as in the obvious example of employees wanting higher wages and customers wanting lowest-cost products. These conflicts, though, because such stakeholders can understand each

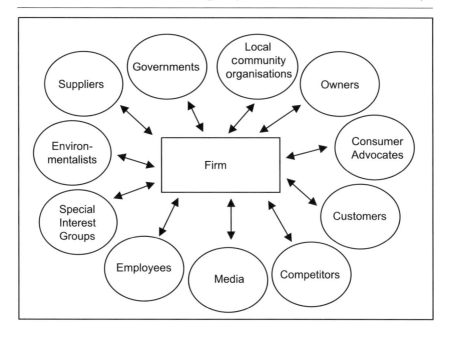

Figure 2.1 Stakeholders of an enterprise. *Source*: Freeman (1984, p. 25)

others' positions, often end in compromises acceptable to all sides, allowing managers to "muddle through" in their approach to these demands (Lindblom, 1959). Additionally, groups may not make their demands simultaneously, in which case managers can give selective attention to the problems. These circumstances create a tolerance zone, or flux, in which managers can manoeuvre.

Of the different stakeholder groups, managers usually assign shareholders and their needs the highest priority. This is the natural result of the fact that in most countries it is legally stipulated that management is appointed by the shareholders to meet their expectations for earnings and growth. Shareholders themselves, too, have become more demanding and aware of their power. As a result, managers are finding themselves squeezed between their shareholders (transition from a "managerial" capitalism to an "investor" capitalism) and the other stakeholder groups.[2]

However, in order to create greater value for shareholders, managers must satisfy other stakeholder relations, at least to a certain degree. These demands may also be experienced differently in different societies. Shareholder influence is stronger in the United States than in many European countries or Asia. Managers in non-US companies tend to place greater weight on societal values, especially labour practices, in part because of the different legal composition of ownership and control of the company. For example, under Germany's co-determination law, employees have specific rights to share in decision-making and elect half of the supervisory board representatives directly.[3] At Volkswagen AG, union members and politicians, which represent the shareholdings of the state of Lower Saxony, have 11 of the 20 seats in the company supervisory board. In Japan, where versions of lifetime employment policies still exist and customers and suppliers are bound together in groups of firms with significant cross-shareholdings (*keiretsu*), managers face even greater constraints.

These different practices represent, to an extent, differences in the values of the respective societies. In the United States, managers work with the "American dream" in mind, having been taught that any individual has a chance to become rich if he or she works hard enough; Europeans tend to put greater emphasis on social security, and tend to be comfortable aspiring to a more moderate standard of living in order for benefits to be spread among all members of society.

Whether a company considers itself to be managed in the European or American style, satisfying major stakeholder demands is crucially important in producing shareholder value.[4]

TRANSACTIONAL VERSUS CONTEXTUAL ENVIRONMENT

To answer the question of where stakeholder power comes from, we split the different stakeholder groups into two categories: groups that belong to the *transactional environment* and groups that belong to the *contextual environment* (Emery and Trist, 1965).

Groups like customers, banks or suppliers, who influence companies through their direct business relations, are part of what is aptly named the *transactional environment*. They can negotiate with the managers of the company about the rules for their transactions, and those rules operate within a formal framework of contracts.

Table 2.1 Possible demands of stakeholder groups and their sources of power

Transactional environment			Contextual environment		
Group	Possible demands	Possible pressure tactics	Group	Possible demands	Possible pressure tactics
				Non-outside-pressure groups	
Customers	Product quality, service value	• Purchasing decisions	Governments	Taxes, employment, environmental protection	• Legislation • Legal fines
Employees	Security, compensation, job satisfaction	• Departure from company • Negative publicity • Reduced performance	Media	Fair information	• Bad publicity
Suppliers	Regular payments, continuity of business	• Refusals to meet orders • Supplying to competitors		Outside pressure groups	
Shareholders	Dividends, capital growth, safe investment	• Voting and inspection rights • Buying and selling	Social activist groups	Employment, no discrimination, social justice	• Publicising issues • Lobbying governments • Influencing consumers
Creditors	Interest, security of capital	• Refusing loans and calling in loans	Environmental activist groups	Preservation of the environment	• Publicising issues • Lobbying governments • Influencing consumers
Insurances	Safe operations, safe products	• Refusing insurance coverage and cancelling contracts	Consumer organisations	Product quality, environmental protection	• Publicising issues • Lobbying governments • Influencing consumers

Groups belonging to the *contextual environment* have no direct market or business relations with the company and use other means to influence company decisions: media, environmentalists, consumer advocates, the government and others. They behave as "referees" of a sort, because they "check" the organisation's activities to make sure it is playing by the rules of the game. Some of these groups create pressure simply as a by-product of their normal functioning, like the media or governments. But other groups in the contextual environment have social, environmental or health-related agendas and exist primarily to create pressure on institutions (companies and governments) to change the way they behave, thus becoming "advocates" for certain interests. In the previous chapter and from now on, we refer to these groups as *activist groups*.

Table 2.1 summarises typical demands arising from both the transactional and contextual environment and shows possible means of influencing companies. It is obvious that groups in the transactional environment, like customers and suppliers, can find ways to "translate" their concerns into business implications ("to buy or not to buy", "to supply or not to supply").[5] Therefore, many managers find it easier to focus on the transactional environment, more or less ignoring or dealing on an *ad hoc* basis with the contextual environment; a dangerous omission. Issues originating from activist groups may lead to important repercussions in the transactional environment.

TYPES OF ACTIVIST ISSUES

Activist demands are almost impossible to categorise, but we can class them loosely into three general types: environmentally motivated, health-related and socially motivated activist issues.[6] What are the differing characteristics?

Environmental issues arise when businesses generate environmentally harmful waste and pollution as well as the goods and services demanded by society. The problems caused by industrial pollution were brought to public awareness during the 1960s in the industrially advanced societies with ground-breaking books such as *Silent Spring* (Carson, 1962) and *Limits of Growth* (Meadows et al, 1972). They came to the forefront in the mid-1970s and reached their peak in the late 1980s after accidents like Chernobyl, the *Exxon Valdez* and Union Carbide (Bhopal). Although companies alone cannot eliminate pollution and waste production, the public is demanding that they at least maintain a certain environmental standard and clean up the pollution they have caused, rather than leaving the burden on society as a whole. Today, the world-wide membership in environmental groups such as the Sierra Club, the National Resources Defense Council (NRDC), the Environmental Defense Fund (EDF), Greenpeace and Friends of the Earth has grown to more than 16 million members and they are gaining more and more credibility with the public.

Health issues normally arise when the consumption of certain products carries a risk of negative side-effects for personal health, or when public and workplace safety are perceived to be threatened. In a typical scenario, scientists discover negative side-effects in a seemingly harmless product, and then report those effects in scientific journals or in the media. In some cases, the publicising of scientists' findings of dangers to human health in itself is enough to bring about a change even before activist groups get involved, especially where public confidence in the credibility of scientists is very high. But in most cases, consumer groups or environmental organisations are needed to push the issues further. Their main interests are to have clear and readily available information on the potential dangers of a product, and safer alternatives.

From a historical perspective, health topics have been of particular concern for the last 30 years, as people have become more aware of factors influencing their own health. One of the first targeted products was cigarettes; in 1962 US President J.F. Kennedy decided to appoint a blue-ribbon group to examine the effects of smoking on health.[7]

Social issues cover an even broader range of situations. Companies may be perceived as increasing their wealth at the expense of society – e.g. lowering their costs through improved productivity and dismissing workers, while taxpayers shoulder the burden of higher social costs. Other social issues include bribery, exploiting workers in or from Third World countries, supporting dictator regimes, promoting animal testing or abortion. Social issues, especially those involving labour standards, are often driven by unions (employment issues)[8]; other social interest groups such as Amnesty International or church organisations may also take up these concerns.

(To paraphrase the Biblical saying about the poor, activists "ye always have with you". When the Hebrew slaves wished to leave Egypt, the activists, represented by Moses and his brother Aaron, demanded freedom. Unfortunately, Pharaoh underestimated the power of the activist group and its powerful ally (God) and therefore did not take Moses' demand seriously. The Hebrew group's incremental pressures on its adversary included turning all the water resources into blood; sending plagues of frogs, lice and flies; killing all the cattle; infecting with a skin disease; sending plagues of hail, locusts and darkness; and finally killing the firstborn of each Egyptian family, including Pharaoh's own son. Egypt, as we know, was forced to capitulate to the Hebrews' demands.)

Labour-related concerns became prominent in the middle of the nineteenth century in response to the growing power of capital following the industrial revolution. Labour unions appeared and discovered strikes, boycotts and other means of achieving their objectives.[9] In the following years, workers' causes advanced continuously in the industrialised countries. However, with the current dynamics of global competition, the balance of power is shifting to employers again, which is in turn generating a renaissance of worker activism such as in the numerous protests in European countries.

TRANSMISSION BELTS

How can groups in the contextual environment, who have no direct business relations with a company, make it change its behaviour? They can use two different strategies.

The first is direct pressure; for example, by protesting in front of the company's gates. However, to quote a senior manager of a large chemical company: "Protesters alone don't make an impact on companies – they will protest for a few days, come and go, and then it's business as usual."

Activist groups have therefore devised a second strategy, which can be far more threatening: galvanise action by seeking allies among the members of the transactional environment which, as we have just seen, may have severe financial implications for the companies concerned. Using banks, suppliers, customers, employees, insurers, etc. as influencers, they apply *transmission belts* of indirect pressure. The impact of this strategy on a company's financial bottom line can be tremendous.

One of the best known such cases in recent years was the Brent Spar incident, to which we referred at the beginning of the book.

SUMMARY OF THE BRENT SPAR INCIDENT

The Brent Spar oil platform was used by Shell Expro (a consortium of Shell and Exxon) as a storage facility in the Brent oil field in the North Sea. Built in the mid-1970s, the Brent Spar had been operational between 1976 and 1991 but became obsolete when Shell Expro constructed a pipeline. Planning its disposal was problematic because of its six storage tanks and complex structure. In the following years, Shell undertook some 30 studies on possible disposal options. The studies concluded that Brent Spar should not be disposed of on land but rather sunk in the North Atlantic where it could not enter the food chain or cause other environmental harm. This option would also be the most cost-effective for the company. Despite the rather confusing legal situation, Shell applied for permission from the UK government in September 1992.[10] In February 1995 the British energy minister, Tim Eggar, announced the British government's intention to approve Shell's plan to sink the platform and informed his European counterparts accordingly. That same day, Shell issued a press release announcing its decision. The announcement went virtually unnoticed by the general public. No country objected to the plan.

But the announcement did not escape the notice of Greenpeace. On 30 April 1995 Greenpeace activists surprised Shell by approaching the empty platform at night by boat, using ropes to climb aboard the huge structure, and occupying it. Greenpeace offices began a huge PR campaign to block the sinking of Brent Spar, sounding warnings that it might serve as a precedent for the large number of North Sea platforms to be decommissioned in the coming years.

The environmentalists sitting on the platform were largely ignored by the media for a few weeks until Shell UK and the British police removed them forcibly from the platform. That was the beginning of high entertainment for the media. With modern communication support, Greenpeace provided reporters – especially in the environmentally-sensitive Northern European audience – with filmed footage of the removal, and of the Brent Spar subsequently being towed to its disposal site in the Atlantic. Meanwhile, Greenpeace activists organised protests on land across Europe. They indirectly incited the public to boycott Shell service stations, to guarantee both high local visibility and a wide impact on Shell.

Back at sea, Greenpeace protesters were following the platform and made several attempts to recapture it, which Shell UK repelled with water cannons. Greenpeace was filming every step and the dramatic footage was getting extensive media coverage through its PR office. These pictures of protests and battles for control of the Brent Spar had a tremendous impact on the public, and as the platform reached the Atlantic, more and more people in Germany, the Netherlands and Denmark joined in boycotting Shell service stations.

Antagonism toward Shell finally became so strong that gunmen fired at a service station in Germany and another service station was damaged by fire-bombing. This led even the highest-level European politicians like the German chancellor Helmut Kohl to urge their British counterparts and Shell UK to cancel the sea disposal. One day before reaching the disposal site, the Royal Dutch Shell group gave up and ordered that the platform not be dumped. This was such a sensation that the issue became the headline of virtually every major news journal. Shell was forced to recognise that even with many technical and legal arguments on its side, it could not withstand such widespread public pressure against the company. (*Source*: Steger et al, 1996.)

We can see from Shell's experience that there are other groups from which activists can draw support to maximise a company's discomfort. Typically, there are two dominant transmission belts that activist groups consider to be their most effective allies: customers and legislators (see Figure 2.2).

INDIRECT PRESSURE THROUGH CUSTOMERS: BOYCOTTS

In the past, customers as a group used to be largely unaware of their ability to influence companies, and chose products based on

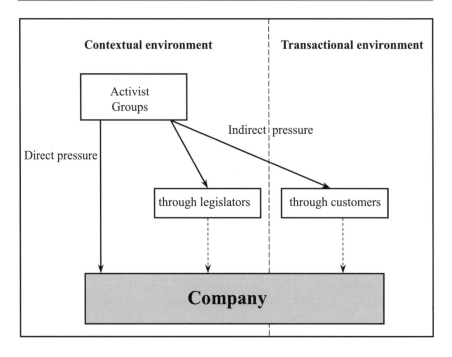

Figure 2.2   Direct and indirect outside pressure

lowest price or highest quality; today's consumers, on the other hand, are becoming increasingly aware of their power and use it for purposes beyond traditional market goals.

One tool for activists to pressure companies is to motivate customers to participate in a boycott. A "boycott" can be defined as the situation in which customers refuse to buy certain products from a particular person or business in order to obtain concessions or to express displeasure (Garrett, 1987). Consumers see boycotts as a way to hold businesses accountable for their activity or inactivity (especially if this implies little sacrifice on their part). They see boycotting as an organised and effective means of communicating complaints to a company, even if some people argue that they are a form of blackmail. Over the years, boycotts have become more and more common and have taken on more varied forms. The ways in which boycotts are used can be sorted into the categories "bargaining chip" and "end in itself" (Gelb, 1995). While in the *bargaining chip* mode, customer pressure is usually advocated or initiated to change the balance of power between certain interest groups and a company; other customer protest campaigns may be organised as *ends in themselves.*

In a *bargaining chip* boycott customers decide not to buy a certain product in order to support a social institution or to increase the bargaining power of this institution. One example is the boycott of California grapes and lettuce from 1965 to 1970, which achieved unionisation for California farm workers when all previous efforts had failed. The boycott against the growers was organised on a large scale with committees operating all over the United States. The growers capitulated when, in some markets, sales went down by as much as one-third.

Many leaders of activist groups have recognised the effective impact they can make on companies through bargaining chip boycotts. Jesse Jackson, a former US presidential hopeful and now president of the National Rainbow/PUSH Coalition, which organises boycotts to try to force companies to reduce a "multibillion-dollar" trade deficit between minority groups who are targeted by companies for consumption and the same companies who discriminate against these minority groups in the workplace, stated it plainly:

> We have the power, non violently, just by controlling our appetites, to determine the direction of the American economy. If black people in thirty cities said simultaneously, "General Motors, you will not sell cars in the black community unless you guarantee us a franchise here next year and help us finance it", GM would have no choice but to comply (Vogel, 1978, p. 9).

If, on the other hand, consumers boycott simply to punish a company or to reduce consumption of a certain product, then their goal is not to increase the bargaining power of a social institution but to show a company that they do not appreciate its way of doing business. In this case it is an *end in itself.* One historical case of such a "boycott" was the Boston Tea Party in 1773, a protest by American patriots against King George of England's plans to introduce a tax on tea exported to the American colonies. The patriots declared they would never pay taxes on British tea, and to emphasise this they disguised themselves as Indians (Native Americans), boarded British ships docked in the Boston Harbour, and dumped all the imported tea overboard. This symbolic act was one of the major events leading to the

American Revolution. In more recent history, the case of the *Exxon Valdez* accident in 1989 produced a boycott of Exxon products in the United States and persuaded 18 000 people to return their Exxon credit cards.

Once consumers became aware of their ability to vote with their dollars, they started to organise boycotts to protest against past accidents and incidents (for example, a boycott against Union Carbide products because of their failure to prevent the Bhopal disaster), as well as to prevent future incidents. For example, in Germany in 1996, Bristol-Myers Squibb Co. (BMS) faced a heavy union protest when it wanted to lay off 560 people from its plant near Munich. While BMS would have easily won the fight against the unions, it reconsidered its decision when the union convinced pharmacies to threaten a boycott of all BMS products.

The effects of such crises can be measured: studies show that calls for boycotts through activist groups triggered significant decreases in the stock prices of the targeted companies over a 60-day period after the boycott was announced (Pruitt and Friedman, 1986). Companies' fear of potential consumer action is also illustrated by a survey of the Control Risk Group among 51 Global European Companies in 1996, which showed that some 20% of the companies surveyed had been deterred from otherwise attractive investment opportunities because of human rights issues; 16% by fears of controversy over corruption; 8% by possible pressure over environmental concerns; and 6% by possible controversy over labour issues (Boulton, 1997).

INDIRECT PRESSURE THROUGH LEGISLATORS

The second transmission belt is through national legislatures, which define the rules under which companies may act: emission thresholds, disclosure rules and social benefit levels, for example. Such regulations can be directly or indirectly imposed on companies. Some are specific to a certain industry, such as airline safety, while others, such as those dealing with discrimination, apply across all industries. Because of these powers, activists often try to influence legislative decisions through lobbying.

If we include the judicial branch as part of the legislature, then the total power of the legislator is even greater, because courts can levy heavy fines against companies that have neglected environmental, health or social concerns. In one year alone during the 1990s, around 1500 product-liability suits are brought against the *Fortune 500* companies in the United States. It is estimated that US companies spend US$300 billion annually on litigation involving environmental claims, product-liability suits, class-action securities suits, medical malpractice suits and Americans with disabilities cases (Grube, 1995). Activists (and, increasingly, companies!) have learned that litigation is a very effective tactic for inflicting financial damage on their adversaries.

Other possibilities for creating indirect pressure – for example, by activating stockholders, who use their voting rights to move company policy toward greater social responsibility – are not yet widely practised, so we will keep our discussion focused on the two main transmission belts.[11]

CONSUMER VERSUS LEGISLATOR TRANSMISSION BELT

The customer transmission belt can be dangerously unpredictable: issues have a much greater chance of "exploding" than through the legislator transmission belt. Why is this?

First, consumers can normally be mobilised more quickly than legislation can be passed and are showing increasing readiness to participate in boycotts. Since successful boycotts have an immediate negative effect on a company's cash flow, and research emphasises the financial disadvantages of losing loyal and therefore profitable customers, it is easy to understand why companies try to avoid this (Reichheld, 1996).

On the other hand, legislators take longer to come to decisions that affect companies. Governments represent highly pluralistic societies and must consider the issues of many interest groups. Contrary to consumers, legislators must agree on agendas, negotiate compromises, etc. before they can act. Also, while officially companies have no direct role in policy decisions, industrial lobbying and other techniques can influence the process indirectly, behind the scenes. And even during the policy implementation stage, individual companies may still influence legislators, e.g. through negotiating on extending deadlines to comply with certain legislation.

Secondly, while in most democratic countries legislative bodies are required to treat all businesses equally, consumers can discriminate without justification and choose freely from which companies to buy their products. The popular trend researcher Faith Popcorn, in her 1996 report, uncovered two trends which she calls "save our society" and "vigilance consumer", describing customers who care more and more about what they buy and express their opinions readily, including on a company's social record.

So, even if customers are unwilling to change their life style (e.g. reduce their car usage in general), they are still able, through the competitor effect, to punish certain companies whose practices are poorly rated, and to do business with preferred suppliers whose ratings show more social or environmental awareness and responsibility. In the Brent Spar case, this right to choose even led to a paradoxical situation: Exxon, which owned 50% of the platform, was actually profiting from the boycott against Shell, because during that time more and more Germans chose to fill up their cars at Exxon stations ("Esso" in German) in order to punish Shell. Meanwhile Agip, an Italian petrol chain, which had a yellow logo similar to Shell's, was losing business. Apparently, customers in Germany confused the two brands, bypassing the Agip stations in their enthusiasm to protest against Shell. In a letter to the *Wall Street Journal* a reader mentioned cynically: "It is apparently easy to drive a Porsche, boycott Shell Stations but fill the car up at the next Aral station and race along the autobahn at maximum speed – all with a good ecological conscience."

Finally, activist issues pushed through the customer transmission belt are more difficult to deflect with scientific arguments. General opinion in society tends to be based on attitudes rather than scientific fact – and working against emotions is an uphill battle for PR departments. The public is usually unable or even unwilling to examine in detail all the available facts of an issue. They tend to react to images, not complexity. Politicians, on the other hand, rely on professional bureaucrats, consultants and scientists to make their decisions. In this environment, scientific arguments have a fair chance of being heard and problems are usually not treated in single-issue form. This makes outcomes much more difficult to predict through the customer transmission belt than through the legislative transmission belt.

Given this range of possible results, what basic early awareness models can companies use to identify a problem in time to keep it from reaching the consumer or government transmission belts?

Notes

1. The stakeholder groups can, of course, be split even further. For example, in the United States, with reference to environmental activist issues, the government could be subdivided into the Environmental Protection Agency (EPA), the Occupational Safety and Health Administration (OSHA), the Federal Trade Commission (FTC), the Congress, the President, etc.
2. The strong shareholder movement of demanding higher returns from their investment gained momentum with the publication of Rappaport's book on shareholder value (Rappaport, 1986).
3. In addition, the workers' council has direct influence on decisions in personnel and social matters. In the case of laying off workers, companies have to develop "social plans" and they must consult the worker's council.
4. From a theoretical point of view the concept of stakeholder management is more inclusive than competing concepts such as public relations, issue management, or employee relations (Savage et al, 1991).
5. These "yes–no" decisions have, in the last years, developed into more elaborate cooperations with groups in the transactional environment. External stakeholders are increasingly becoming included in product design, quality training and other business processes (Harrison and St. John, 1996).
6. Another interesting attempt to sort and categorise activist issues was done by the Institute for Crisis Management (ICM) in Louisville, Kentucky, which then ended up with no less than 16 different crisis categories: industrial accidents/natural disasters; casualty accidents; environmental damage; class action lawsuits; consumerism; defects and recalls; discrimination; executive dismissal; hostile take-over; labour disputes; mismanagement; financial damages; sexual harassment; whistle-blowing; white collar crime; and workplace violence.
7. The real "consumer movement", which covers many health aspects as well, took off in the 1960s when the US President John F. Kennedy passed the consumer bill of rights, which entitles consumers to four different kinds of protection: *the right to safety* – to be protected against the marketing of goods which are hazardous to health or life; *the right to be informed* – to be protected against fraudulent, deceitful or grossly misleading information, advertising, labelling, or other practices, and to be given the facts to make an informed choice; *the right to choose* – to be assured, wherever possible, access to a variety of products and services at competitive prices, and in those industries in which competition is not workable and government regulation is substituted, to be assured satisfactory quality and service at fair prices; and *the right to be heard* – to be assured that consumer interests will receive full and sympathetic consideration in the formulation of government policy, and fair expeditious treatment in its administrative tribunals.
8. In some countries like the United States or Japan there are individual unions organised for each company, and therefore in those countries unions cannot really be considered as activist groups.

9. The term "boycott" was coined during this period. Charles Boycott was known for growing rich while treating Irish land-tenants harshly. In the late 1800s the peasants decided to flex their economic muscle and stopped paying him rent, repairing his shoes, mending his trousers and doing business with him. The leaders of this peasant rebellion in Ireland named this tactic after its notorious target, Captain Boycott, and the word has since come into popular use.

10. The International Maritime Organisation (IMO) guidelines state that decisions for platforms like the Brent Spar should be made on an individual basis, taking into account such factors as environmental impact, safety, occupational health, other marine users and economic considerations (however, these guidelines are not legally binding). The 1992 Oslo–Paris Convention (signing Countries were Belgium, Denmark, Finland, France, Germany, Iceland, Ireland, Luxembourg, Netherlands, Norway, Portugal, Spain, Sweden, Switzerland, the United Kingdom) stated that sea disposal would be allowed in exceptional cases. Another international law, the United Nations Convention on the Law of the Sea (UNCLOS Treaty), which requires removal of redundant structures, was not ratified by the British government. Under the UK legislation on abandonment – covered by the 1975 Petroleum and Submarine Act – operators must submit their abandonment proposal for government approval, together with full supporting documentation and a review of the other options considered.

11. This does not mean, however, that companies need not worry about other groups in the transactional environment. Sometimes banks or insurance companies may use their direct pressure possibilities, because of the fear that one of the two transmission belts – customers or legislators – will work against the concerned company thereby creating an adverse effect financially (e.g. lawsuits) on the loan or insurance risk.

3
Corporate Early Awareness Models

THE INADEQUACY OF THE TRADITIONAL MODEL

Why do so many managers handle pressure from activist groups less professionally than they handle other business issues? We believe that the main reason is that their methods of analysing these issues at an early stage are not adequate. Most managers begin by identifying the company's stakeholders, as we saw at the beginning of the previous chapter.

Traditionally, such an analysis starts with the interest groups or stakeholders: first, identifying the groups, then analysing their respective demands and finally linking them to single issues. One stakeholder, for example, could be a union trying to maintain a high level of employment (demand) with reference to the planned restructuring of a production site (issue).

Typically, however, the generic stakeholder groups of a company are fairly similar within industries, and an analysis based first on these groups and their demands usually leads to rather static, narrow and generalised assessments. For example, environmentalists are seen to be always fighting for the same thing – a higher level of environmental protection. Similarly, unions are always expected to want the same thing – more money for their members and higher employment; the media to want good stories, and so on. How can managers evaluate challenges on such a general, if not stereotypical, basis?

The reality is that similar activist groups do not always want or demand the same things. Take, for example, the question of job cuts. In most cases, employees and unions accept (although they certainly do not like it) that companies sometimes have to cut back the workforce and to close unprofitable plants in order to maintain competitiveness. But in early March 1997, when Renault announced plans to close a plant in Belgium, something totally unexpected happened: employees and customers simply balked. The situation exploded beyond the borders of Belgium into a Europe-wide protest and calls for boycotts. The tenor of the customer protest in Belgium soon became: "They want to produce Renaults abroad? They should sell them abroad as well, then." This launched a national boycott of Renault cars. Obviously, management had touched on a symbolic issue: the fate of the only Renault site in Belgium, which was the difference between this particular plant closing and others.

Using traditional stakeholder analysis, this degree of public reaction would not have been forecasted. It would simply have shown that "employees want job security". This illustrates one of the main weaknesses in the research that has been done so far on similar crises. An analysis based on evaluating general stakeholder demands can easily become irrelevant to management practice because the following variables change constantly over time:

- *The agendas of different stakeholder groups.* For example, environmental groups are increasingly shifting the debate from toxic emissions as by-products of industrial processes to the question of energy usage in itself and the problem of the greenhouse effect. Even Greenpeace, which has been synonymous with bold environmental activism (e.g. "Save the Whales" and protests against French nuclear testing in the South Pacific) is beginning to include more "passive" techniques of activism on its agenda, such as the use of scientific studies and dialogue to influence the governments and corporations it targets.
- *The importance and degree of influence of different groups.* Public perception is a major factor in this area. The power of consumer organisations in the United States first peaked in the 1970s with Ralph Nader's successful crusade against General Motors (he initiated the "Unsafe at any Speed" campaign against safety defects in General Motor's Chevrolet

Corvair). The 1980s saw these same groups losing the public's attention, but they are back in the 1990s, raising new issues such as bans on animal testing by cosmetics manufacturers.

- *The company position and exposure within the industry.* Activist groups prefer to single out symbolic opponents rather than take on an entire industry. They will target companies whose position within the industry is exposed. The oil industry presents a perfect example: after the *Exxon Valdez* accident, Exxon was the preferred target of environmental groups until the Brent Spar incident was in the spotlight. Then Shell became the scapegoat of the oil industry, not least because of the Nigerian government's hanging of the human rights and environmental activist Ken Saro Wiwa only weeks after the Brent Spar incident.
- *Societal values.* Obviously, as societal values change, so does the importance of each issue. An example is surveys regarding the attitudes of German citizens concerning the most important problems in the country. These surveys show that certain problems that have been perceived as significant in the past, like politics (with reference to the former USSR and East Germany), have almost disappeared, while others, like unemployment, have regained importance.

ADVANTAGES OF THE NEW MODEL

Given all the disadvantages of the traditional model, there is obviously a need for a new approach. When we reviewed examples where activist groups were able to make a strong impact on companies, it became obvious that powerful stakeholder involvement is almost always linked to special projects such as product launches, production changes, political discussions on new issues, new scientific discoveries, etc. We found that activist groups rarely protested against the *existence* of a company or what it stands for, but on special issues, which consequently should be at the centre of the analysis. The idea of analysing activist demands on the basis of the *characteristics of the issues* themselves can give managers more relevant results. Consequently, our model examines the problem not from a stakeholder perspective, but from an issue perspective.

In the new model, managers begin their analyses by defining current issues (using our last example, the restructuring of the production site) that might attract opposition. In a second step, we analyse the characteristics of the issue. We introduce the categories of characteristics themselves in the next chapter. (It is possible that there will be so many issues that managers do not even know with which issue to begin. In this case, a helpful rule of thumb is to begin with new projects or issues rather than older or ongoing ones. This is because fresh issues always incite more interest among the public than old ones.) In the new model, the activist groups are no longer the focus of the analysis. The strength of the so-called *key activist group* is just one of the eight characteristics of an issue that determine whether or not it can be a problem for the company. Other characteristics – media-friendliness, the isolation of the company and connections to other issues – will be discussed in later chapters.

Figure 3.1 shows the difference between the traditional model and the new model. Key activist groups are those that have the potential to generate broad public awareness of an issue of direct relevance to their organisations' purpose. Rather than get involved in every issue, they concentrate on certain key topics. For example, Greenpeace is active in the fields of toxicity, nuclear energy, atmosphere protection and biodiversity; Friends of the Earth concentrates more on environmental degradation, preserving biological, cultural and ethnic diversity, and empowering citizens. Other groups focus on very specific issues, like the Franz Weber Foundation, which is involved in nature conservation and animal welfare issues, or the Rainforest Action Network, which, as its name implies, exists to protect rainforests. In social issues, one can find similar examples, like Amnesty International fighting for victims of grave human rights violations, People for the Ethical Treatment of Animals, whose goal is to prevent animals from being exploited by man, or Jewish organisations defending the interests of the Jews and Holocaust victims.

So although many activist groups may declare sympathy for a certain project of their peers, an issue has to be a direct match with the key concerns of an activist group in order to merit any significant action. In our empirical research we found that the *key* activist group had much more of an impact on the outcome of an issue than the combined efforts of less important groups that

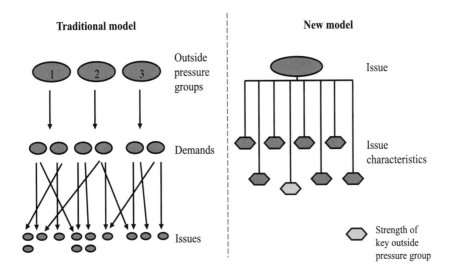

Figure 3.1 Traditional model and new model for evaluating outside pressure

might be also be involved in an issue. The different groups may be protesting from different angles or with very different goals in mind. Take, for example, companies in the paper industry that were confronted in the 1980s with campaigns from several institutions like Friends of the Earth, Greenpeace and the WWF. Each of these groups had its own message: rain forest protection; right of indigenous communities; conservation of wildlife habitats; containment of water emissions; safety of feminine hygiene products; and decreases in landfill and in energy consumption.

The reader should remember that the involvement of a key activist group is only one of the eight characteristics of an issue.

EARLY IDENTIFICATION VERSUS LATE INTERVENTION

How can managers use this checklist to avoid potential market share loss and reputation damage?

First, it is important to repeat what we said in the beginning: in the long run, the best crisis prevention policy is to "do the right thing". Managers must consider the legitimate interests, including ethical concerns, of the stakeholders of their company. It is in the company's best interests to establish decision-making processes that take into account societal norms on social, environmental and health-related criteria, as well as focussing on the company's own mission. However, even the most conscientious companies in this regard can come under fire and thus need to be prepared.

Today, most companies have a "fire department" – public relations, communications – which deals with issues that have already erupted. In this case, the main hope for winning is good communications to influence public opinion. A better strategy is to aim for the early identification of potential or budding issues in order to avoid confrontation crises later on. Early identification aims at systematically scanning the business and social environment for danger signals to recognise issues in time (Ansoff, 1975). Such early identification may exist for *past accidents*, as well as *past, present* and *future incidents*.

Accidents are, by their nature, sudden and unexpected and therefore they cannot be predicted. What *can* be predicted is *public reaction* to an accident. Industrial accidents happen every day, but few result in a public outcry. Those that do are not necessarily the ones that create the most harm, but are more likely to be those that fit the criteria necessary to provoke the public, such as the cluster of accidents that occurred in the production of Hoechst's Frankfurt site in 1993.

Incidents, whether they are *past, current* or *future*, are more controllable than accidents, and therefore the sensitive ones can be identified with more lead time. An example of a *past incident*, which has come back to haunt Hooker Chemicals and Plastics Corporation, is the pollution of the Love Canal in the United States, a neighbourhood that had been built over an abandoned hazardous waste site. Investigative reporting discovered that between 1942 and 1953, Hooker Chemicals and Plastics Corporation (now Occidental Chemical Corporation) dumped over 21 000 tons of toxic chemicals, including Dioxin-tainted trichlorophenols, at the Love Canal site. During the mid-1970s, contaminated leachate migrated to the surface of the canal, to some residential basements adjacent to the canal, and through sewers to area creeks. In

1978, because of an abnormally high rate of miscarriage, birth defects and cancer, New York State evacuated over 500 homes near the dump site. Although the company had discontinued its toxic waste disposal decades earlier, it suffered severe financial consequences (the company was forced to pay US$102 million for the clean-up) and Occidental Chemical's reputation was badly damaged.

Current incidents attracting activist concern include the case of the automobile industry, which has come under increasing attack for not producing more fuel-efficient models. Finally, *future incidents* can be expected as a result of the current discussion about genetically engineered food products, which some groups are trying to have banned or, at least, to include enforced labelling.

In principle, managers have a choice as to whether they nip issues in the bud or intervene only when they are reaching the discomfort level. The advantage of early identification and preventive measures is that the company can often avoid a confrontation with activist groups from the start. The advantage of late intervention is that the company does not "waste" its effort on issues that may not justify the attention – the difficulty, of course, is to recognise the difference.

STRONG VERSUS WEAK ISSUES

The up-front handling of activist demands is usually advantageous for "strong" issues, which would eventually have to be handled anyway:

1. companies have more freedom of choice in terms of possible solutions;
2. they may be able to avoid damage to their public image;
3. management time can be better invested in other areas of the company's business rather than eaten up with crisis management.

"Weak" issues, which can be handled without a large public outcry, can possibly be responded to later in the process.

If Shell had realised that the Brent Spar case had the potential of becoming a "strong" one, it would have had more freedom in trying to find a solution for disposing of the platform than it did finally. Although to date the company has not made a final choice, it has basically no option but to dispose of the platform on land. The contrast between the up-front and back-end approaches is illustrated by Ross Laboratories, the nutritional division of Abbott Laboratories, and Nestlé (the infant formula sales in the Third World). Abbott foresaw the potential danger to its image and quickly co-operated with UNICEF and WHO when the first negative reports appeared, whereas Nestlé delayed its handling of the issue and therefore suffered through the boycott and the resulting harm to its reputation.

It is, of course, difficult to know in advance which issue will be "strong" and which "weak". What makes the difference?

The main difference between "weak" and "strong" issues is that they go though different stages and different levels of public interest:

- *concern*: a matter of interest or importance;
- *issue*: an important subject of debate or litigation;
- *crisis*: an unstable or critical time or state of affairs in which a decisive change is pending;
- *scandal*: a thing causing general public outrage or indignation.

Strong issues will normally go through all of these stages, eventually becoming a *scandal*. Therefore, they require immediate attention, because the company's degree of decision-making freedom declines with time. Weak issues do not present an immediate need to take far-reaching actions. In most cases they remain at the *concern* and *issue* stages, and often disappear in a "spiral of silence". Weak issues can exist for a very long time without affecting the company's degree of freedom in decision-making.

In the following chapter we present a systematic approach to support managers in their categorisation of issues as weak or strong.

These tools may help managers to calculate the less-evident aspects of an issue: the *pattern and structure* (Senge, 1990). Most managers see only the tip of the iceberg, i.e. the daily events themselves, missing the more dangerous patterns and structures beneath the surface. The tools can also be used to help decide which issues should be responded to immediately.

There are two checklists – one to help the company evaluate the relative risks of upcoming issues, and the second to estimate the probability that a key group will act on the issue.

4

Company Issue Checklist

We have argued that issues should be at the centre of an analysis of activist group demands. The following example illustrates how to do this. In 1996, the British–Australian company RTZ-CRA decided to build, at a cost of 1 billion Australian dollars (around US$750 million), a zinc mine in the Australian state of Queensland. The zinc mine project and a project-related pipeline would contribute 10% of world zinc output over a 20-year period. However, management recognised that there was an issue brewing with the Gulf Aborigines, who claimed that the territory in which the mine would be located belonged to them, and that the mine would mar and destroy their land. From a legal point of view RTZ-CRA knew it could have legislation enacted to secure title over the land, but management needed to ask itself what the ramifications of such an action might be. Would the issue go away after RTZ-CRA gained title? What damage could be done to the company's image? Could it suffer financial damages that might cancel out or reduce profits from the mining project?

In our research we identified the following relevant checklist items (Box 4.1) that RTZ-CRA managers could use to evaluate the issue.

We then take a detailed look at the eight points on the checklist. At the end of the description we will see how RTZ-CRA could have applied the checklist.

---

1. Are the arguments against the issue plausible?
2. Does the issue evoke emotion? Is it understandable – visual, touching – by the public?
3. Is the issue media-friendly?
4. Are there connections to other issues of the company or other companies?
5. How strong is the key activist group?
6. How isolated is the company?
7. How far have the dynamics of the crisis already evolved?
8. How easy is the solution?

Box 4.1 Company checklist

COMPANY CHECKLIST

1. Are the arguments against the issue plausible?

Two factors determine whether activists' claims are plausible: if (i) it is connected to some understandable concerns, and (ii) it is communicated through a reliable and credible source.

People can have very strong opinions that are not based on logic, but on values and beliefs. Therefore, companies should not evaluate activist claims only on the basis of whether they are scientifically or technically justified, but consider instead whether there is a certain degree of plausibility in the eyes of the public. Even if sometimes public opinion seems capricious, unpredictable or irrational, managers should try nevertheless to look further than their own scientific data and internal issues. They should, as a rule, listen carefully, even, and especially to, their harshest critics. Falling into the trap of labelling activist demands as irrational from the beginning limits companies' ability to gain additional insights and understand the concerns of the public. Managers should also consider that the reference system for evaluating the plausibility of an issue through an activist group may be very different from the company's own reference system. For example, in the European debate over the use of gene-manipulated maize, industry assumes that the existing intensive, monocultural farming systems will be the norm in the future, and evaluates the benefits of biotechnology with this in mind. Conversely, most environmental activist groups, which are against the use of biotechnology, see it as binding agriculture to monocultural farming systems, and as a big disadvantage to the multicultural farming system that they favour. Furthermore, managers should realise that rather than the activist groups having to prove companies guilty of harmful practices, society is demanding more and more that companies first give proof of their products' safety.

The second factor that determines the plausibility of claims is whether people trust the information source. In general, if the source is trustworthy in the eyes of the public, then the information is less likely to be challenged. In the Western world, trust in large corporations is generally quite low. Before US legislation forced companies to report their emission levels of 300 hazardous chemicals in the so-called Toxic Release Inventory (TRI),[1] firms were constantly pushed by activist groups to publish their emissions. Even when they did, however, nobody believed the data. Since the information has been published through this trusted (relatively) government agency, pressure to disclose the data has subsided.

Philip Morris learned this lesson of trust and non-trust the hard way in 1996 when the company began an aggressive advertising campaign against the "secondary smoke" issue in Europe. While the tobacco industry has long defended the idea that smokers were exercising their freedom of choice, pressure in recent years has turned to the passive, involuntary exposure to secondary smoke. In their advertising, Philip Morris argued that inhaling secondary smoke is less dangerous than eating cookies or drinking milk, citing a scientific study by the US Environmental Protection Agency (EPA). From a statistical point of view, the study of the EPA from 1994 – which was based on a combination of 30 other studies – concluded that exposure to secondary smoking could not be identified as a significant risk.[2] These results were highly controversial in the scientific community.[3] The way Philip Morris used the results infuriated many readers and, as a result, the company was accused by a large number of activist groups, especially anti-smoking organisations, of distorting scientific evidence. Almost nobody considered Philip Morris a believable source for discussion on the health effects of secondary smoking, because the tobacco industry is notorious for its attempts at creating doubt about scientific findings. One tobacco manager boasted back in the 1970s: "Doubt is our product, since it is the best means of competing with the 'body of fact' that exists in the mind of the general public" (Hilts, 1994). As a result of this criticism, Philip Morris was forced to discontinue this particular campaign and, in an interesting aside, faced several lawsuits from producers of cookies. In France, a Paris court decided in July 1996 that Philip Morris should be fined US$195 000 every time the advertisement appears.

In contrast, Johnson & Johnson was twice able to recover public trust after the company's Tylenol capsules were poisoned. In the first case, the leaders of the company's Tylenol division decided to order an immediate recall and removed bottles of Tylenol from the shelves of stores after seven deaths were linked to it in Chicago in 1982. They acted even before the government could force a recall and before the public perceived the company as being defensive, despite the US$100 million anticipated cost. Similar actions were taken after a second attack in 1986. Although it lost large amounts of money in the short term, the company gained public trust and obtained loyalty for new forms of Tylenol with tamper-proof seals and other health care products of the company. Consequently, Tylenol was able to regain its former leading position in the market. Since the incidents, surveys show that Johnson & Johnson is considered a trustworthy institution by the public. This example also shows that trust can be built on a long-term basis.

Other accusations could never be considered plausible and therefore lead only to minor disruptions. For example, the gossip and chain letters about Procter & Gamble's (P&G) connection with satanism began in the early 1980s when certain groups claimed that P&G's president spoke in support of satanism on a television talk show. As proof of their arguments, these groups mentioned the company's old moon-and-stars trademark, which has 13 stars and could therefore be seen is a satanic symbol connected with devil worship. However, the fact behind this symbol is that in 1850, P&G marketed Star Candles, utilising a man-in-the-moon trademark consisting of a popular figure of the 1800s, and 13 stars representing the original 13 colonies of the United States. (They can also be found on the US dollar bill.) Despite the fact that this rumour came up again and again over the years, the issue never affected P&G's business seriously – it was simply not plausible. To avoid mushrooming negative publicity, P&G has sued rumourmongers and sent letters to churches and the news media denying any connection with devil worship. (The company has now also discarded its traditional trademark.)

In summary, managers should consider: (a) whether an issue is connected to plausible concerns, and (b) whether the company or the activist group is a trustworthy information source in the eyes of the public.

2. Does the issue evoke emotion? Is it understandable – visual, touching – by the public?

This question is probably the most important one on the checklist. Emotions can be the most powerful motivations for action. Emotions are not necessarily negative – they are simply a fact of life, helping people to reduce the complexity that they have to face in their decisions. Only a small number of issues are able to arouse the interest of large numbers of people at a time, but when they do, the momentum is difficult to counter. Issues that evoke emotion have several characteristics in common. They are:

- easily understood by the public;
- visual;
- touching.

People become excited about things that they can see, understand, and love or hate. Environmental or health-related disasters achieve inclusion in international media when pictures or films of suffering animals or ugly piles of waste are available to create good visuals and touch people's emotions. Social issues become strong when they show a great visual injustice. Everyone can understand the message, and possibilities for public reaction under these conditions are high.

One example of a very emotional issue has been the US debate on "dolphin-safe" tuna fishing. After research revealed that at least one million dolphins died in fishermen's nets between 1972 and 1990, dramatic advertisements with headlines like "Kill a Dolphin Today – All You Need is a Tuna Can and a Can Opener" were used by animal rights groups to encourage consumers in a boycott against tuna canners who trapped dolphins in their nets. Although there are healthy numbers of dolphins on the planet and the animal is clearly not on the endangered species list, this dolphin-by-catch quickly became a hot issue for the public and resulted in a tremendous outcry. First, teenagers became active spokespersons against dolphin killing, then their parents caught on and started boycotting tuna as well. The major contributing factor to this was the fact that most human beings like dolphins – highly intelligent and sociable creatures typified by the friendly character in the *Flipper* television series. The issue of dolphins dying in fishermen's nets is an emotionally distressing one with all the necessary characteristics – it is understandable, visual and deeply touching.

Attempts at other fishing techniques are fraught with problems, because in each of them the number of young tuna or tuna in reproductive stages caught increases. Arguments based on hard data that the tuna themselves are much more likely than dolphins to be added to the endangered species list do not have the same emotional value with the public, and therefore pressure on companies for a solution for dolphins will always be heavier than that for tuna. Sharks, which are crucial to marine eco-balance, get no more public sympathy than tuna. Despite activist groups' protests against overfishing and endangering the existence of these predators, the United States is still a major supplier and consumer of shark meat and fin as well as an importing, exporting and re-exporting nation for shark products. In short, everyone wants to save the whales and the dolphins, but who feels sorry for a shark or a tuna?

Public outcry in the United States and the threat of legislation, forced Star-Kist, the tuna subsidiary of Heinz, and other major tuna marketers to switch to "dolphin-free" fishing methods. In announcing his company's shift to dolphin-free tuna, Heinz's CEO, Anthony J.F. O'Reilly, was able to take pressure off the issue and use emotion to his own advantage. Heinz agreed to accept a ban on dolphin-unsafe tuna throughout its operations world-wide. As a consequence, the market share of Star-Kist in the United States rose to a record 40% after the announcement. The whole issue finally resulted in a labelling programme for tuna cans that became one of the most popular labelling programmes ever.

This case also shows that emotionally charged issues not only attract the public, but often lead to legislative action. In April 1991 the United States placed an embargo on the import of

Mexican tuna because of its non-compliance with dolphin-safe fishing methods. As of 1998, after seven years of tuna boycott, the economic effect on the Mexican tuna industry has been devastating and the damage appears irreversible. During this period, the sector has suffered a 55% shrinkage. Economic losses have been estimated at over US$500 million, the fishing fleet has been reduced by more than 50%, and 30 000 direct and indirect jobs have been lost, while tuna exports have dropped by 70%. In the United States, Congress also prohibited the import of tuna products from other countries that had been purchased previously from banned countries (the World Trade Organisation (WTO) later ruled this legislation illegal).

However, one should not conclude from this example that animal rights in general are high on the consumer's agenda and are always able to evoke emotion. If many people really felt strongly about animals being driven around the country for long periods, some supermarkets might gain market share quickly by announcing that they buy only local meat. But this issue is not as emotional, probably because of missing aesthetics (mistreatment of pigs leads to far fewer and less exciting protests than does mistreatment of horses or dogs). What the example also shows is that emotions do not depend on scientific evidence only, but are subject to personal bias.

Another emotional issue is the mad cow disease scandal, which has taken a heavy toll on British farmers and the beef industry. At the end of March 1996, airwaves and newspapers around the world were filled with stories: "Mad Cow Disease Claims 10 Human Victims!", "British Government to Slaughter 11 Million Cattle!" These stories appeared immediately after the British government admitted that scientists had found a link between bovine spongiform encephalopathy (mad cow disease) and the human Creutzfeld-Jakob disease (CJD). The issue was complex from a scientific point of view, but on a visual level it was easily understandable: television news clips of diseased, disoriented cows falling over said it all. These images caused panic among many Europeans, who feared one of the greatest public health calamities since the Black Death, with hundreds of thousands of people dying from a horrific brain disease. Because people's health was directly affected and the vast majority are extremely sensitive about what might happen to their brains (second only to reproductive organs!), the mad cow disease scandal had a great emotional impact.

A negative consequence for Britain was that continental Europeans banned British beef from their tables, and it was decided that millions of cows in the United Kingdom had to be culled and burned. Additionally, European consumers reduced their total beef consumption significantly; in some European countries by as much as 30% (for example, Portugal –31%, Greece –25% and Italy –21%).

This case also illustrates the possibility of national or cultural differences in emotional reactions to an issue. In France, for example, where personal health is not as high on peoples' list of concerns, overall beef consumption fell by only about 9% in 1996 as compared with the 30% continental average. The French example also shows that emotions can be calmed by symbolic acts, as when French President Jacques Chirac announced publicly that he was sticking to his favourite dish, tête de veau (calf's head stew).

Similar national differences exist concerning other issues. For example, nuclear power finds a much broader acceptance in France, Japan, Korea and Taiwan and stirs up far less emotion than in the United States or in Germany. But even in Asiatic countries, which up until recently experienced few activist group demands and where public emotional reactions are generally frowned on, the trend for public pressure on companies seems to be gaining a foothold. Green Cross, a Japanese company, is currently accused of having sold HIV-contaminated blood products in the 1980s. In September 1996, the Green Cross Corporation had to announce that it will probably see a net loss of 6.5 billion yen (US$ 59.1 million) and a 14% sales decline, largely because of a boycott of its products by medical institutions. The issue was a strong one for the company because of the emotional impact it had on the public (humans could easily understand the deadly effects of the Green Cross's negligence concerning the HIV menace).

3. Is the issue media-friendly?

Highly emotional issues are those most likely to be media-friendly. The importance of the media in raising issues cannot be over-emphasised, because media involvement is the way to bring an

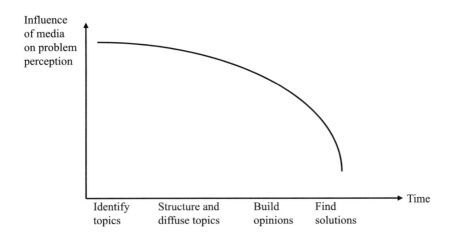

Figure 4.1 Stages of media influence

issue to prominence. Only the mass media are able to disseminate a topic of discussion instantaneously throughout society. John Jennings, the chairman of Shell Transport and Trading UK, one of the managers who suffered most from the Brent Spar incident, came to this conclusion: "It's a CNN world. And that means it's a show-me world, and not the trust-me world of the past" (Wagstyl and Corzine, 1997). The media determine which topics will receive attention, how problems are structured and diffused and sometime even solved. However, the media's decisive strengths are in identifying and structuring issues, while they are less involved with diffusion and finding solutions.[4]

> The press may not be successful much of the time in telling people what to think, but is stunningly successful in telling its readers what to think about (Cohen, 1963, p. 13).

Figure 4.1 shows the stages of media influence. For example, when several tourists were killed in Miami in 1993, the international media pounced on the story because the victims were from Germany and Canada, where the murders received wide coverage. The media itself identified the issue (violence in Miami), structured it (danger for tourists), built the opinion (especially in Germany and Canada) and even helped to find a solution (change the licence plates of the cars rented through rental companies, so that people are less easily recognised as tourists). But each year there are more than 1200 murders of locals and immigrants in Florida – this is not an issue internationally because the media did not include it in the "tourist murders" structure of its story. It is, however, interesting to note, as illustrated by this issue, that the European media appear more "solution-oriented" than their US counterparts, who tend to focus more on sensationalising a problem.

There are many issues that fulfil all the emotional requirements and still do not gain media attention. That is because it is also very important that an issue is somehow *new, extraordinary* and *accessible* to media reporters.

When the media began reporting on environmental and health disasters about 20 years ago, interest mounted quickly because the issues were new. Blazing rainforests, slaughtered elephants, oil-slicked otters, and forced child labour made good stories. This rising interest led to the fact that in the 1980s virtually every consumer magazine was running cover stories on the environment, on health and social injustice. In 1975, during the infant formula debate, the US Interfaith Centre on Corporate Responsibility (ICCR) sponsored a film entitled *Bottle Babies* in which the negative effects of using infant formula in the Third World were shown. Among other images, the film showed a child's grave with a Nestlé infant formula can in place of a headstone. The powerful film was shown at church gatherings, and protest gradually spread to the general public. Media appeal grew even stronger when the Nestlé boycott escalated in the United States, and in 1978, US Senator Edward Kennedy, Chairman of the Senate's Subcommittee on Health and Scientific Research on Infant Nutrition, opened public hearings on the controversy. The US television network CBS and other stations reported regular updates on these hearings, because they were the first of their kind.

In the following years, one boycott group called INFACT, a Boston-based activist group that spearheaded a boycott against General Electric for manufacturing nuclear weapons parts, even won an academy award for their documentary video on the subject. However, in the 1990s, these stories became commonplace and interest declined. Today, issues have to be different or extraordinary in some way to get media attention. If a particular issue, or even a similar one, has already been reported, people tend to skip the story and look for something more interesting.

The media industry is one that, like any other, has to make profits in order to survive. Therefore, they report stories that sell, such as the Brent Spar case, which was the first time that journalists had reported on a platform disposal issue. The dramatic North Sea battles between the Greenpeace vessel and Shell's water cannons were also a first for the novelty-hungry media public.

New is not always enough – in order to be media-friendly, an issue has to be accessible to the reporters as well. If something happens in an out-of-the-way place that is difficult for even reporters to reach, they are not likely to expend their energy and resources to get there. While, in 1976, there were many areas in the United States with much worse hazardous waste problems than those at the Love Canal, few were less than one hour by air from the headquarters of the television networks in New York. So, when families had to move after the toxins began to resurface, there was media saturation of the issue.

Today, however, the accessibility problem has decreased as activist groups learn how to work with the media. Greenpeace makes and provides "video news releases" free of charge to the media, which present issues from the Greenpeace point of view. Other activist groups provide material for the press through their Internet servers. So the media can use the material provided by the activist groups rather than sending their own reporters to the scene. Many stations broadcast this material without even changing the accompanying voice-overs.

The media today include the national and international press, technical journals, television, local radio programmes and popular new forms like the Internet. Activists' concerns may first appear in local or highly specialised media, then may – or may not – succeed in moving into more general publications. When a small community uncovers a waste site scandal, this might be highly interesting to the local media, but an old and unimportant story for the national media. The same negative correlation may exist for highly specialised scientific publications. Health and environmental issues are discovered typically by scientists and first published in small, highly-specialised, limited-circulation journals. Mention of a pollution issue might first appear with very limited exposure as an article in the Sierra Club's *Sierra*. A consumer issue might appear first in *Mother Jones* and a medical issue might first appear in the *New England Journal of Medicine*. These issues may be relevant and even earth-shattering for some scientists, but all too often they are meaningless to the general public and not suitable for the mainstream media. Still, despite their limited circulation, the local and technical media can sometimes be the catalysts that bring issues to broad public awareness. Especially if the issue in question is both new and extraordinary, it might be taken up by national newspapers or less-specialised scientific sources such as the *New York Times* Tuesday section, Science Times, or the *Washington Post*'s health care section, and from there become a household topic.

The growing popularity of the Internet is helping truly to make the world into a "global village".[5] Internet-caused crises will be an increasing problem for companies, because media coverage can be generated by a single person with a complaint. Anyone from a disgruntled former employee to a dissatisfied customer can spread his or her own messages, such as in the case of the Intel Pentium computer chip. When what the company termed an "insignificant" flaw was found on Intel's Pentium chip by a mathematics professor in late 1994, Intel did not take it overly seriously. Small flaws were at that time considered routine with the release of a new microprocessor, so the company blocked the first complaint about the chip. The professor went public on the Internet, spreading the news throughout the on-line community with lightning speed. Despite the fact that Intel had been considered best-practice in assessing potential problems through regularly monitoring the Internet, the company seemed in this case not to appreciate the "real time" dynamics of the Internet. As Intel was beginning to respond to untruths and identify outspoken critics who might be assuaged, the dynamics of the Internet and on-line chat groups became overwhelming.[6] Finally, Intel offered to replace the chips at a cost of US$475 million.

Boycotts and protests generally spread much faster through the new Internet. It took more than a decade for boycotts against South Africa to take hold, but organised protest against Burma and companies that continue to do business there has gained support rapidly in only two years, mainly through the Free Burma Coalition Web site, which averages 36 000 visitors a month. Activists use the Internet to monitor Burma on a daily basis and report to the world what streets the demonstrators are on, where they are arrested and how the government reacts, thus drawing international attention to one of the world's most brutal and repressive military regimes, the Burma State Law and Order Restoration Council (SLORC). This Council has received severe condemnations from the US Congress and State Department, the European Parliament, the United Nations Human Rights Commission, the International Labour Organisation, and Amnesty International.[7] The group also runs listservs, which are e-mail chat groups.

One of the last US companies to remain in Burma, the Pepsi Corporation, was finally forced by these and other organisations to leave in January 1997. Only Texaco stays behind with its gas-drilling operation in the Gulf of Martaban 260 miles south of Burma's capital city, Rangoon.

The Internet is also taking on corporations directly, with pages combining text, graphics, video and audio, to spread information on a company's questionable practices. Activist groups can use the Internet to challenge claims of companies point-for-point, as the Rainforest Action Network (RAN) is doing with Mitsubishi. RAN's Web site links its rebuttals back to Mitsubishi's site, so that readers can check RAN's rebuttals directly against the statements they refute.

Shutting down offending Internet pages has proven to be next to impossible for companies. In McSpotlight, a Web site containing case details and campaign photographic material on a lawsuit between McDonald's and a handful of activists, McDonald's is accused of promoting ill-health, destroying animal welfare, causing environmental damage and exploiting children through advertising and employees through low pay. The site has been accessed by an average of more than 600 000 people *monthly* since its February 1996 launch. To prevent its pages from being forcibly closed under libel law, McSpotlight has identical sites in the United States, the Netherlands and New Zealand. In addition, the site maintains a "McInformation kit"; that is, the entire site compressed and ready for downloading into a single Internet file to any site in the world, making it impossible for McDonald's to make the site disappear. Allan Hunt-Badiner, RAN's chairman argues:

> We're all learning how the architecture of the World Wide Web has taken the game into a new arena. Unlike TV where corporations bought attention

with impunity, suddenly it's the consumers that decide who they want to listen to. The magic of the ever-encircling web should clarify for corporations that there is, in fact, a "wash," and that, indeed, everything will "come out in it."

Despite these new forms of communication, however, companies themselves can still influence the media through their advertising expenditures, and in most countries the media depend on their advertisers. Therefore, heavy advertising can sometimes improve a company's position in a conflict, or at least force the media to be more objective in their reporting.

This happened in the case of Deutsche Telekom in January 1996, when, on New Year's Day, Deutsche Telekom changed its tariff structure, raising the price of local charges to pay for more competitive long-distance rates. However, because of a software error, 550 of Telekom's 8000 telephone exchanges failed to recognise New Year's Day as a holiday and overcharged customers. At first, the company was strongly criticised, because of the perceived social injustice of the new rates, coupled with the seeming incompetence behind the software failure. A few weeks later, the focus for criticism against the company shifted to telephone sex lines. However, a few months before Telekom went public in November, it seemed as though all the media were reporting positively on the company. Perhaps one of the reasons was Deutsche Telekom's multi-million-mark advertising budget that would be spent on the media.

This strategy can sometimes backfire, opening debate on the misuse of company financial power. This happened to P&G when the company decided in 1990 to remove its advertising from a television station in Boston that broadcast advertisements from a liberal political group called "Neighbour to Neighbour", which called for a boycott of P&G's Folgers brand coffee. In the advertisement, Neighbour to Neighbour said that the money spent on the coffee beans went to support El Salvador's civil war. The ensuing public criticism was less concerned with where P&G's coffee bean money went than with what the public saw as the company's misuse of financial power.

On the other hand, in several Western countries the public are beginning to distrust the media too. In a 1995 poll by the American Bar Association, 41% of the respondents said they had lost respect for defence lawyers when watching the heavily televised O.J.

Simpson trial, but 56% said they had lost respect for the news media as a whole for its behaviour during the trial (Jurkowitz, 1995). They felt that the media presence was disruptive – polarising the debate, oversimplifying arguments and turning the quest for justice into a circus. This perception obviously goes beyond the O.J. trial. Some of US television's hottest talk shows (down-market television) have come under criticism for low ethical standards. In late 1995, a number of important advertisers in the United States put pressure on the media by refusing to air advertisements during these shows. Similarly, Ford and Chrysler have begun to monitor the contents of magazines such as *Esquire, New Yorker* or *Vanity Fair* for potentially controversial topics and political incorrectness, before releasing any advertisements. The automobile manufacturers fear boycotts should their advertisements be seen in connection with these topics. Obviously, the media themselves have lessons to learn about potential repercussions when they feature gratuitous sex, foul language, references to violence and other "entertainment" to which segments of the population object.

4. Are there connections to other issues of the company or other companies?

Managers must be aware of the connections among controversial issues, because these may give some issues prominence out of proportion to their limited direct environmental, health or social impact. Activist accusations may take on huge proportions, perhaps beyond all rationality from a company's point of view, if, in the eyes of the public, they are connected to other events. The list of possible interconnections can be very long. The connections may lie *within the company, with other companies within the same industry*, or *with related effects* or results.

One example of connections *within the company* is the Swiss food giant Nestlé. Since the infant formula case, every new issue that comes up for Nestlé is tied back to that one. Most recently it came back to haunt Nestlé in the 1996 controversy over the planned usage of genetically engineered soya in many of its products. Another example can be found with the European women's lobby waging a battle against Perrier–Vittel to remove pictures of women's nipples that appeared on bottlecaps in Belgium. This issue was blown up further by reference to an earlier issue, when traces of benzene were discovered in Perrier in the early 1990s.

The paper industry is a good example of one that suffers constant interconnections *within the same industry*, because paper producers are accused regularly of being environmental laggards. Past insensitive behaviour regarding logging practices, bleaching systems, water and air pollution and recycling and disposal is brought up constantly every time there is a new issue, such as the current question of forest certification and sustainability.

Finally, activist concerns over *related effects* may be found, for example, in the case of endocrine mimicking, where several plastics are suspected of causing a reduction in male sperm count and fertility. The different plastics have different characteristics and are produced by different companies, but they may lead to the same damaging effects on the population. If these findings are confirmed scientifically, all companies in the chemical, packaging, and even food industries will come under public pressure.

Connections can be especially troublesome for managers in the case of accidents. It may be nearly impossible for the company to communicate its point of view to the public, because they are outraged by linkages over which the company has no control. One such example could be seen in December 1993 when the Swiss chemical company Ciba lost 160 000 water-tight 10 g sachets of Apron Plus, an insecticide, during sea transport from Rotterdam to West Africa, where it was supposed to be used by farmers to dust seeds (Haour and Miller, 1995). Although this accident had no real dangerous environmental or health effects, since the sachets were water-tight and could be collected easily from the beaches around the North Sea, Ciba suffered extensive public criticism, especially in Germany and the Netherlands – this despite the fact that the *Sherbro*, the ship that transported the insecticides, was not even owned by Ciba but by a chartered French transport company named SCAC Delmas Vieljeux. Viewed independently, it seemed to Ciba that public outcry was unfounded and would die down because:

- there was no direct impact on the environment;
- Ciba could not be held responsible for the accident;
- Ciba could not be considered guilty of negligence; and
- Ciba had reacted very responsibly by providing the resources for clean-up.

Although this transport accident was Ciba's first major incident in years, and the company declared that it would shoulder the costs for cleaning up the beaches and for the safe disposal of the chemical, public reaction was strong because of a much-publicised series of accidents throughout 1993 at the German chemical company Hoechst. When the Ciba accident occurred in December, the media pounced on it, and the public drew the connection to the Hoechst accidents. Immediately after first reports of the accident, German television crews travelled to the northern German islands hoping to catch sight of some sachets drifting ashore. Scandal-hungry reporters were looking for pictures of clean-up crews wearing face masks, goggles and protective spacesuit-type clothing. For them, the shipping accident became a big event because it was so visible. Ciba became the scapegoat for the accident, proving in the eyes of the public once more the dangerous ignorance and irresponsibility of chemical companies when dealing with environmental issues.[8]

Similarly, the 1979 accident at the Three Mile Island nuclear plant in the United States stirred up public hysteria, partly resulting from a totally unexpected and unfortunately coincidental interconnection: at the exact time of the accident, a film about a nuclear power plant disaster, *The China Syndrome* with Jane Fonda and Jack Lemmon, was released in American cinemas everywhere. As a result, communication delays by the managers of the nuclear plant had severe consequences for the entire US nuclear energy industry.[9]

Sometimes connections can be non-specific, but related to general public attitudes or other events in society. These are very difficult to predict; however, managers at General Motors (GM) successfully foresaw danger in a case of alleged industrial spying against Volkswagen (VW). Four ex-GM executives, including Jose Ignacio Lopez de Arriortua, VW's chief of production, were accused of stealing GM documents when they left the US car-maker for VW in 1993. GM might have been able to win huge compensation sums in two trials in the United States and in Germany from the German car-maker, but, instead, it settled the issue outside court. Hurting VW was a threat to many Germans' job security, and seen by the German public as provoking general economic decline. So when GM received the results of a December 1996 survey in which a third of Germans said that they might boycott US goods if high damages were ruled against VW, GM managers saw the danger of the interconnection and possible repercussions for its own image in Germany and that of its German unit, Opel.

On the other hand, in the Brent Spar case the managers did not take into account the connections between Greenpeace's protest and the upcoming North Sea conference that would take place in the Danish city of Esbjerg while the platform disposal process was under way. Greenpeace used the event as a springboard for their campaign, constructing a 7.5m tall model of the Brent Spar at the entrance to the conference. Attention was diverted from algae blooms and dying seals to the Brent Spar issue. Media coverage of the conference was extensive; Shell's actions were criticised intensely.

Of course, companies can sometimes profit from the fact that there are no suitable connections, and a potentially explosive issue surfacing at a time when other controversies are dominating may be ignored for an indefinite period.

How Can Managers Deal With These Connections?

A *cross-impact analysis* can be very effective in identifying the outcome of possible connections between different events to use for contingency planning. A cross-impact matrix contains several possible future events, listed both down the first column and across the first row. For each field within the matrix, a "+", "−" or "0" symbolises positive, negative or no interconnections between events. Each matrix field is divided into two parts. The upper part symbolises the probability of occurrence of the event that is listed in the row, should the event occur that is given in the column. The lower part tells us the probability of occurrence of the event in the row if the event given in the column does not occur. So, for example, a 3×3 matrix for three possible events contains 12 usable matrix fields. A hypothetical example of such a matrix could look as follows.

A subsidiary of the German chemical companies Hoechst and Schering, Plant Genetic Systems International NV (PGS) is producing genetically engineered (GE) rape to be sold on the European market. However, there are a number of activist groups that question GE food because of its unknown long-term dangers to the environment and human health. PGS should identify the three most significant possible events to occur on the basis of stakeholder involvement:

1. European legislation will require tougher surveillance of PGS's activities and products.
2. Labelling of all GE food as such will be enforced, reducing the market opportunities of these products.
3. Activist groups are able to increase public concern about GE food.

To develop contingency plans and to understand better possible developments in the external environment, the managers of PGS could try to find connections between these events that they may put into the cross-impact matrix. They should think, for example, about the effect of a labelling programme on public concerns about GE food. Is the public's fear going to increase or decrease if people know which products contain GE substances and which do not?

In the PGS case, the cross-impact of the three events may look, for example, as Table 4.1. On the basis of this cross-impact matrix, PGS can then start to make plans to fit different scenarios. For example, the managers can develop a contingency plan in case legislation concerning surveillance becomes tougher. From the matrix, they determine that this will not necessarily have an impact on labelling programmes, but most probably will increase consumer pressure. If these connections are understood by the managers, the company can plan how to deal with them ahead of time rather than dealing with the iceberg after they have already hit it.

Table 4.1 Example of a cross-impact matrix

Impact from / to:	Legislation	Labelling	Consumer Pressure
Legislation	*(shaded)*	+ / 0	0 / 0
Labelling	0 / 0	*(shaded)*	+ / −
Consumer pressure	+ / −	+ / −	*(shaded)*

These examples show that planning should take into account possible activism resulting from connections to: their own company history, the industry's history and the issue's history, as well as society's general agenda (upcoming events, conferences, etc.). This kind of analysis should be done with an open mind, and from the perspective of "the man in the street" (not just company employees).

5. How strong is the key activist group?

> So the rule for use of the military is that if you outnumber the opponent ten to one, then surround them five to one; attack, two to one; divide. If you are equal, then fight if you are able. If you are fewer, then keep away if you are able. If you are not as good, then flee if you are able (Sun Tzu, 1991).

At the beginning of this book we explained the importance of the key activist group, or advocate, which can take ownership of an issue away from the company. At this point in the checklist, managers should evaluate the strength of this group (and eventually *all* groups involved). On a case-by-case basis, power is relative; the same group can be very powerful on one topic, but weak on another.

As we argued in Chapter 2, we believe that the importance of an issue in the eyes of the public is determined by its own particular characteristics, only one of them being the power of the key activist group. However, even if a certain issue has all the ingredients to become a strong one, if there is no activist group powerful enough to push it to public attention, then the company involved may escape extreme negative effects. Despite the fact that the number of these groups has risen dramatically in recent years, only a few have the power to make a strong impact.[10] Among these are the larger environmental groups such as the Sierra Club, the National Resources Defense Council (NRDC), the Environment Defense Fund (EDF), Greenpeace and Friends of the Earth, some very powerful social issue groups such as Amnesty International, People for the Ethical Treatment of Animals, certain unions and Public Citizen, a powerful group that focuses on health issues.

These groups share a few common characteristics: they are large, international and highly professional, staffed by expert lawyers and scientists. Other groups are staffed by only a handful of people and rely largely on volunteer efforts. So a company that finds itself on Greenpeace's hit list would understandably take the threat much more seriously than if it were attacked by a smaller, lesser known group.

But what makes an activist group able to affect companies through media access and customer and legislator influence? In general, their strengths are:

1. a broad base of support, and
2. their internal structure.

Bases of Support

Activist groups provide their sponsors, members and supporters with the opportunity to support certain ideals or goals. Supporters can give the activist group financial or other donations, thereby "voicing" their concerns without necessarily becoming active themselves.[11] The more supporters, the stronger the voice. Managers should therefore assess whether the activist group represents the feelings of a large or small part of the population. The Consumer Federation of America brings together over 200 groups that represent some 30 million Americans and defends consumer interests. Amnesty International has over 1.1 million members from more than 150 different countries around the world. Even a very large corporation would have to think twice about fighting with either of these organisations.

Besides its own members, support is also determined by the general attitude toward a group by society at large. While some activism concerns issues that affect the general population (humanitarian issues, ethnic discrimination, environmental destruction, torture, etc.), other issues affect individuals on a very personal level, such as when they fear for their jobs or feel they are being treated unfairly. Public support for those groups is often inconsistent. For example, unions may be seen as solely concerned with their own interests, disregarding the good of society as a whole. As a result, despite the fact that in almost every democratic country the majority approve of unions, they are blamed for inflation and even driving some companies out of business (Lipset, 1986).

The power of an activist group, however, is also related to its financial power. The more spectacular campaigns, like the one around Brent Spar, are often extremely expensive and very few activist groups can afford them. This gives unions, who regularly collect dues from their members, power related to their own financial resources (as well as to the number of members), despite the ambivalent public attitudes described above.

Many activist groups act on an international level, and therefore have different degrees of power depending on their support in different countries. Greenpeace, for example, had, in 1995, 2.9 million members world-wide and an income of US$152 million. The biggest membership base and contributions were from Germany, the United States and The Netherlands. So, of course, Greenpeace's power is the highest in these countries as well – with more campaigns taking place in these countries in order to satisfy the contributors.

But a purely quantitative evaluation of the support for an activist group does not say everything. Some groups have learned very well how to bring issues to public awareness and are considered very influential; others are still in the learning process. High-visibility tactics such as full-page advertisements, videotapes, mass mailings, Web sites on the Internet and newsletters can attract celebrity support against targeted firms. In general, action-oriented groups have a much better chance than the ones that try to win issues by focusing on scientific debate. For example, consumer groups' testing of products, publishing product information and giving recommendations for shopping are a far cry from the often spectacular feats of environmental organisations; their media impact is therefore often lower.

Internal Structure

Managers should also look at activist groups' internal structure. The organisational structure of these change-oriented groups (Greenpeace calls itself a "catalyst for change") tends to be different from corporate organisations, which are shareholder-oriented and exist to make money. Non-profit organisations are judged by other criteria. According to Peter Drucker, the product of these non-profit organisations is "a changed human being" (Drucker, 1990). Contrary to companies, non-profit organisations do not measure their market share in monetary units, but in degrees of change. To change people normally requires a more democratic structure in an activist organisation as compared with a commercial organisation.

We think that the key criterion for evaluating the power of an activist group as a function of its internal structure is the *degree of centralisation* in decision-making. In most businesses, when management takes a decision, it is then carried out. This is not necessarily so with not-for-profit organisations. In many organisations of this type, the managing director is required to have every decision reviewed either by committees or by a board. And while boards of corporations tend to be small and efficient, they are usually larger and less efficient in non-profit organisations (Fisher, 1995). Often, in activist groups, the board is very strong and tends to over-control. Managers in activist groups often do not have a clear command authority, which creates many inefficiencies and takes away the possible surprise effect. So being able to catch a campaign target by surprise depends largely on the existence of central power structures, not least because of the financial flexibility of a centralised activist group. Greenpeace International, for example, always keeps part of its budget available for contingencies such as the Brent Spar campaign in order to be able to strike quickly.

While some activist groups like Greenpeace have recognised the advantages of central decision-making, and have a powerful steering committee that can take decisions on campaigns quickly with little backtracking, other organisations are strongly membership-driven. In these cases, local groups have an influence on all key decisions; obviously, discussion takes longer and the probability of compromise is higher. Examples of these kinds of structures are the national chapters of Friends of the Earth. Naturally, these groups can have only a limited surprise effect, needing much more consensus-building before stepping into action than a highly centralised group. Sometimes groups even require unanimity, which makes the process of consensus-building long and tedious.

To centralise their decision-making process and move faster on upcoming issues, some groups, like companies, decentralise themselves into "business units" that can act with flexibility in their "market". The American consumer advocate Ralph Nader formed groups that act under the umbrella of "Public Citizen" to defend consumer interests. Founded in 1971, Public Citizen works in Washington with the support of more than 150 000 people interested in fighting for safer drugs and medical devices, cleaner and safer energy sources, a cleaner environment and a more open and democratic government. It has a total of six divisions:

- *Congress Watch*: legislative lobbying.
- *Health Research Group*: fights for safe foods, drugs and medical devices and for universal access to quality health care.
- *Litigation Group*: public interest law firm. Its attorneys bring precedent-setting lawsuits on behalf of citizens in order to protect the health, safety and rights of consumers.
- *Critical Mass Energy Project*: anti-nuclear activism and alternative energy.
- *Global Trade Watch*: trade issues related to job security, environment, health and safety issues and democratic accountability.
- *Buyers Up*: volume discount buying of heating-oil products.

Another way of centralising the power of decision-making is to give national organisations a high degree of independence from the international headquarters. Greenpeace, for example, has worked to manage this balancing act of central and decentralised power. Most decisions of the organisation are taken locally through the national offices, rather than Greenpeace International's headquarters in Amsterdam. These local offices run campaigns on national pollution issues, and are responsible for building contacts with national politicians and journalists. However, when it needs to, Greenpeace can act like a centralised organisation. In 1986, its offices were wired up to an international computer network and, although national offices are given relative freedom from Amsterdam, they are never allowed to change Greenpeace's world-wide policy to suit local tastes. Greenpeace Norway, for example, is obliged to oppose whaling in spite of the protests of local fishermen.

6. How isolated is the company?

Activist groups prefer not to attack entire industries. Especially in long, drawn-out debates, industries usually take a common position, making it hard to single out "sinners" and to move them into the public spotlight. If activist groups can target a single, isolated company as a scapegoat, they can frame a case as a symbolic fight.

Many companies try, therefore, to accomplish a "common front" by joining industry associations, which protect them to a certain extent through common lobbying and communication initiatives. Others voluntarily sign agreements such as the International Chamber of Commerce's Business Charter for Sustainable Development or the Chemical Manufacturers Association "Responsible Care" programme, in which they agree on general values and attitudes,[12] or to neutralise resistance by industry-sponsored constructive approaches (e.g. a recent "drink and we pay the taxi" programme of some night-clubs in Switzerland).

Front-runner companies are obvious targets for pressure. Activists find it easy to concentrate on this one company, in part to give the media a clear symbolic fight that can be relatively easily covered. Any company pursuing a project that could be interpreted as being a bad precedent for the whole industry should therefore be aware of the high danger of drawing activist attacks. This is exactly what happened to Shell in the Brent Spar case. Although the owner of the Brent Spar was, in reality, Shell Exploration and Development (Shell Expro), a joint venture between Shell and Exxon, Greenpeace levelled its criticism solely at Shell. This made the message easier for the public to understand, and the environmentalists had one isolated opponent on which to focus. When the Greenpeace campaign began, the entire industry left Shell to defend itself alone. Even Exxon, their 50% partner in the venture, would not make any public statement in favour of Shell, and tried to maintain a low profile throughout Greenpeace's campaign, despite the fact that the Brent Spar incident was going to be used as a precedent for bans and moratoria on decommissioning a growing inventory of offshore facilities around the world.

Another good example of isolation, this time on a social issue, was the reduction in sick payments in 1996 in Germany, where the industrial giant Daimler–Benz, the largest company in Germany, found itself suddenly in the role of the scapegoat for German industry in general. In this case, the German government tried to cut sick pay by reducing the statutory entitlement of workers to 80% of normal wages for sick days from the previous 100%. The new law became effective in October and Daimler–Benz was the first German company to attempt to apply it. This front-runner activity was, of course, an ideal battlefield for the unions. An immediate wave of protest was unleashed among employees, with workers staging brief strikes at various companies' sites across the country. The discussion on German television began to concentrate more and more on Daimler–Benz as an isolated opponent of unions and workers' rights. Other big industrial companies shied away from the issue and told the media they would wait before taking any decision to apply the law – waiting to see whether Daimler–Benz would survive or be ripped to shreds. In December, after weeks of hefty criticism, Daimler–Benz announced it would hold off implementing the new law until it had reached a "contractual clarification" on the issue with the union.

Of course, in accident cases, companies are automatically isolated and this is probably why public outrage can become so fierce. For example, in the Union Carbide gas leak in India, only the company was attacked, not the entire chemical industry. Similar situations may arise when a product is found to damage people's health (Johnson & Johnson's Tylenol capsules).

To be singled out from among a large group of other "sinners" is seldom only a question of bad luck. Besides size and visibility, the attitude a company projects can make it a target for activists. After a 1991 call by the Church of England to boycott Nestlé products to protest at the continuing sales of breast milk substitutes in Third World countries, many church-goers stopped buying Nestlé products. When, in 1992, Nestlé announced that its sales had increased despite the boycott, the church felt that Nestlé had not taken seriously their concerns about the health of children in Third World countries. Nestlé will, therefore, inevitably be a target for future campaigns, and activists will try to single them out at the next available opportunity.

The German chemical company Hoechst was very successful in doing an analysis of its risk of being forced into an isolated position. In April 1997, Roussel Uclaf, their French pharmaceuticals subsidiary, agreed to stop the production of the abortion pill RU

486, which terminates pregnancies without surgery. This decision was taken in light of an on-going battle with anti-abortion campaigners who lobbied against the drug sales, particularly in the United States. Hoechst declared that it no longer wanted to be involved in moral arguments on abortion. The company was afraid that its image would be tarnished and did not want to risk being hit with a boycott, especially in the US market. According to one Hoechst manager, the company saw the United States "on the verge of a civil war over abortion". Just one week prior to the final decision to drop the drug, some US anti-abortion groups had already called for a boycott of a new Hoechst allergy drug unless the firm dropped RU 486. The logic behind Hoechst's decision is clear: it would be the only company producing this abortion pill; hence, it would have become isolated easily and a perfect target for anti-abortion groups. Hoechst, however, foresaw the danger that pro-choice movements, who advocated sales of RU 486 in the United States, would attack it from the other side. So, finally, in order to wash its hands of the whole debate, it made two very calculated moves: in Europe, it agreed to transfer "without remuneration" the patent rights for the drug to a newly formed company headed by Edouard Sakiz, who had been Chief Executive of Roussel Uclaf until 1993. In the United States, at the request of the government, Hoechst transferred the rights for the drug to the pro-choice organisation "The Population Council" which is now trying to get RU 486 approved for sale with the Food and Drug Administration (FDA).

7. How far have the dynamics of the crisis already evolved?

As we have mentioned, issues go through different stages, from their first identification to the point where the problem is eventually resolved or disappears.

Once an issue is identified, the task for managers is next to analyse how far it has already developed and what might be its future dynamics. Doing so may help them to predict what may trigger the next stage. In general, there are two tools that support managers in such research: diffusion curves and scenario analysis.

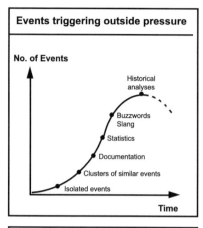

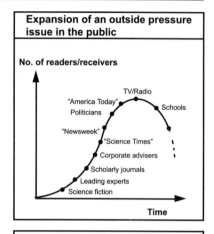

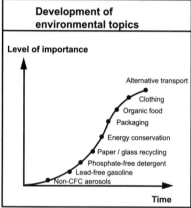

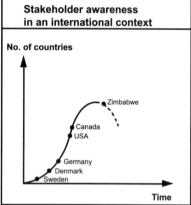

Figure 4.2 Diffusion curves

Diffusion curves

Every new idea is developed by only one or a few individuals and has then to find its way into overall awareness. Some new ideas get stuck in this process and disappear silently, while others become an important "trend". As in fashion, ideas may make their way to mainstream trends or become adopted only by some "avant-gard" buyers.

Diffusion curves (see Figure 4.2) describe a pattern of transmitting new ideas into overall awareness by moving along some predictable patterns. Diffusion theory assumes that from one specific subject (i.e. the carrier of new knowledge), a ripple effect will bring the new knowledge to an ever greater number of subjects (bandwagon effect). So an idea is born and then grows in importance. This growth can be measured in different ways: the number of related events, people informed, countries involved, etc. In practice, diffusion functions allow a systematic and continual observation of relevant themes and indicators and can help managers to understand the dynamics. The growth of an issue's importance is thereby traced against time. The diffusion curves can be either cumulative or non-cumulative, but after a slow start, diffusion curves typically climb steeply and then taper off at the saturation level.[13]

Keeping these typical patterns in mind, managers should try to identify potential diffusion curves for their issues. They should list the sequence of issue-related events that have already occurred and think about possible future events/developments from an intrinsic logic. Additionally, they should consider which events might alter the situation to such an extent that the company will no longer be able to maintain its current position (the steep climb). This point can be referred to as the "take-off" point. The take-off point can be compared with a "critical mass" that is reached at that time. If the predicted diffusion curves are consistent (events naturally follow each other), they may be able to predict future dynamics and which may be the next group, country, media or event to come up and are then able to prepare action plans.

A good example of strong dynamics in an issue that could have been analysed using a diffusion curve is the case of chlorofluorocarbons (CFCs) and refrigerators, where Greenpeace was able to promote a major market change after new solutions became feasible. When, in 1985, the connection between the ozone hole over the Antarctic and CFCs became scientifically confirmed, the producers of refrigerators argued long and hard that it was impossible to build refrigerators without using CFCs as a coolant. However, in Germany in 1991, Greenpeace began promoting a hydrocarbon mix called "Greenfreeze" as a substitute for CFCs. The "Greenfreeze" refrigerant uses a propane–butane mix, which has no direct impact either on the ozone layer or global warming. Its main potential drawback is flammability, which, some argue, makes it unsafe.

As the traditional producers of refrigerators were not ready to use this technology, the dynamics of diffusion took over. In early 1992, Greenpeace injected much-needed support by bringing together scientists and representatives of a former East German company named Foron, and entrusted the company with the development of propane–butane refrigerators. Greenpeace's part of the deal was to obtain 70 000 orders for this refrigerator by actively promoting it. By 1992, the company was producing "Greenfreeze" in commercial quantities and other manufacturers lost market share. In July 1992, Greenpeace went further to campaign for CFC-free refrigerators all over Europe and demanded that the seven West German manufacturers should use the same technology. For a short time, the industry remained sceptical and argued about significant risks to consumers and workers, but the real dynamics of this stakeholder involvement took off when the retailers ordered and marketed it and when Greenpeace presented "Greenfreeze" on a political platform in November 1992 in a meeting of the signatory states of the Montreal Protocol on the Protection of the Ozone Layer, which imposed tougher restrictions

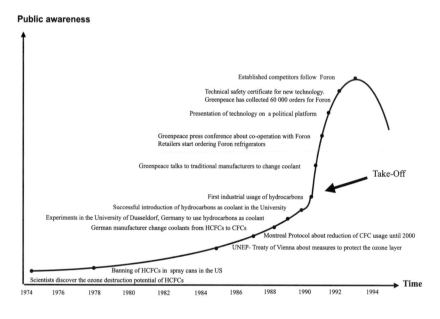

Figure 4.3 Diffusion process for hydrocarbons as refrigerator coolants

on CFCs.[14] This added impetus to international diffusion and a world-wide campaign for conversion. Within one year, all German producers of refrigerators such as Bosch, Siemens, Miele and AEG were forced to exchange their coolants for "Greenfreeze".[15] In 1995, three of the four largest refrigerant manufacturers in China switched to the "Greenfreeze" technology. The diffusion curve for this issue can be seen in Figure 4.3 (not time-proportional).

The clear indicator of imminent take-off was in 1991 when CFCs were first substituted in environmental settings. The white goods manufacturers could foresee at that moment that the substitution in household appliances was from then on only a question of time, because the basic technology was ready.

The decisive forces behind the take-off of a diffusion can be either single- or multi-factored. The refrigerator case involved the interaction of several accelerators: environmental movements, several international protocols, available technology and readiness of the retailers to order it. In the mad cow case, which we mentioned earlier, media attention to the scientific findings alone sufficed.

Scenario Analysis

A second tool to identify the possible development of issues is scenario analysis. The idea behind scenario analysis is that, given the impossibility of knowing precisely how the future will play out, a good decision is one that works well across several possible futures. Scenarios can be developed to identify and understand uncertain future dynamics that refer to the transactional environment of a company (customers, suppliers, banks and insurance policies, etc.), as well as to the contextual environment (political developments, activist groups, etc.). Most companies use the scenario technique to understand the dynamics of the contextual environment (e.g. macroeconomic developments caused by political decisions). Shell has used scenarios as means to try to understand the future for more than twenty years (van der Heijden, 1996). The following simplified discussion of scenario development is drawn largely from Shell methodology.

To reach "robust" decisions and understand many possible dynamics, scenarios are created in the plural, with each scenario

diverging from the others. They are accordingly suited to express-
ing the often divergent views of managers, as well as to examining
fundamental alternatives and the joint impacts of many uncertainties. Thus, the purpose of scenario planning is not to pinpoint
future events, but to highlight large-scale forces that may push the
future in different directions.

A scenario analysis begins by identifying the issue that one
wants to address. Let us take as an example the decision over a
hypothetical chemical company's possible investment in the biotechnology field in order to produce genetically engineered (GE)
raw food material. The company managers want to know whether
the public will perceive GE food as an environmental or health
threat, and what the general attitude to genetic engineering will
be in the years to come.

Today, as genetic engineering becomes feasible on an industrial
scale, scientists are worried about two kinds of risks from GE
organisms: risks to human health and risks to the environment.
Health risks are generally considered low, as few of the micro-
organisms used in research or industry are pathogenic to humans.
Perhaps the only danger would be to someone allergic to peanuts
or shellfish, for example, because he would never know if a tomato
or other food had been altered with proteins from these allergens.

However, there is more substantial risk that undesirable environmental effects could be caused by novel organisms released
into the environment. GE products are inherently unpredictable;
once released, they would be virtually impossible to confine to the
laboratory. A report published by 100 top American scientists
warned that the release of gene-splitting organisms "could lead to
irreversible, devastating damage to the ecology". Recent evidence in Europe shows that GE plants such as rapeseed, the
source of canola oil, can spread their herbicide resistance quickly
into weeds, creating "superweeds", damaging crops and the ecosystem. Some of these effects may be difficult to predict accurately or may become apparent only in the longer term. Other
environmental risks include unanticipated effects on non-target
species, negative influence on the interactions among species, unanticipated involvement in biogeochemical cycles and the transfer
of undesired characteristics to other organisms.

However, for companies like Monsanto, Hoechst, Novartis or
Novo Nordisk, biotechnology promises great financial prospects,

and for many governments it seems to be the solution for feeding the future global population of 10 billion.

Since scenarios are a way of understanding the dynamics shaping the future, the next step is to identify the primary "driving forces" at work. These driving forces often fall into four categories:

1. *social*: quantitative, demographic issues (population growth; immigration rate; minority development); softer issues of values, lifestyle, demand or political energy.
2. *economic*: macroeconomic trends (How will the population growth affect the price of food commodities?); micro-economic dynamics (What will my competitors do? How will the structure of the industry change?).
3. *political*: electoral (Who'll be the next environmental minister?); legislative (Will research policies change?); regulatory issues.
4. *technological*: direct (How will biotechnology develop?); enabling (Will quantum physics bring in the next biotechnological revolution?); and indirect (Will substitutes for genetically engineered food production become available?).

The point of examining the driving forces is to look past the everyday business that typically occupies managers' minds and to examine long-term external forces. Some of these can be called "predetermined". They are completely outside our control and will play out in any story of the future; for instance, demographics. However, not all forces are so evident, nor so easy to calculate. An example of a less predictable event is the expected erosion of soil in a certain country and the resulting need of more intense agriculture.

After identifying the predetermined elements from the list of driving forces, the next step consists in analysing uncertainties, and identifying those that are key to the problem. To identify these uncertainties, managers generally work in teams, using some variation of the following procedure:

1. each group member writes each major trend or uncertainty he/she sees on a separate Post-it note.
2. each participant, in turn, explains what he has in mind with each trend or uncertainty and the group collectively rearranges the Post-its into common trends and uncertainties.

3.   after prioritising the uncertain factors, the group focuses on the two most critical ones and begins to sketch out alternative scenarios.

The goals of this group work are to understand better all the uncertain forces and their relationships with each other, and to support managers in identifying the developments that are the most difficult to predict. When trying to group the different uncertainties, it often seems at first that no two are alike, but it is usually possible to tie uncertainties that have some commonality to a single spectrum, an axis of uncertainty. Ideally, it should be possible to simplify the entire list of related uncertainties into two orthogonal axes, which define a matrix (two axes crossing) allowing a definition of four very different, but plausible, quadrants of uncertainty.

In our GE food example, chemical company managers could have identified the following two key uncertainties: (i) the level of support and acceptance of this technology by a broad public: from broad acceptance to blunt refusal of processed food, and (ii) the

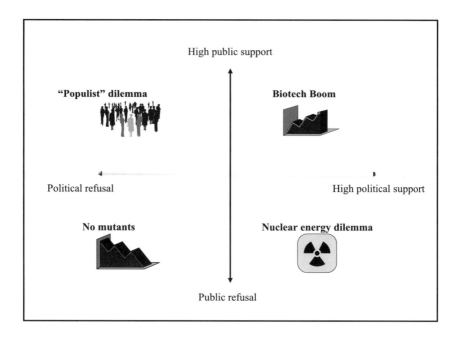

Figure 4.4   Scenario analysis for genetically engineered food

uncertain level of political and governmental intervention in genetic engineering. Will governments encourage the bio-technological industry or will they stop it? The second uncertainty might seem at first glance an outcome of the first, but in fact, while they are related, they are "separately" uncertain. This can be seen in a number of activist cases where government ideas differed greatly from those of the broad public (e.g. nuclear energy generation). The two uncertainties combine to create four scenarios – different "future spaces" to explore. In Figure 4.4 we give them some names so that they can be referred to more easily.

The goal is to tell four stories; not with the hope that one of them will become true, but to pin down the corners of the plausible futures. Note also that different scenarios do not fall neatly into "good" and "bad" worlds, desirable and undesirable futures. Like real life from which they are built, the scenarios are mixed bags. The four developed scenarios can be described as in Box 4.2.

Given that managers do not know which – if any – of these scenarios will unfold, what can they do to prepare?

Some of the decisions companies make today will make sense across all of the futures. Others will make sense only in one or two. Once the planners have identified those implications that work in all of the scenarios, they can confidently get on with their plans. At Shell, for example, projects are evaluated against different scenarios with the ultimate goal being to undertake only those projects that give positive returns under all scenarios (van der Heijden, 1996).

Companies also need to identify "early warning signs" (as, for example, with the proposed checklist) that give clues as to which of these scenarios are beginning to unfold. At the same time, the identified key uncertainties show managers along which lines the dynamics of an issue may change. For example, in our GE food case, managers of the chemical company may come to understand that future dynamics will be driven by changed attitudes of legislators and the general public. In some cases, the leading indicators for a given scenario are obvious, but often they are subtle – a piece of legislation, a technical breakthrough, or a gradual social trend. It is important to monitor these critical signs closely; for example, through contacts with opinion leaders.

To summarise up to this point, pressures on companies emerge through dynamic processes, usually possessing some common

Biotech Boom:	In this scenario, irreversible environmental damage creates a global environment so hostile that agriculture becomes difficult even in former fertile areas. Over-population adds to the problem. As Third World famines worsen, affluent countries are hungry for good quality produce. Desperate to replenish its food supply, the public accepts genetic engineering (GE) as its only hope for a new generation of crops which can survive in the deteriorated conditions. Business prospects for biotechnology shoot way up. Consumers demand high-quality food and refuse to buy puny, spotted produce. Governments encourage the biotech industry with subsidies and research grants.
Nuclear energy dilemma:	In this possible future, governments strongly support GE as an improvement to food supply to last into the future, but the public remains suspicious about the new technology's health effects and disagrees with their political leaders. Similar to the 1980s No Nukes movements, large masses of protesters march in front of the biotech company's gates, break into laboratories and chain themselves to the fixtures, dress up in Mutant Creature costumes and parade in front of TV cameras, etc. Some scientific findings support the public's disapproval. As people are unable to change legislation, consumer movements will advocate food companies who can guarantee their products are GE-free, and will try to enact a labelling system.
No mutants:	Research findings manage to prove serious environmental and health dangers related to GE food. GE food and further researching and experiments in the area are outlawed in most countries. Former GE advocates are publicly humiliated in the press. Biotech companies suffer severe image loss. Lawsuits run rampant and most of the smaller firms are wiped out.
"Populist" dilemma:	In this scenario, governments shy away from GE food as a solution and hold back support until research can prove beyond the shadow of a doubt its safety for the environment and to human health. Meanwhile, the general public snaps up novel and attractive GE products at the grocery store. Crops are altered to be able to grow well in deserts, and Third World countries suddenly have a cheap and plentiful supply. Despite government and some scientists' warnings, no one can give up GE food.

Box 4.2

patterns: discussion is sparked on a newsworthy item, the topic is triggered further, the issue "takes off" and finally matures to broad awareness. Managers can use diffusion curves to visualise the processes by which the issues with which they are concerned might develop, and try to understand possible future dynamics. Through the use of scenario analysis, they may identify additionally the driving forces and key uncertainties that will determine the dynamics.

8. How easy is the solution?

Experience shows that both the public and legislators prefer solutions that do not put the company's existence at stake. But if a "perfect solution" does not in most cases exist, what are the possible solutions?

Solutions to activist issues can refer to changes in production processes (mostly environmental issues), in products (environmental and health issues) and in the company's behaviour in general (especially with reference to social issues).

A change in production processes could be, for example, taking measures (e.g. build filters) to reduce the amount and toxicity of emissions resulting from a certain process. Two such examples are that of the paper industry, which was forced by environmental activists to switch to chlorine-free bleaching methods, and of refineries that had to make major investments in new filter technology. In such cases, usually the entire industry is affected, and competitive disadvantage occurs only on an international basis (if at all).

Whenever a product is attacked by consumers, the easy (although not necessarily cost-efficient) solution is often to take the product off the market and substitute it with another product, or to change the product formula. A typical example occurred in 1984. P&G Germany launched a laundry booster sheet "Top Job" to enhance washing power. The product reached sales of about US$30 million some months after its introduction, until the German government told P&G that "Top Job" was unnecessary and harmful to the environment. While the German Federal Environmental Office had no power to remove the product from the shelves, it decided to persuade and educate consumers through press releases. As a first response to these releases, P&G bought space in regional newspapers that said: "Many homeowners use Top Job in order to save money and of course it is compatible with the environment". But after calls for a boycott, P&G decided to take the product off the market and cancelled the planned European roll-out. The solution was easy to find, since P&G wanted most of all to avoid damage to its public image.

Similarly, Source Perrier was faced with a severe crisis in early 1990 when traces of benzene were discovered in its product. The discovery led to an immediate world-wide product recall, which was a feasible, even if expensive, solution.[16] Sometimes, product changes refer not to the product formula itself, but to other product features, like packaging. A good example of such a solution can be found in the Tylenol case where Johnson & Johnson introduced tamper-proof seals on its packaging after the recall.

Solutions to social issues refer in most cases to changes in general attitudes and behaviours. An example can be found in the 1997 racial discrimination case against Texaco. In this case, six black Texaco employees complained that they were discriminated against in promotions, and this could be proven clearly by a secret tape that caught Texaco executives belittling blacks. As a consequence, the company fired the managers and started a programme to improve the career opportunities of all minorities working in the company.

What Level of Change is Demanded?

As we have already mentioned, legislators normally do not demand economically impossible actions from companies, because this would go against some of their own interests. They generally know what is feasible and are aware of the fact that they cannot improve companies by imposing crippling demands on them. In the current environment of global competition for jobs and wealth, politicians' success also depends more and more on the health and success of businesses in the regions they represent. So, for example, legislation for tighter pollution control is often passed only if the concerned companies are not suddenly put at a great disadvantage when compared with foreign competitors. Companies are heard in the legislative process and are given the opportunity to communicate their opinions on a piece of legislation. Today's politicians also rely less on the command-and-control rationale, but prefer to work out "voluntary agreements" where industry can exercise some choice in how it will change its practices to comply with legal and political requirements. So normally legislators do not make demands on companies where there is no solution in sight. This trend for consideration of business interests has been growing, especially in recent years, as governments around the world attempt to make more intelligent legislation.

The situation with respect to the broad public is a bit more complicated. Even though the public evaluates issues more on an emotional basis, they can usually tell the difference between a feasible solution and an impossible one. Often, the public compares the perceived behaviour of one company with the behaviour of another and evaluates possible solutions on this basis. For example, animal testing is still publicly accepted as an unpleasant necessity for products that fight disease or save lives. People understand the need for guinea pigs in this context. But animal testing for cosmetics or other products is perceived as unnecessary; protests are more powerful because many people believe that other solutions are possible. The Boston-based Gillette Company, for example, learned this lesson when the company was affected in 1995 by a call for a boycott on all Gillette products and the products of its subsidiaries (e.g. Oral B) through concerned schoolchildren, who wanted the company to stop animal-based safety tests of their products. Gillette argued that the best available safety tests – and the ones most likely to hold up in court in cases of liability claims, will sometimes involve animals. Still, while Gillette and P&G have so far not been able to forswear animal testing, other companies such as Avon, Bennetton, Chanel and L'Oréal have given up the practice and therefore become peers against which Gillette has to measure itself. And some best-practice companies go even further: instead of using animals, Body Shop conducts patch tests of products on human volunteers at its head office. Rabbits and mice, the company points out, do not have a choice. So, according to public perception, solutions are available, and they expect Gillette to find one as well.

As we can see from this example, solutions that are pushed by public opinion should be benchmarked against practices in other companies in the same industry. Companies should identify significant differences between their own products/processes/ behaviour and that of their benchmarking partners.

What About Cost?

Companies usually know very well which of their problems can be solved at what cost. Even if they do not communicate this to the broad public, they should use this knowledge as a basis for evaluation of the checklist point. Many managers will probably be surprised that activist groups can then be quite reasonable. In some cases, however, it may happen that there are really no feasible cost-efficient solutions. When benchmarking reveals problems, but other constraints stand in the way of a solution, managers must be ready to stand fast, wait until the pressure has died down, and keep alert for alternative steps they can take. We return to this point in Chapter 8.

SUMMARY

The eight points of our checklist are the characteristics that are central to issue analysis in the new model as we have introduced it in Chapter 3. Together they determine whether a certain issue might become "strong" enough to be a threat to the company.

When managers have analysed these eight points of our checklist, they may make a qualitative summary. They can evaluate an issue from an overall perspective by evaluating the results of the different checklist items and then assessing the overall danger resulting from the issue. In such an overall evaluation, they also rely on their industry expertise and background knowledge to judge the issue in its context.

In general, a quantitative measuring of issues; for example, by assigning percentage values to the different questions and then aggregating the value of each checklist item in an overall value, would be possible. However, we believe that in most cases managers tend to rely more on their judgement and not on fixed percentage points. Additionally, as we have seen, there is some overlap in the different checklist items that would produce inconsistencies in an overall aggregation of all questions.

A Sample Evaluation

Let us now come back to the example at the beginning of this chapter, the company RTZ-CRA and its problem with the Australian Aborigines. Using the checklist points, we can make the following evaluation of the activist issue.

1. The claims were *plausible* because the Aborigines have land rights that have been seriously neglected so far. In Australia a recent court judgement has raised the prospect that 80% of the entire land might be subject to claims by the Aborigines – and 40% of the landmass has already been subject to native claims. Australia's now open society has increasingly recognised that the Aborigines have been treated unfairly ever since the first European settlers arrived.
2. It is an *emotional* issue, certainly a touching one. Questions involving Aborigines, and indigenous people in general, are strongly visual because of cultural roots that differ from the West's.
3. The *media-friendliness* is not the most influential factor, because the entire issue consists only of discussion and little action is involved. However, as mentioned, the cultural specialities may be a little bit media-friendly. It is not a new topic for the Australian media, however it is of general high importance.
4. There are some strong *interconnections* to other projects of RTZ-CRA. The company knew that if the confrontation got ugly it would suffer also in other projects like that in Irian Jaya, Indonesia, where it was already under attack with regard to a copper and gold mine. And RTZ-CRA did not want to risk deterioration of its relationships with aboriginal communities across the country, which would threaten its vast coal, iron ore and alumina operations. There are also connections to the question of Aborigines in general. The most recent reports of government- and community-sponsored child-stealing (taking Aborigine babies away from their mothers and placing them with white families to dilute and assimilate the Aborigine population), which was practised as recently as the 1960s are getting media attention – certainly RTZ-CRA would be seen as harming a people that has already suffered enough.

5. The *strength* of the activist group was high, as the Aborigines had just appointed a new charismatic leader, Murrandoo Yanner. He enjoys the support of the 200 000 Aborigines in Australia and can take many decisions on his own. And liberal forces in the general public tended in the last years to have more sympathy with the Aborigines. Transmitting the issue further on, to consumers, will be difficult for the Aborigines, because zinc is a commodity product and only industrial customers are involved.

6. RTZ-CRA was a front-runner and therefore an *isolated* opponent of the Aborigines. This mine project was the only current project of that size; in fact, it would have been the biggest zinc mine in the world.

7. The *dynamics* in the issue were already very developed when the RTZ-CRA management had to take a decision. The plight of the Aborigines and their land rights has been a frequent focus of the overall political discussions in Australia. The decision to build the mine could easily become the "take-off" point for strong protests against RTZ-CRA as the isolated opponent.

8. A *solution* to this issue was easy to find; namely, to postpone the decision on the mine building. This decision, taken before work on the mine even started, did not endanger the company as a whole.

Under these circumstances, RTZ-CRA decided to drop its request to secure title over the land, and decided to begin direct talks with the Gulf Aborigines under the right-to-negotiate provisions of the Native Title Act. So the Aborigines have been able to postpone the zinc mine project indefinitely. The unilateral decision to stop pushing for enabling legislation has underlined the growing realisation of a new political phenomenon in Australia: the emerging power of an increasingly knowledgeable aboriginal entity. However, now the company is under fire from white Australian politicians, who accuse RTZ-CRA of a double-cross after it dropped its request for special legislation. The government was embarrassed, because before the decision it had agreed to introduce special legislation to secure pipeline corridors for the site.

Table 4.2 Visualised company checklist

Assessment criteria	Rating					Comments
	++	+	0	–	–	
Plausibility		•				Aborigines have land rights.
Potential for emotions		•				People and their cultural roots are strange to modern society, but very visual.
Media-friendliness			•			So far only discussions.
Connections with other issues	•					Other projects of RTZ-CRA and general question of Aborigines.
Strength of the key activist group		•				Aborigines have charismatic leader who can take fast decisions.
Degree of company isolation		•				Only project of that size.
Dynamics		•				Mine project could be "the take off" point in the diffusion process.
Ease of solution		•				Company survival does not depend on this mine.

Overall assessment

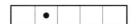

Summarising the Evaluation

One neat way to support a qualitative conclusion is to assign ratings from "no danger for the company out of this checklist criterion" (––), to "very high danger from this checklist criterion" (++). Then a summary chart like the one in Table 4.2 can provide a visual and immediate guide to an overall assessment of the problem.

The example shows how the company checklist can help managers to analyse the dangers from approaching activist issues. However, even if this checklist were completely comprehensive, it still leaves a number of questions open. For example, what can managers do if they know that they will identify an approaching problem using this tool (for example, having to close one production site and lay off the workers at that site), but so far no activist group has taken the lead on the issue?

First, managers should make absolutely certain that each project is handled in an acceptable way, with consideration to environmental, social and health factors. They should initiate for this purpose a scientific or social assessment of the risks to stakeholders and match the results with corporate standards and the acceptance criteria of society.

Only if, after this assessment, they are still convinced that they have taken the best possible decisions, should they then consider which activist groups might be against the project, and which of these might decide to build a campaign on it. To help judge whether or not an activist group will pick up the issue and attack, we propose that managers employ a second checklist, which analyses an issue from the perspective of an activist group. Using this list, a company may anticipate what the potential adversary might do.

Notes

1. The TRI was federally mandated and all manufacturing facilities with 10 or more employees that meet the established thresholds for manufacturing, process or otherwise listed chemicals are required to report emissions data in it.
2. These study results were somehow contradictory to what the EPA had declared in 1993 when the agency found that "the widespread exposure to environmental tobacco smoke in the United States represents a serious and substantial public health impact." At that time, the EPA declared that in adults, secondary smoke is a Class A (known human) carcinogen responsible for approximately 3000 lung cancer deaths annually in US non-smokers. Also, other studies of the EPA have shown higher risks from secondary smoke in some European countries than in the United States.
3. The critics attack the EPA's guidelines of statistical significance; namely, their 95% confidence level, which was violating accepted epidemiological standards. Besides that, the study was criticised for ignoring the effects of secondary smoke in triggering other conditions, such as asthma, breast cancer and heart disease.
4. A number of research projects like the "Project Censored" of the Sonoma State University in California tried to explore and publicise the extent of censorship in the United States by locating stories about significant issues of which the public were unaware. Each year the project selects the 25 "most under-reported" stories.
5. The term "global village" was created by the Canadian philosopher McLuhan.
6. One of the most embarrassing developments was the on-line jokes about the new microprocessor. For example:
    Q: How many Pentium designers does it take to screw in a light bulb?
    A: 1.99904274017, but that's close enough for non-technical people.

Q: Why didn't Intel call the Pentium the 586?

A: Because they added 486 and 100 on the first Pentium and got 585.999983605.

7. The military, who in 1996 renamed the country "Myanmar", is accused of having forced elected officials to flee for safety, and other offences such as forced labour and institutionally sanctioned rape and torture.

8. In Germany, chemical manufacturers have begun to recognise that the mysterious nature of the manufacturing plants created fear and suspicion among community residents. With the hope of overcoming these suspicions, manufacturers embarked on an openness campaign, conducting plant tours for local residents and interested parties.

9. In this case, for one entire day no spokesman could be found to make any statement or give more details on the accident.

10. If we take the number of non-governmental organisations (NGOs) as an indicator for the number of activist groups, we can observe that there were 48 in 1948 that gave recommendations to the Economic and Social Committee (ECOSOC) of the United Nations (UN). Since then they have mushroomed to no fewer than 1000 in 1995. At the first environmental conference of the UN, NGOs were non-existent. At the environmental conference in Rio de Janeiro in 1992, there were 1500 NGOs present, and at the Conference on Social Issues in Copenhagen in 1995, the number reached 2400 NGOs. The total number of NGOs today is estimated to be about 25 000, with an annual growth rate of 4%.

11. Here one can see clear links to one of Hirschman's (1970) models. He argues that while consumers can simply "exit" and stop buying the company's products, they can also "voice" these concerns and try to pressure the company. This voice option can trigger a process further and lead more consumers to choose an exit or voice option. People can exit the NGO that supports issues with which they disagree and give no further donations; and by giving donations they can voice on issues that are of particular interest to them.

12. The "Responsible Care" programme includes the following six sets of guidelines:

- *Community Awareness and Emergency Response* – to work with nearby communities to understand their concerns and to plan and practise for emergencies.
- *Pollution Prevention* – to achieve ongoing reductions in the amount of all pollutants released into the environment.
- *Process Safety* – to prevent fires, explosions and accidental chemical releases.
- *Distribution* – to reduce the potential for harm posed by the distribution of chemicals to the general public, employees and the environment.
- *Employee Health and Safety* – to protect and promote the health and safety of people working at or visiting company sites.
- *Product Stewardship* – to make health, safety and environmental protection a priority in all stages of a product's life, from design to disposal.

13. Similar diffusion curves had already been developed by Post (1978).

14. The Montreal Protocol says that the use of CFCs, which were until recently the most widespread refrigerant in use, is going to be phased out by 2000. Hydrochlorofluorocarbons (HCFCs), which were initially touted as CFC replacements, are banned from 2020 in developed countries and from 2040 in developing countries.

15. Abroad, after their European success, Greenpeace started playing the role of enthusiastic broker between the German manufacturers and potential customers in India, China and Latin America.
16. The immediate cost to the company of US$100 million was not the end of the story. Shortly after, it faced further controversy about whether labelling accurately portrayed its product.

5

Activist Issue Checklist

Companies should try to understand activists' thought processes in addition to their own in order to get a feel for their "world view" and anticipate which issues they are likely to pursue. Persevering with projects that attract powerful antagonists can involve companies in tough and damaging campaigns.

Advocates cannot act on every issue that comes to their attention; like every social organisation, they focus their energy and resources on the ones that relate to their current agenda. Naturally, they prefer to take on issues where their chances of making an impact, being a catalyst for change or otherwise "winning" are high.

To analyse the likelihood of coming under attack for a project or decision, we recommend the following procedure: first, analyse the issue against the company's own checklist. One of the characteristics in this analysis is the "strength of the key activist group". To determine whether the identified key activist group might pick up on a potential "hot issue" (according to the other seven criteria), the company must next analyse the issue against the key activist group's own priorities. If the issue characteristics are high on this list as well, then the company is facing a situation that demands immediate attention. Figure 5.1 shows the connections.

The checklist can exist either explicitly or implicitly within the activist group, and represents factors determining when it will take action. To get an idea of these rules, managers can read the mission

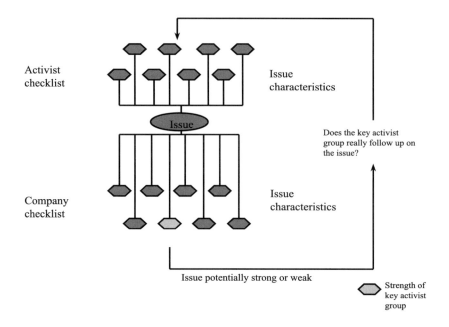

Figure 5.1   Link between company and activist checklists

statements of the groups, look at their recent campaigns and do a media analysis of their recent projects. What the checklist might look like also depends on the type of group, which can be loosely categorised as follows:

1. *large groups with massive membership bases and emphasis on active membership involvement*. e.g. church organisations like Caritas, the National Wildlife Federation, or the Brazilian social movement "Movimento Sem Terra". These groups tend to emphasise social justice.

2. *large groups with strong action-orientation and little direct participation by supporters*: e.g. Greenpeace, People for the Ethical Treatment of Animals and the National Urban League. These groups focus on issues that have strong pictures and clear symbols in order to create a "wake-up" effect on the public.

3. *quasi-scientific groups*: e.g. Foundation for Development and Peace, Ocean Voice, Environmental Defense Fund, etc.

These groups generally do not run campaigns, but focus more on communicating their scientific findings and influencing opinion leaders.

4. *project-specific organisations*: e.g. the Infant Formula Action Coalition (INFACT), which was founded to organise consumer boycotts against infant formula producers selling in Third World countries. These groups are often formed around a single issue and exist only for the duration of the campaign (until the issue is resolved).

With reference to the attitudes and modus operandi of activist groups, the environmental consulting company SustainAbility Ltd has developed a matrix comparing these groups to sea animals. Managers may feel a bit silly using these labels, but the matrix can actually be very helpful in constructing the Activist Checklist.

The first axis of the matrix is the extent to which the activist group seeks to integrate the role of businesses and public interest into its own goal system. At one end are the "integrators" – groups that place high priority on developing productive relationships with businesses through identifying win–win solutions. On the other end are the "polarisers" – groups that work single-mindedly to achieve their goals and do not try to cooperate with companies.

The second axis shows whether the activist group discriminates between different companies within an industry with respect to their real or perceived commitment to environmental, health and social issues. At one end are the "discriminators" who track the progress of individual companies compared with industry benchmarks. On the other end of the spectrum are the "non-discriminators", who focus on the problems caused by entire industries, not identifying which companies are the "good guys" and which are the "bad guys". Table 5.1 shows what the matrix looks like.

These four different kinds of activist group have different rules concerning which issues they tackle and how they run their campaigns. *Sharks* tend to run campaigns in which they attack companies arbitrarily and often criticise society as a whole. Their campaigns are not very target-specific and they currently pose little threat to individual companies. *Sealions* are even less

Table 5.1 Comparison of different activist groups. *Source:* SustainAbility Ltd

	Polariser	Integrator
Discriminator	*Orca* (Killer Whale) • highly intelligent, strategic • can adapt behaviour, strategy to context • fearsome, uses fear to coerce • uncertain in behaviour • likes deep water, can cover great distances • associates with own kind • eats sealions (and, sometimes, dolphins)	*Dolphin* • intelligent, creative • adapts behaviour and strategies to context • can fend off sharks • equally comfortable in deep or shallow waters, can cover great distances • can be a loner – or intensely social • empathy for other animals
Non-discriminator	*Shark* • relatively low intelligence • tactical • acutely responsive to distress signals, blood in water • poor eyesight, peripheral vision • undiscriminating in terms of targets • swims, often attacks, in packs	*Sealion* • moderate intelligence • tactical • popular spectacle • friendly • menu item for sharks and orca • tends to stay in "safe waters" • believes in safety in numbers • uneasy if too far from group

dangerous for companies because they tend only to involve themselves in "weak" discussions about societal values in general. Then there are the *dolphin* activist groups, which focus on single issues, but actively cooperate with companies to try to find solutions. They realise and understand the different interests and needs that exist naturally between a company and society, and try to support companies in bridging some of these differences. The really dangerous activist groups for companies are *orcas*. They isolate their prey, and try to humiliate them publicly for their sins. They choose symbolic issues and make great use of symbolism in their campaigns.

Today, more activist groups are moving in the direction of becoming orcas or dolphins. They discriminate among targets and single out the biggest sinners within an industry. In some cases, they try to meet with the companies and work together on solutions; in others, they just want a victory over their opponents.

In our empirical research looking at a large number of issues, we found that many activist groups, especially orcas or dolphins, use a set of guidelines for when to involve themselves in an issue. We also found some patterns in these guiding rules that state the requirements for a successful campaign, as listed in Box 5.1. Companies worried about activist groups should note that when a certain issue fulfils the requirements of this (or a similar) list, the danger of a confrontation rises sharply.[1] Each point is now explained in further detail.

---

1. The campaign should have a clear aim or goal.
2. The issue is easily understood by the general public.
3. The issue has a high symbolic value.
4. The issue has the potential to damage the image of the company.
5. The opponent is strong enough (no "underdog" effect).
6. The issue can be "packaged" in a campaign in which the public can get involved.
7. There are solutions that are confrontational, not gradual (political concepts, management concepts, product or process concepts that are competitive in price and quality).
8. There could be a dramatic element to the campaign to engage the media.

Box 5.1 Activist checklist

ACTIVIST CHECKLIST

1. The campaign should have a clear aim or goal

In most cases, activist groups prefer issues where they can identify a clear and specific goal. People are more realistic today about what they can expect from companies and the general tendency is not to target individual companies for general problems such as global warming or loss of biodiversity (although *sharks* will sometimes attack on these general issues).

One determining factor for the goal of an activist group is, of course, the time frame. In the case of an accident, for example, activist groups can fight for fair compensation of financial and other losses, or they may just try to punish the company for its imprudent behaviour (as in the case of the boycott against Exxon after the *Exxon Valdez* accident). On the other hand, in the case of a possible present or future incident, the goal is often to prevent the company from undertaking the project in question, or to damage a company's image. So, to a certain degree, goals are predetermined.

Clear goals are strongly related to possible solutions. Solutions are especially easy to find when the issue is about a particular product. One such example was the Natural Resources Defense Council (NRDC) forcing the chemical and tyre company Uniroyal to remove one of its products, "Alar", from the market. Alar was the trade name for a pesticide used on apples in the United States. In 1989, the EPA announced that according to one of its studies, over a 70-year period, five out of 100 000 persons exposed to Alar would get cancer. Even higher risks were projected for children who ate and drank apple products. Yet, the EPA announced, the chemical would not be banned because studies did not show an imminent hazard. While Uniroyal quickly refuted the EPA's warning, stating that Alar posed no significant risk to public health, the NRDC reported in an ominous-sounding publication entitled *Intolerable Risk* that five out of every 20 000 children might eventually get cancer prior to their sixth birthday because of exposure to Alar. Soon after the issue appeared on a segment of the American television news show *60 Minutes* with a skull and crossbones overlaying an apple, everyone from consumer groups to apple growers was testing for the presence of Alar in apple products. "Am I killing my children by feeding them applesauce or applejuice?" became the pre-eminent question in many American parents' minds. Within months, the NRDC had reached its goal, and despite protests from apple growers, Uniroyal withdrew Alar from the market (Susskind and Field, 1996).

In health issues like the Alar case, the goal for activist groups is obvious – they can campaign for a product to be taken off the market or to be changed. Environmental and social issues are generally more difficult to link to a specific goal. In these two areas, single projects that are perceived to threaten the environment, or are socially unjust, can be targeted, but for a debate on general industry behaviour, it is difficult indeed for activist groups to target companies. This is also the reason why such groups often go for single-issue campaigns in environmental and social areas, thus attracting critics who blame these "one-sided" approaches.

In many cases, the main goal of environmental and social activists is to create awareness; the goal of solving a specific problem is only secondary. Still, there are some examples of campaigns with clear goals that go beyond creating awareness in the environmental and social areas. In the issue of animals rights, for example, the "Coalition for Consumer Information on Cosmetics" formed by nine animal rights groups launched in 1996 what it calls The Corporate Standard for Compassion for Animals, to standardise industry's claims regarding animal testing (mainly by pressuring suppliers to pledge that they will abandon animal testing of their ingredients). And in the environmental field we have mentioned already the success of Greenpeace in pushing the white goods industry to produce CFC-free refrigerator coolants. Still, goals such as "protect animal rights" and "save the ozone layer" are by their nature less specific and more difficult to control than product-specific goals.

In summary, activist groups know that they stand a higher chance of winning single issue campaigns with clear goals. Such clear goals are in scarce supply for activist groups. But if a company has somehow created a target and a goal for activist groups, it should be on the alert for danger.

2. The issue is easily understood by the general public

Most people are confronted daily by a vast number of messages, only a few of which will cut through the confusion and make an impression. These few messages are usually the ones that are plain and easy to understand.

Therefore, many activists prefer issues where they can point the finger clearly at "good guys" and especially "bad guys". It should be neither too technical nor abstract, and relatively free of complex details.

Take, for example, the 1996 case of racial discrimination at Texaco, where the discrimination was clearly proven by a secret tape that caught Texaco executives belittling blacks. In this case, the American public could easily see who the "bad guys" were and therefore relate to the issue. Later, Jesse Jackson, the leader of the National Rainbow/PUSH Coalition, called Texaco "the Mark Fuhrman of Corporate America" (referring to the detective in the O.J. Simpson criminal case who was accused of using racial epithets). The issue was plain enough to understand. On the other hand, many scientific discussions, like the recent one on endocrine mimicking, are simply too technical and too abstract and the "bad guy" is nowhere in sight – it is everybody and nobody. This level of abstraction produces a less attractive issue for activists.

Very technical issues, even when they do get attention, tend to be misunderstood, and, in addition, people often react to them in irrational ways. If companies could count on people consistently behaving in a rational way, they could predict public reactions easily by calculating the risk of negative effects of a certain action. From a technical perspective, risk is defined as the likelihood of a hazard occurring multiplied by the impact of the event. The impact of the hazard can be measured in terms of dollars, health impacts or lives lost. While this formula is theoretically correct for calculating risk, it has little to do with the way the public perceives risk, and is by no means an indicator of how the public will react to a certain issue. Some companies have nevertheless tried to predict issues by assessing risks involved with environmental and health issues. This turned out to be rather unhelpful from a public relations point of view, because what they calculated had little to do with what the public understood as risk.

Risk calculation in itself is a tricky and confusing business, even for the experts, and, realistically speaking, there are weaknesses in risk measurement methods. Just choosing the parameters by which to calculate the risk can lead to great frustration, as seemingly small differences cause large variances in the result. The examples below illustrate the extent of the problem.

- In the case of breast implants, the probability of an implant going awry was estimated in ranges from 0.2% to 35% (Susskind and Field, 1996). Reasons for these differences may be differing assumptions (different models of analysis), errors of omission (short-term versus long-term effects), unknown latent effects, subjective bias and the difference between animal studies versus human effects (Conservation Foundation, 1985).

- In a study on the risk of PCE, a solvent used in dry-cleaning, choices about the type of test animals to use (mice versus rats), the methodology of extrapolating results to humans by body surface or weight, and the selection of one dose–response model over another (linear or quadratic) can change the resulting risk assessment by a factor of 35 000.
- The US Nuclear Regulatory Commission estimated the risk of a core melt-down of a nuclear power plant in a range of 1:10 000 to 1 000 000 depending on the assumptions (Covello, 1991).

Given all these technical variables, activists obviously prefer to focus on easy-to-understand issues. The causes of a problem do not necessarily have to be easy to understand, but the effects should be clear for the average person.

Because the "man in the street" does not examine all of the scientific data surrounding an issue, activist groups can influence the public's risk perception through modifying, magnifying, and channelling public knowledge about possible effects. This is why they are sometimes accused of communicating their point of view selectively, by misusing scientific data, or by ignoring scientific arguments altogether. We can refer once again to the Brent Spar case.

A number of scientists were convinced that a deep sea disposal at the North Feni Ridge, where the Atlantic was more than 2000 m deep, was indeed the environmentally most sound solution. At that depth, contamination would neither enter the food chain nor cause other environmental harm. Shell UK had, for example, explicit assurance from geologists at the University of London that the sinking of a platform at such a depth would have no environmental impact. They pointed out that natural physical processes on the sea floor produced more dangerous substances than the whole of Brent Spar and its contents. The studies argued that the quantities of metals in the platform were very small compared with the releases from natural sources such as the Broken Spur hydrothermal vent field in the North Atlantic, which emitted between 500 000 and 5 million tons of different metals a year. Some scientists even suggested that "the bacteria of the ocean-floor would have greeted the arrival of Brent Spar as if all their Christmases had come at once." Many deep-sea microbes require heavy metals as electron or energy sources in their metabolisms.

Of course, there were also renowned scientists who took Greenpeace's position arguing that deep sea disposal would have more negative environmental effects than the land disposal option. But what really convinced the public that Shell was wrong was a simple argument that was easier to understand. The Greenpeace campaign director, Ulrich Jürgens commented: "I don't care about scientific arguments. I don't care if there are ten or a thousand tons of hazardous waste on the platform. The question is, how does our society cope with its waste? And our message is: don't litter!"

What About Difficult Issues?

When an issue is difficult to understand, some groups make use of the "customer segmentation" technique. They target their campaigns to a specific audience that will both understand the issue and be instrumental for the campaign's success. For example, the issue of genetically engineered wheat may be too technical for the general public; therefore, some activist groups begin their campaign with paediatricians who will then advise parents against feeding baby cereals containing genetically engineered wheat to their children.

One way for managers to weigh how understandable the issue might be to the public is to write an imaginary news headline about the issue from the activist group's point of view. If the headline is easy to phrase, the issue might impose a real danger. If the managers in some of our examples had done this, they might have had a better idea of what they were getting into: "Shell Dumps its Rubbish in the Sea" or "Nestlé: Babykiller". A headline like "Dow Chemical Contributes to Biodiversity Loss" just does not have the same impact. As a result, the Dow issue stands less of a chance of becoming "hot".

3. The issue has a high symbolic value

The power of symbols in management was recognised for the first time in the debate over corporate culture in the early 1980s (Deal and Kennedy, 1982). At that time, researchers and practitioners found that symbols can represent many of the hidden agendas in an organisation and show the culture in a visible form. Our research has shown that symbols have the same kind of importance for activists as well, being the visible parts of much wider concerns that they represent. An issue is symbolic if it represents a "picture" to the public that facilitates media communication and public involvement. For example, the Brent Spar platform was a symbol in itself that seemed to epitomise oil companies' lack of respect for the environment, tossing their junk into the sea.

Table 5.2 Selected industrial sector's public image for environmental consciousness. *Source: Environment USA.* Angus Reid Group, Toronto, Canada

Industry / Perception	Very careless (%)	A little careless (%)	A little careful (%)	Very careful (%)	Unsure (%)
Environmentally conscious sectors					
Gas and bottle industry	7	26	43	11	12
Electricity utilities	9	27	41	11	11
Banks and other financial institutions	9	24	34	9	24
Hospitals and health care facilities	14	29	37	12	8
Newspaper industry	11	32	36	7	14
Careless sectors					
Retail stores	11	33	32	4	20
Nuclear energy industry	22	28	27	14	9
Public transportation services	13	40	33	5	9
Quick service restaurants	21	35	34	5	5
Forestry and pulp and paper companies	20	36	28	7	9
Waste management industry	21	36	27	8	8
Automobile manufacturers	21	37	30	6	7
Cosmetic manufacturers	17	33	22	5	23
Packaged good industry	18	39	29	5	9
Environmentally dangerous sectors					
Mining industry	24	33	22	5	17
Agricultural chemical industry	23	39	25	5	8
Household cleaning product manufacturers	24	41	22	4	8
Plastic industry	31	38	21	3	7
Oil and gas companies	39	31	19	5	5
Chemical industry	34	37	18	4	6

Most activist groups make active use of symbols in their campaigns because they can be used to change society's overall value system. Finding and using symbols can create a "wake-up" effect for problems that have so far not been recognised. Symbols that are used in campaigns can generally represent "mistakes" of entire industries or single companies.

Some industries that have made very bad images for themselves can easily be used as symbolic opponents, while other industries are perceived in a more positive light. Table 5.2 shows some examples from the United States in the environmental field.

So any issues arising in industries that find themselves in the "Environmentally Dangerous Sectors" are much more likely to be seen publicly as symbols of general villainy.

A recent example of the power of symbols in a strongly exposed industry could be seen in 1996 in Germany, when the nuclear industry wanted to transport spent nuclear fuel to the Gorleben nuclear waste storage facility in special yellow containers called "castors". The dread-evoking containers and the fact that the nuclear waste was "escaping" its maximum security prison became powerful symbols for the German public's anti-nuclear feelings in general. The issue resulted in severe protests against the transport, mostly peaceful but also including sawing through railways, setting fire to signal boxes, toppling a power line and making bomb threats. Finally, the transport required a mobilisation of 30 000 policemen, the largest post-war operation in Germany.[2] In contrast, in France, transported nuclear waste is normally quietly escorted by two policemen as nuclear energy has less of a symbolic value in France.

An issue with high symbolic value that represents "mistakes" of single companies is the discussion surrounding fashion designers and fur. One of the strongest animal rights groups, People for the Ethical Treatment of Animals (PETA) generally tries to protect animals from being worn, eaten, experimented with or used for entertainment. They run general campaigns against eating meat or keeping pets. But their real successes were with the anti-fur campaign and the fight against animal testing in cosmetics firms. Furs are visible symbols of human conspicuous consumption. Even many meat-eaters disagree with the idea of killing small furry animals, or inflicting cruel experiments on them for reasons of human vanity and fashion. After fur sales reached a peak in the 1980s, animal rights activists were able severely to damage the business through their protests (see Case Study 4 in Chapter 7). Afterward, PETA continued its campaign only against designers that continued using fur, rather than the entire fashion industry.

In the absence of inherent symbols in the issues, activist groups may be able to "invent" symbols themselves. Greenpeace activists always wear their famous protection suits and goggles whenever they protest against toxic waste. In the Netherlands in 1996, Amnesty International published an advertisement showing a sheet of carbon paper separating two documents – a business contract with China and a death warrant – symbolising violations against humanity by suggesting that the signature on one implied, or would lead to, approval of the other. Other groups like to get children involved in their protests because they are seen as both highly sympathetic and as symbols of hope for the future.

In recent years, groups that historically did not focus on symbolic issues for their protests have begun to recognise the power of symbols in mobilising support for their struggle. In the United States, for example, even unions are changing the way they protest, moving away from general strikes and choosing symbolic actions or people to get their message across. One of the new heroes used as a symbol is the Latina housekeeper Margarita Salinas, who was fired from the New Otani Hotel in Los Angeles after she had worked there for 16 years. The reason: she and others were fighting for better wages, real job security, respect and affordable health care. In 1997, more than 2000 people protested in front of the hotel to get her hired again.

4. The issue has the potential to damage the image of the company

Corporate image, especially for large and well-known companies, is one of the most important assets to safeguard. Therefore, it is an ideal target for an activist group wishing to make such corporations into villains. For example, in 1996, Asea Brown Boveri (ABB) was commissioned by the Malaysian government to help in the construction of a dam in Malaysia (see Case Study 8 in Chapter 7). ABB was supposed to be the major outside contractor and responsible for the overall project management and supply of electrical equipment. However, the dam project has been condemned by many international activist groups as being socially destructive, environmentally disastrous and economically misconceived (for this reason it was eventually delayed indefinitely in September 1997). While some activist groups were trying to persuade the Malaysian government to scrap the project, it was ABB as the big, rich corporation that bore the brunt of the criticism. This was, of course, because ABB's image is much more vulnerable than the Malaysian government's. This was also recognised by ABB's Development Director, Richard Fenning:

> As long as domestic political and regulatory systems in emerging markets remain fluid, pressure groups will increasingly enforce some kind of corporate accountability on ethical issues (*Financial Times*, 14 January 1997).

Even though many firms that have been targeted by activist groups publicly report that their sales were not adversely affected, executives will often complain off the record of the damage the company suffered to its image. Once a company's image has been tarnished by one issue, the public will be even more distrustful of them the next time around. Multi-brand companies facing negative issues surrounding one product often experience negative consumer attitudes toward their other products as well. For example, Weinberger (1986) showed in a laboratory experiment that when people were given hypothetical information about health risks related to Budweiser beer, opinion of the company's related Michelob beer brand became negative as well.

While companies fear negative images among the public, there is also a less evident, but also powerful, effect – employee motivation and a company's ability to attract good employees. Employees who have a good image of their company take pride in working there, trust their future to it and assume that they will be treated fairly. Hiring highly qualified people is therefore easier, suppliers and subcontractors prefer to do business with a company that has a renowned reputation, and, of course, customers prefer to deal with it as a supplier. The opposite is true when a company's image has been destroyed. Employees may even be confronted socially: "You work for THAT company?"

A company's image can be damaged in two ways: first, as a result of its behaviour before the pressure campaign starts (the issue itself) and secondly, by its reactions and behaviour during the campaign. For example, Texaco's image was damaged because of the publicising of managers' racist statements. However, when activist groups began to attack the company, Texaco was wise enough to react quickly to resolve the problem. Only two weeks after the appearance of the issue, the company agreed to pay more than US$175 million in reparations over the next five years. In so doing, Texaco avoided further damage to its image in a long media war.

Shell did not take into consideration that activist groups take delight in strong retaliation by companies, some even trying to provoke a physically violent reaction, because it only helps to weaken further the image of the company. In the Brent Spar campaign, Shell's use of water canons to protect its platform from further Greenpeace attempts at boarding it only made Shell appear brutal, and the Greenpeace protesters gained the public's admiration for their bravery. Companies are expected by society to behave properly at all times, while public opinion seems to permit and even applaud a certain degree of roguishness on the part of activists.

Even in less dramatic instances, simple court actions against protesters can backfire severely for the company through adverse publicity. Many activist groups therefore welcome lawsuits by companies, because it shows that they are being taken seriously and creates public sympathy. In the Nestlé infant formula case, the company filed a lawsuit against the Third World Action Group for translating into German and reprinting the new paper article entitled "Nestlé: Baby Killer". Even though Nestlé won the suit, its image only worsened, giving the impression of a huge corporation bullying a small social welfare organisation.

Another well-known case is that of McDonald's, who took an organisation called London Greenpeace (not affiliated with THE Greenpeace) to court in 1985, when London Greenpeace distributed leaflets entitled "What's Wrong with McDonald's". The leaflet criticised the famous burger chain on the grounds of diet and ill-health, animal welfare, environmental damage, its exploitation of children through advertising and of employees through low pay. McDonald's identified five members of the group who had helped to distribute the leaflets. Three apologised, but the other two, a bartender and an unemployed postman, chose instead to defend themselves against the charges. Despite their lack of legal training, the two managed to keep the American super-corporation's lawyers busy for a record 314 days at the High Court and a final judgement in favour of McDonald's was made only in June 1997. McDonald's won a US$98 000 libel award (which the two activists will probably not be able to pay) in a case that it spent roughly US$16 million to pursue. If McDonald's had not taken this action, the pamphlet would probably have been skimmed over by a few hundred people in London instead of now attracting world-wide attention. David Morris, the unemployed postman, related to a newspaper: "It doesn't matter what the verdict is because we've already won."

These two examples show that even "slap" lawsuits, which a company may bring against an activist group with the sole intention of draining the group's resources (time, money, momentum, etc.) and to intimidate opposition, may backfire.

Which Companies are the Preferred Targets?

Activists naturally prefer to attack companies that have high-profile images. Therefore, consumer companies that are well known to the general public are preferred targets for campaigns. Badges of success – brand names like BMW, Chanel and Shell – automatically attract a high level of attention and groups know they stand a chance of gaining consumer allies in their campaign. Once the negative spotlight turns on a popular brand, years of painstaking image-building can be destroyed. Companies that have popular brands are living in a glass house, and should be well aware of the danger that comes with the territory. In the just-mentioned McDonald's lawsuit, one of the activists argued in an interview: "McDonald's spends US$1.5 billion a year on advertising. We think people should have an opportunity to hear the other side."

Sometimes, activists use one strong brand as a target for an issue that has nothing to do with the company. This happened in 1997 to Burger King in New Zealand. The country's anti-smoking lobbyists encouraged consumers to boycott the restaurant chain, which had put up large posters depicting James Dean smoking a cigarette, arguing that the practice encouraged smoking, especially in teenagers. Obviously, Burger King's objective was not to promote cigarettes. It declared that the boycott was ludicrous and merely a publicity stunt by the lobby group, desperate for any popular brand to target as a symbolic opponent. New Zealand Burger King's Director of Marketing complained: "We have Marilyn who died of a drug overdose, James Dean smoking and Elvis who died of whatever. Where does all this stop?"

However, a recent poll by Walker Information (Indianapolis, Indiana, USA) reflects consumers' feelings and actions in the United States and may serve as a good warning sign for the importance of social issues on the image and sales of a company.

- Seventy-eight percent of all consumers are currently avoiding or refusing to buy from certain businesses because of negative perceptions about them. These include both organised boycotts and individual refusals to buy.
- Of that number, 48% said that unethical or unlawful business practices play a significant role in determining their decisions.
- Forty-seven percent indicated they would be much more likely to buy from a company that is socially responsible and a good corporate citizen if the quality, service and price were equal to that of competitors.
- A growing group – 16% – said they actively seek information about a company's business practices before purchasing.

This survey shows that consumers are consciously making choices about companies from which they will buy, which also explains the recent success of companies such as Body Shop and Patagonia, which are considered best-practice examples of socially responsible companies. Consumer guides, which provide information on products made by companies whose policies and practices are deemed ethical by the organisations that publish the directories, are widely available today: for example, *Shopping for a Better World* from the Sierra Club and/or the Council on Economic Priorities (CEP). On the basis of these information sources, customers can not only find out which company makes which products, but they can also examine at a glance the parent company's social record. *Shopping for a Better World* "grades" each company (using the US school system's A–F scale) on each of the following eight major areas of corporate responsibility: *environmental performance; charitable giving; community outreach; advancement of women; advancement of minorities; family benefits; workplace issues;* and *disclosure of information.*

Even if a company is not considered a consumer goods company with a popular brand name, some activist groups may try to get at the company through any related brand they can find. For example, in the US–Vietnam war, the most symbolic product that protesters could find to target was Napalm. Obviously, a large-scale consumer boycott on Napalm would not have much effect on its producer, Dow Chemical, so the activist groups encouraged consumers to hurt the company by boycotting another product for which Dow contributed only the raw materials – Saran Wrap (the most widely used plastic food wrapping in the United States).

Intel faced a similar problem. After heavy marketing efforts, the company was able to shift its product from a commodity to a consumer goods brand. With its famous "Intel Inside" campaign, the company had begun marketing its semiconductors increasingly as consumer products. Consequently, the market had come to expect Intel to behave like a consumer products company. But when, in 1994, Intel refused to exchange the flawed Pentium processors against new ones, its behaviour resembled more that of an original equipment manufacturer that is unconcerned with end users. Because it now had a famous brand name, it was consequently easy for the computer community to damage Intel's image.

Logically, companies that produce only industrial products or commodities with no generally recognisable brand name are to a certain extent safe from public image attacks through the consumer transmission belt. Still, these companies have a vested interest in staying on good terms with the government, as politicians are often their key "customers"; for example, when it comes to purchasing decisions on infrastructure or energy projects – and politicians are, of course, influenced by the opinions of their voters.

5. The opponent is strong enough (no "underdog" effect)

Activist groups like to engage with strong opponents so that they can position themselves as righteous Davids against corporate Goliaths. The group may spur on the public with an underlying envy argument: "Look at this company. Not only are they taking all our money, but now they are harming the environment/health/ social rights." Of course, activists can attract more attention for their causes by attacking big and famous companies rather than small businesses or end users.

The Rainforest Action Network (RAN) is currently spearhead- ing a broad international coalition of organisations to boycott Mitsubishi and its subsidiaries until the company stops logging or purchasing timber or timber products from operations harming the environment or native communities (see also Case Study 5 in Chapter 7). The Mitsubishi Group is a great adversary, consisting of 190 interlinked companies, and hundreds of related firms, which together form the world's largest industrial and financial empire. Among these companies are the Mitsubishi Corporation, Mitsubishi Bank, Mitsubishi Heavy Industries, Mitsubishi Elec- tronics, Mitsubishi Motors, Kirin Beer and Nippon Kogaku (maker of Nikon camera equipment).

Activist groups usually refrain from attacking "weak" com- panies, because this could cause an "underdog" effect. In such a case, the public may change sides and argue in favour of the company, which they see as having enough problems to deal with already, without being hassled by activists in addition.

Most groups especially try to avoid attacking companies where a high number of jobs are at stake. In many European countries, the problem of job security is uppermost in the public mind, and public opinion could turn against the activists if job losses are threatened. The Ruhrkohle company, Germany's leading coal ex- ploration company, operates in regions with high unemployment rates and relies heavily on government subsidies. Despite the many ecological disadvantages of coal, no environmentalists dare to pick a fight with Ruhrkohle. The North Rhine–Westphalia state's government, in which the Green party is part of the coali- tion, seems to treat the endangered company with kid gloves and has even agreed to raise its subsidies. So, while serious financial problems may be uncomfortable, at least managers can console themselves that there probably will not be any major environmen- tal groups knocking down their doors for a while: "For envy one has to work, compassion, one can get for free."

This last statement does not apply to pressure in the form of liability suits. Here, people are looking for personal recompense and do not care about the company's balance sheet. These cases tend to be individual ones, and activist groups normally play a less important role. Dow Corning, a joint venture between Dow Chemical and Corning, produced breast implants. Problems found with their product included the implants falling apart in the body, dead tissue in the nipple area, contracting of skin around the implant, infections, chronic pain and implant leakage. As a result, 44 000 US women brought a class-action suit against Dow Corning for over US$4 billion.[3] In 1995, Dow Corning declared Chapter 11 bankruptcy, which has allowed it to continue operating. However, if Dow Corning loses in court, it will be wiped out completely.

6. The issue can be "packaged" in a campaign in which the public can get involved

Activist groups have become highly sophisticated in their ability to package stories. Interesting campaigns contain a combination of several characteristics – possibility for physical action rather than scientific discussion, symbolic fights and a visual and attackable adversary. Such campaigns are more likely to inspire public involvement. Groups prefer issues in which their contact with the public is not restricted to simply informing the world of the presence of the issue, but where they are able to enlist public involvement in stopping or solving the issue. The easiest and most obvious is through the customer transmission belt with a consumer boycott. Large numbers of people can easily and almost passively participate simply by not buying the product of the company in question or substituting a product category in general. It has become the most widely used form of getting the public involved in an issue.

However, as activists have to compete like everyone else for public attention, they need somehow to differentiate themselves from the other activist groups and try, where possible, to initiate creative or more active ways for the public to get involved in a campaign. Protesting on the street, being invited to a forum, or even writing a letter to the chairman of a company or an important politician can be stimulating life experiences, and activists attract this kind of commitment from people on the issue in question.

Activist groups can even use the public to offer the company a "carrot" rather than threaten with the "stick" on an issue. There are cases where these groups have induced large parts of the population to accept paying higher prices in exchange for a company's agreement to improve its social/environmental/health issues.

One good example of this is the case of the "Five cents more" campaign of the American union organisation AFL-CIO. The union asked consumers to "Please tell your grocer to support strawberry workers' basic rights." Apparently, many consumers did this and even agreed to pay five cents more per basket, with instructions to use the extra profit toward strawberry workers' rights, including a living wage, health insurance and clean drinking water and toilets in the fields. As a result, the living conditions of the farm workers improved significantly.

Some campaigns are too difficult or complex for general public participation. An example is the debate on endocrine mimicking, which focuses on the question of how far chemicals, such as those found in a variety of products like plastic packaging, fertilisers, etc. are threatening mankind through massively disturbing reproductive cycles. In this case, it is difficult to pinpoint blame on a single chemical, and there are just too many products and companies involved to organise any sort of consumer or other public action.

The level of public involvement an activist group is able to galvanise also depends largely on its talent for motivating people. Some of them purposefully drive an almost overly-aggressive campaign to attract attention and gain popular involvement. For example, People for the Ethical Treatment of Animals (PETA) spokesman Michael McGraw argues in favour of the organisation's aggressive, or sensational, approaches to public relations, saying that we live today in a tabloid age where things have to be sensational and flamboyant to get people involved. To attract people to the animal rights issue and to encourage them to write protest letters, the group launched, for example, in March 1995, an advertising campaign against fur-coat designer Karl Lagerfeld and celebrities well known for their fur coats and mink stoles. Parodies of Lagerfeld, Sophia Loren, Ivana Trump and Catherine Deneuve appeared as fashion dinosaurs in PETA's "Furassic Park" advertisement. Additionally, the group encouraged famous top models to participate in the campaign: "We'd rather go naked than wear fur." And, in order to discourage people from eating meat, PETA is now running a vegetarian campaign with a mascot called Chris Carrot. This person visits elementary schools in the United States and Europe, giving children buttons that ask them to eat their veggies – not their friends. If the message gets through to the children, they might influence their parents to cook with less meat and in the long run they might decide for themselves to reduce their meat consumption or even become vegetarian. These methods of imposing the group's morals on the population certainly spark discussion and often do get people directly involved.

7. There are solutions that are confrontational, not gradual (political concepts, management concepts, product or process concepts that are competitive in price and quality)

We have mentioned before that activists prefer to attack on issues for which they have a clear goal. However, this does not necessarily mean that society shares the same goal. It may very well be that society on the whole is averse to this goal because it would mean a certain loss of personal comfort. For example, people could do a lot of good for the environment simply by reducing their meat consumption. But this solution is unattractive to most people and the chances for success in any major "Eat Less Meat to Save the Earth" campaign would be marginal.

Activists, therefore, try to provide attractive, publicly acceptable solutions for the problems that they are attacking. They are realising more and more that they have to become part of the solution instead of just pointing the finger at the problem, knowing, however, that a perfect solution does not always exist. For example, in energy supply, not only are fossil fuels and nuclear power widely criticised, but even the "clean" alternatives that have been promoted by environmental organisations have come under criticism: in California and Wales, wind turbines are accused of having killed birds, wave machines are said to disrupt marine habitats and hydro-energy is destroying valuable landscape. As Chris Rose, the Brent Spar Campaign Director of Greenpeace UK puts it:

We have to move from being hunters, hunting out and spotlighting problems, to becoming farmers, nurturing solutions (*The Times*, 27 September 1996).

Most groups, however, are not looking for gradual solutions that involve changing habits, processes or products incrementally over time, but prefer, instead, confrontational solutions. Means for reaching these solutions could be political concepts, such as energy taxes, management concepts, such as the introduction of a committee that reviews a company's equal opportunities employment policy or even alternative product and process concepts.

One example of this search for solutions is the case of the "SmILE" car designed by Greenpeace. Many people today are aware of the environmental problems caused by cars. The transport sector is responsible for 22% of the world's greenhouse gas emissions, and the 500 million cars world-wide contribute 80% of this. However, to date no activist group has succeeded in reducing automobile traffic even marginally. Even in environmentally sensitive countries like Germany or the Netherlands, people will continue to prefer their cars because they do not see viable alternatives. Arguments in favour of more environmentally friendly public transport do not have much effect because this alternative is seen by many as a gross inconvenience. Citizens are still not ready to give up their cars.

Greenpeace set out to prove that while we cannot convince people to give up their cars, automobile manufacturers could at least make cars that pollute less. To prove that automobile companies have failed to take even the first steps toward the production of more environmentally sound vehicles, Greenpeace designed and built an eco-efficient car themselves. The SmILE is a modified Renault Twingo, which is almost 50% more energy-efficient than its conventional counterpart and other cars of similar size. SmILE stands for "Small, Intelligent, Light, Efficient" and describes the car of the future according to Greenpeace: light, compact, efficient and intelligently built. The modifications were done by a Swiss engineering company and financed by Greenpeace. According to Greenpeace, the SmILE confronts the automobile industry's denials that halving petrol consumption is feasible.

Many groups are unconcerned with finding solutions for their adversaries because their level of critique is fundamental. Internally, Greenpeace had problems with its more fundamentalist activists for trying to come up with the SmILE solution, who argued that the SmILE is still not totally clean, healthy and environmentally benign. So the official view of the group is that the SmILE is not a solution in itself, but serves merely to prove that automobile petrol consumption can be cut in half with contemporary technology.

Managers should ask themselves whether their adversaries might be able to offer solutions that are acceptable to the general public. In such a case, the chances for coming under strong pressure to adopt these suggestions will be high. Likewise, some groups may drop an issue, because they cannot come up with a better solution themselves. However, managers should not rely on the lack of a viable alternative as an argument to force a group to back down, because activists reply, "Coming up with a solution is your problem, not ours."

Solutions, of course, are relative, and depend on one's point of view. In the controversy over ABB's involvement in the Bakun dam project, ABB argued that pulling out of the project was not a solution because another company would pick up on it anyway. One manager stated:

> ABB's involvement in the project is even preferable to the involvement of other companies, because their environmental, health and social practices are inferior to ours.

Even though managers may believe sincerely in the "if we don't do it, someone else will" argument, an activist group may see the situation very differently. For them, the solution is to harass the first company and, if they manage to turn it away, to harass the second company that takes its place, and so on until no company wants to be involved in the issue. So, even if from the point of view of the company there is no solution, this might not be the case from the activist point of view.

8. There could be a dramatic element to the campaign to engage the media

Media coverage is essential to a successful activist campaign, but the media already receive more information than they can use. Unless groups can bring dramatic elements into their campaign, they will not have a chance of making the headlines.

Using the attention-getting "striptease method", groups sometimes present the situation in small doses and with each dose the media has something new to report. They do not give away everything they know all at once. Like theatre, public interest builds slowly until a climax is reached. Therefore, if possible, many activists employ "escalation steps" in their campaigns for dramatic effect. For example, they may start a campaign with scientific discussion, which then builds in intensity and plays more and more on emotions, with a few action elements thrown in for effect.

Take again, for example, RAN in its battle against Mitsubishi. In May 1993, RAN launched a dramatic advertising campaign in the United States with a full-page advertisement in the *New York Times*. As the next step in the escalation, they encouraged supporters to send telegrams and letters to the prime minister of Japan, the president of Mitsubishi Corporation and the premier of Alberta. Then, to increase the drama, RAN produced a 20-minute video showing Mitsubishi slashing away at rainforest growth and hauling off precious rainforest wood. To gain allies and keep media interest high, the group then launched an intensive campaign to get other environmental groups to join forces with them against Mitsubishi. Finally, the group distributed powerful brochures denouncing Mitsubishi's rainforest activity to high school and college students in the United States and Japan.

Activist groups are well aware that dramatic elements cannot always be planned in advance, and they hope that they do not have to contribute all the drama themselves. They count on provoking their opponents to "bite back" in order to add to the drama. As Thilo Bode, the Director of Greenpeace International, reflected after the Brent Spar campaign, "Every time we were stuck and didn't know what to do next to keep interest high, Shell helped us."

No matter how the drama is created, when there is potential for it, the probability that an activist group will get involved is higher.

SUMMARY

An activist issue that fulfils a majority of the points of the Checklist will almost certainly attract the attention of at least one group, and this group will try somehow to build a campaign around the issue. As a result, if an issue can be identified with the company's checklist as potentially "hot", and a majority of the above-mentioned checklist items are true as well, then the company is potentially facing severe problems and should immediately develop an action plan.

We are not implying that companies should only behave responsibly when they fear confrontation. But if a company is convinced that it has given social, environmental and health concerns every possible consideration, believes it has come up with an acceptable decision, and analysis shows that there is still a high risk of running into strong opposition, then contingency planning for responsive action is justified.

The usefulness of the activist checklist can be seen, for example, in the Shell Brent Spar case. The eight checklist items show why Shell was so strongly affected by the Brent Spar incident. If Shell had used this checklist, it might have foreseen that its platform was an ideal target for Greenpeace, and that Greenpeace stood a high chance of coming out as the victor in the campaign. And Shell would have been able to see from Greenpeace's point of view what Thilo Bode later said: "Something as good as the Brent Spar won't come again soon."

1. The clear goal of the campaign was to prevent deep sea disposal of the platform. Even if Greenpeace was unsure whether they would accomplish this goal, they were quite positive that they could at least spark serious debate on the practice of deep-sea platform disposal.
2. The public was able to understand that dumping 14 000 tons of steel into the sea (an equivalent of 6000 cars) is not necessarily environmentally friendly. The Greenpeace message that Shell was in effect "littering" was easy to get across to the public.
3. The huge platform was a strong symbol, as were the water cannons and the physical struggles for control of the platform.
4. Shell is a well-known consumer brand with a high-profile image. It is vulnerable to boycotts. The public perception that Shell brutalised Greenpeace during the campaign and that it was insensitive to the environment took its toll on Shell's image.
5. Shell is one of the largest companies in the world and is the most profitable; hence, it is the ideal "strong" opponent. In

the year before the campaign the company had a mammoth turnover of US$116 billion with earnings of US$6.3 billion.

6. Greenpeace was able to package the campaign for the media in a way that would encourage public involvement: occupying and freeing the platform, vessels following the Spar, helicopter attacks, etc. inspired the public to boycott Shell stations, organise protests, write letters, etc.

7. From Greenpeace's point of view, the "solution" was a simple one; namely, not to dump the platform. They also suggested alternatives to deep disposal, with Shell retorting that these were not satisfactory alternatives.

8. The campaign was chock-full of dramatic elements – the surprise occupation, the water cannons, the struggles, Greenpeace's daredevil at-sea harassment techniques, the protests at Shell service stations, etc.

A visualisation of these eight points can be reached by using a rating table. For the Brent Spar case this might have looked as in Table 5.3.

Table 5.3 Visualised activist checklist

Assessment criteria	Rating					Comments
	++	+	0	–	––	
Clear aim or goal	●					Stop sea disposal.
Understandable by public	●					Platform is equivalent of 6000 cars.
Symbolic	●					Platform, water cannons, physical struggles.
Image can be damaged	●					Shell acted brutally, Shell is consumer brand.
Strong opponent	●					Shell is the most profitable company in the world.
Public can get involved	●					Public can boycott Shell stations.
Confrontational solution	●					Land disposal.
Dramatic elements	●					Occupation, struggle, water cannons.

| Overall assessment | ● | | | | | Perfect object for outside pressure campaign. |

On the other hand, these checklist points explain also why the pollution of an aquifer in Turkey by Shell was not a suitable target for the Greenpeace campaign, even though the very same opponents were involved. Greenpeace accused Shell of systematically polluting a huge underground reserve of potential drinking water between 1973 and 1994 in an aquifer near the city of Diyarbakir in Southeast Turkey where two million people live. Greenpeace criticised Shell as having double standards and non-existent ethics. But as the company had already ceased these practices, Greenpeace's campaign was only focusing on past sins. In addition, Shell had sold the exploration company in Turkey to the international firm Perenco in 1994 and kept only its stake in a refinery. The public could not get involved in the campaign and there were no real dramatic elements. Therefore, the debate never really got much attention.

Identifying Different Activist Groups

As we stated at the beginning of this chapter, each activist group has its own priorities by which it evaluates and prioritises issues, and there is a marked difference according to the type of group – *shark*, *sealion*, *orca* or *dolphin*. The checklist presented here reflects the current direction that most groups now seem to be taking (orca and dolphin-type behaviour) and can be adjusted to a specific case. Managers may well be confronted by groups who evaluate issues differently from the way we have done. For example, some do not require public involvement, preferring instead legislative lobbying tactics.

Managers can also benefit from taking the activist checklist a step further by looking at issues from the point of view of the activist groups' stakeholders. By understanding the external environment of the activist groups, managers can even better understand their rationality. For example, a company in the food industry might try to understand the rationale of the financial donors to PETA. What do they expect from PETA and what do they want in return for their donations? For what reasons do they give their support? The answers to these questions might be valuable guidelines for evaluating possible issues in which the group might get involved.

Checklists as Tools

The discussion of the use of the company and activist checklists for increasing strategic awareness of activists' issues has shown that there are a number of tools that can indeed be helpful for managers in order to predict approaching conflicts. It should be remembered that these tools are only a support for managers and are not meant to replace their judgement, expertise and knowledge of their industry and its broader environment.

In the last two chapters we have described the relevant characteristics that define whether an issue might become a serious threat. But if such issues are too numerous and a company has to track too many of them, managers might feel overwhelmed by their sheer variety and therefore be unsure about how to track all of them. In the next chapter we present a way to track developments systematically so that managers are informed at an early stage about possible threats.

Notes

1. Of course, in the case of organisations that have only one purpose related to a single issue, the question cannot arise as to why they pursue this issue. But in this case the checklist can be used by companies to work out which form of campaign might be the most promising one to the activist group.
2. In 1996, one state alone, Lower Saxony, paid DM 46 million (US$27.3 million) for the protection of one Castor container transported by rail and road to Gorleben. The state is now trying to get a reimbursement from the nuclear power industry.
3. A class-action suit is filed by one or more individuals on behalf of a group of plaintiffs who have a common cause of action against the same defendant. A class-action suit facilitates a fair trial because the legal issue is decided by one court and then the decision is applied to all cases, thus avoiding inconsistencies in the legal system.

6
The Checklists Applied: Early Awareness Systems

If a company decides to apply our methodology and regularly scans its environment for possible controversies, one option is to track these issues systematically using an early awareness system. These systems are most likely to be based on a company's existing information technology network.

Computerised scanning systems are not new; most originated in military environments, such as the Airborne Warning and Control System (AWAC) used in Bosnia and other regions. In medicine, computerised early awareness systems are used to detect cancer, and, in national economies, scientists use systems of "leading indicators" to forecast ups and downs in economic cycles. The Food and Agriculture Organisation (FAO) of the United Nations runs the "Global Information and Early Warning System on Food and Agriculture", which aims to provide policy-makers and policy analysts with the most up-to-date information available on all aspects of food supply and demand. Earthquake warning systems are currently under development hoping to provide information on when the next major shock will occur, and surface currents of the sea are calculated by some researchers using circulation models to predict the paths of icebergs and warn ships.

These systems have two characteristics in common: first, they do not require an unassailable chain of scientific evidence before a recommendation is made or an action taken. What counts in scanning is not established causality, but the plausibility of the findings. Waiting until the danger is confirmed beyond the shadow of a doubt means that in all likelihood disaster already will have struck. The second characteristic is that all of these information systems require a capacity for large databases in order to produce meaningful information. Therefore, they can most effectively be run with the support of computers.

All awareness systems (computerised or not) can be classified as aiming for either operational or strategic awareness, depending on the object and the time dimension. The difference between the two is that in the case of operational early awareness the potential identified through strategic awareness already has turned into reality. In the military, for example, strategic early awareness wants to know the number and types of enemy weapons before they are even in the arsenal. Operational early awareness systems, on the other hand, evaluate risks that are known already in principle, but where details are still missing (e.g. precise enemy troop movements). In medicine, strategic awareness of cancer probabilities may be achieved by screening genes, and operational awareness by looking at a patient's skin.

WHAT MIGHT EARLY AWARENESS SYSTEMS FOR BUSINESS LOOK LIKE?

In general, they can be described as a special application of existing information systems that, by providing early indicators, draw attention to approaching opportunities and risks, whose significance has not yet been commonly recognised. They can help a company to stay on track operationally and strategically by taking timely and appropriate action.

Examples of operational early awareness systems in business include tracking current stock, incoming orders, sales and market shares, etc. Strategic early awareness systems, on the other hand, observe long-term developments (interest rates, general consumption patterns, consumer attitudes, etc.) that influence a company's long-term strategy. They support managers in scanning and monitoring their general business environment. Since activist groups belong to the contextual environment of an organisation, and can influence the company's future without being involved in direct business relations or transactions, monitoring of these groups clearly should be part of the scanning process.

Strategic early awareness scanning requires computer support just as much as operational early awareness systems that trace stock or incoming orders. A corporate headquarters can only with difficulty stay on top of all possible developments in all of its different operating countries and connect all information from all different business units and all different markets at any time. So, in the world of business there is a growing need for computer support in strategic early awareness.

How might strategic scanning systems support managers in their task of anticipating activist group demands, when pressure on companies can come from very different sources? And how can managers make sure that all relevant information for the checklists is collected on a regular basis and not only when the issue has already crossed the threshold of public attention?

Computerised early awareness systems need to help managers to collect and aggregate data in a systematic way. Even if data collection sources are decentralised, sensors must distribute the processed data to any managers who might need it. The tasks of such a system can therefore be divided into data collection and transfer, information processing and information distribution.

DATA COLLECTION AND TRANSFER

Data collection for early awareness of developments in a company's business environment can take place using five different information sources. First, employees may enter data "by hand". In this case, people at the peripheral elements scan the information environment in their special area of expertise, which might be customer groups or scientific fields, for example. Observations of interest to the company are, in the former case, entered into the system; for example, sales managers enter information referring to customer attitudes.

Secondly, data can be collected through the monitoring of press agencies and information services (e.g. Reuters) by using key words to sort out the topics of interest for them.

A third source may be specialised databases, i.e. scientific databases for the newest research findings or legal databases for court decisions. Similarly, by using search engines (AltaVista, Webcrawler, Yahoo, etc.), managers can scan the Internet for key words on topics that might be important for the company. Internet chat or newsgroups on certain topics can also help to discern public attitudes.

Finally, company internal information sources provide valuable information. Customer information systems of consumer goods companies, based on toll-free 800 numbers, where companies like Coca-Cola monitor consumer attitudes, provide feedback on issues ranging from product quality to the noise of automatic vending machines. Such systems often do reveal important signals at a very early stage. Complaints and questions from consumers may contain valuable information about developments in the company's business environment.

Once data are entered, they have to be communicated in order to be combined usefully with other data. This communication can take place at the corporation's headquarters, through the

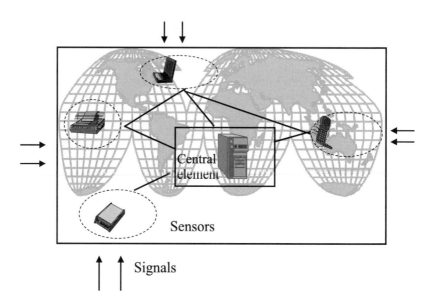

Figure 6.1 Data collection and transfer in a computerised early awareness system

company's own network (e.g. an Intranet)[1] or using public networks like the Internet. This basic design philosophy of the data collection and transfer is represented in Figure 6.1.

INFORMATION PROCESSING

Once the data have been communicated to the organisation, they have to be checked, aggregated and stored. This check includes a review of the logical consistency, a sorting procedure by which the data are assigned to certain issues and storage in databases. Groupware programs may help managers to structure the incoming data, as in Box 6.1.

Any central database should facilitate flexible queries such as a full-text search (to find all data related to one issue), queries on attributes (key activist groups, time distribution, media, etc.) and trend reports. To provide managers with trend reports, the system should be able to calculate, for example, distribution functions for

---

Issue: ENDOCRINE DISRUPTORS – SCIENTIFIC FINDINGS
Title: AGGREGATE EXPOSURE, ENDOCRINE DISRUPTORS
            KEY PIECES OF EPA-OPP SCIENCE AGENDA FOR 1997.
Date: 27/1/97
Source: FOOD CHEMICAL NEWS
Key words: Pesticides, EPA OPP, Endocrine disrupting assessment
Full text:

Assessing risks from aggregate exposures to pesticides, estimating the endocrine-disrupting potential of both active and inert pesticide ingredients and developing a multidimensional risk assessment process "will be keeping us [EPA's Office of Pesticide Programs] busy" in 1997, EPA OPP Deputy Director Penny Fenner-Crisp told the executive committee of the agency's Science Advisory Board Jan. 15. The deputy director laid out OPP's science agenda to SAB at last week's meeting, asking them for help and recommendations. Because the Food Quality Protection Act requires that all 9300 existing tolerances and exemptions from tolerances be reassessed by Aug. 3, 2006, with 33% due by August 1999, another 33% due by August 2002 and the remainder in 2006, OPP will have to work very hard to complete the reevaluation process on time, Fenner-Crisp said. One SAB member pointed out that the agency would literally "have to approve two to three tolerances every single day of the year" in order to meet the deadlines. (. . .)

Box 6.1

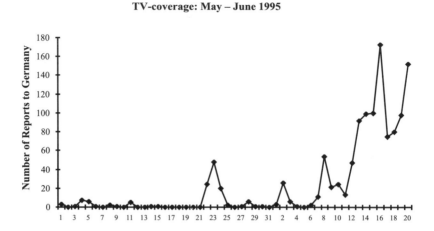

Figure 6.2 Possible information processing result in a computerised early awareness system

factors like media coverage of various controversies. An example of this is shown in Figure 6.2.

INFORMATION DISTRIBUTION

Information distribution can take place in a pull or a push form. In a pull system managers have to access the information system themselves and pull data of interest out of the system. Examples of these kind of systems are Intranets or groupware programs.

In a push system, managers get the information that is relevant to them in an automatic form. They might, for example, get a daily update on an issue in which they are involved through e-mail. To build such a system, the central processing unit has to possess user profiles that identify user interests.

EXAMPLES OF COMPUTERISED EARLY AWARENESS SYSTEMS

A number of companies are already successfully running computerised early awareness systems.

Ciba/Novartis

One excellent example is a system developed by the Swiss chemical company Ciba under the name Issue Support & Advocacy Network (ISAN), which can now be found at Novartis (a merger of Ciba and Sandoz). This system links the Novartis operations in 60 countries. ISAN has two "scouts" in each of the operating countries, who scan their information environment carefully for weak signals on potential activist issues. These staff members usually belong to the communication, environment and safety or legal departments. When they identify a development that might be of importance to the company (a risk or an opportunity), they access a Lotus Notes database, which connects all Novartis facilities world-wide, write a full-text description of this early awareness signal and sort the issue into different categories. The template for signal description contains the following fields.

1. What is the issue?
2. Who is affected (internally/externally)?
3. Who has discovered the issue?
4. When did the signals appear?
5. Where did the signals appear?
6. Why can it become an issue relevant for Novartis?

In addition to the country organisations, the different Novartis divisions at headquarters add information to this database, and an automatic wire monitoring of all international press agencies and review of Internet pages through key word searches completes the selection. A group of managers in corporate headquarters regularly accesses the database. These managers make a qualitative as well as a quantitative analysis of the possible impacts using a checklist tailored to their specific needs.

If the managers in the headquarters believe that certain signals might cause an issue to "take off", the group identifies the responsible line unit, who is the "issue-owner" and informs them. A very important decision for every activist issue within this process is whether the issue is considered to be local or corporate. Local issues are limited to single countries in which Novartis is operating. They achieve the status of a global issue whenever there is a risk that Novartis' reputation could be damaged. In this case, issues are handled by the headquarters in Basle.

One case where the company put its ISAN-system to good use occurred when Ciba moved the production site for one of its eye care products from the United States to Indonesia. Through information that had been scanned into their early awareness system, Ciba found a risk – that sales of the products in Portugal might provoke strong stakeholder opposition. Portugal has been waging a political battle with Indonesia since 1976, when Indonesia occupied the Portuguese enclave of Timor. The occupation was unrecognised by the United Nations, but Indonesia still occupies Timor, which continues to be a sore point between the two nations. Naturally, if it were to sell Indonesian-manufactured products in the Portuguese market, Ciba's image would be endangered, possibly leading to a complete national boycott of all Ciba products. So Ciba planned for eye-care products to be delivered to Portugal from another production site. In theory, this connection could, of course, have been made without a special computer system. But in actual practice, given the number of possible cases and links (it is not obvious to think about Portugal when evaluating a production site change to Indonesia), an automated early awareness system facilitates this tracking of stakeholder issues significantly, and increases the chances of catching the less obvious danger signals early on. It is very difficult for a central unit to perform effective crisis prevention without fast access to information.

In addition, the ISAN system helps in the analysis of the information acquisition behaviour of key stakeholders, because it contains information about all persons who have ever been in contact with Novartis. Whenever somebody makes an information request, the name and the request are stored. ISAN also includes information on journalists, authorities and politicians and on every question that Novartis has ever been asked in any of their country organisations.

With this complete information support, Novartis can handle issues early in the game. They are able to identify issues in time, make better informed decisions and ensure that the source of information for the media and authorities is the company itself and not the activist group. At Novartis, the corporate communications department has prepared question-and-answer sheets and

2000 position papers for pre-crisis communication on almost any emerging issue. At the moment, ISAN is still a pull system, but, in a later stage, Novartis is planning to build up an automatic e-mail system that will ensure that line managers in every division receive early awareness information in their field of responsibility by routing this information automatically to them every morning.

Dow Chemical

A system similar to that of Novartis is currently under development at Dow Chemical. The company is going to use its worldwide Intranet system as a technical platform for a corporate early awareness system. Dow Chemical is using this system to identify, store, distribute and evaluate information on current activist issues such as the discussions on breast implants (Dow Chemical is 50% owner of Dow Corning, one of the major producers of breast implants), chlorine chemicals and endocrine disruptives. Besides their Intranet (pull system) Dow Chemical is also using e-mail for an information distribution to selected managers (push system). However, the Intranet at Dow has a less external orientation than the system at Novartis, as the data tend to be presented in a "scientific" way, showing the latest research findings. It is less concerned with evaluating the reaction of stakeholders on activist issues.

Eurochlor

Eurochlor, the industry association of the European chlorine industry, has started a pilot project for an early warning system named "Co-ordinated Orbital Monitoring Programme Alarm Security System" (COMPASS).[2] The objective of this system is to evaluate ecologically pertinent findings on the (chlorine) industry at the preliminary stage of scientific, public and political discussion. The purpose of the data evaluation within the system is an early recognition of risks from aspects of eco-toxicology and human medicine, so that measures to control environmentally relevant exposures can be taken. The evaluation of issues is being done using scientific methods. The view of the assessment within the system is, however, not the review of certain chemicals, but the eco-systematic changes in the environment and the effects on human health. The technical character of the COMPASS system can be seen when we look at the sources of information used:

1. global networks of experts, consisting of scientists;
2. databases;
3. managers from various industries; in particular, the chemical industry;
4. public authorities;
5. national and international organisations;
6. workshops, congresses, scientific conferences.

One of the discussions currently tracked by COMPASS concerns research on endrogenic mimicking, which might potentially be caused by chlorine chemicals. Besides the technology versus activist focus, the difference between this system and Novartis' is that COMPASS works in a centralised way. Information is collected centrally in Brussels by people who scan the six types of information sources and feed the data into the system. The reason for this centralised approach is that COMPASS does not deal with social issues but with scientific findings. As a result, closeness to the market and local activist groups is of less concern. Relevant questions are whether the risk connected to a certain chlorine chemical is scientifically plausible, significant, related to long-term impacts or endangering human life.

SUMMARY

The computer systems mentioned above are nothing new from a technical point of view and rely largely on existing information systems. What is new about them is their content orientation toward activist issues as one important development in a company's environment.

Obviously, our examples are mainly focused on highly exposed industries. Companies in these industries have to fear activist campaigners more than their counterparts in other industries and are therefore highly interested in receiving support in their issue management tasks. However, as we have seen in a number of our examples and case studies, formerly non-exposed industries are now increasingly involved in these types of issues, giving managers in these companies more of an incentive to take an interest in strategic early awareness systems.

Notes

1. Intranets are an Internet technology "spin off" – a kind of internal Internet, using the advantages of the existing low cost Internet technologies. An Intranet is usually built on an organisation's internal computer network and can serve as a communication platform replacing, for example, printed documents or process descriptions.
2. Currently, Eurochlor tries to find a partner to implement COMPASS in an advanced form on a more neutral platform.

7
Case Studies

To show the effectiveness of the checklists, we have selected some useful case studies in which we analyse a total of nine issues (social, environmental and health). We have chosen examples not only from Europe and North America, but other regions as well. This analysis is, of course, now in the "late-awareness" stage, since we as researchers identify topics after discussion has already begun. At any rate, the examples can also be applied in the "early-awareness" stage. The order of case studies is shown in Table 7.1.

Where it seemed appropriate we decided to use all of our proposed tools, including diffusion curves and scenario analysis, while in other cases we applied the checklists without using these tools. Some of the examples we use here are looking back and we are analysing whether the company *could have foreseen* the crisis they ran into, while others are actual live cases that are still running as we write. In these life cases we use our checklists to examine the potential impact of the issue on the company.

Choosing cases where events are still unfolding is a gamble. The reader can take our analysis and compare it with what has actually happened by the time he or she reads our book. We took this gamble to make the case studies more interesting, and to test the effectiveness of our methodology.

Table 7.1 Case study structure

Type of pressure \ Location	Europe	North America	Other continents
Social pressure	1. Union Bank of Switzerland and the Nazi gold	4. Fashion designers using fur and animal rights activists	7. Landowners in Brazil and the "Movimento Sem Terra" (Landless Movement)
Environmental pressure	2. Nestlé and the use of genetically-engineered soya	5. Mitsubishi and its world-wide logging operations	8. ABB and the Bakun Dam
Health-related pressure	3. British farmers and BSE	6. Cellular phone companies and electro-smog	9. Dow Chemical, Shell Oil and Occidental Chemical and the pesticide DBCP

CASE 1: UNION BANK OF SWITZERLAND AND THE NAZI GOLD

During World War II the German military needed constant imports of new supplies to keep the war machine running. To finance them, they looted gold from the countries they overran and scavenged gold jewellery and dental fillings from the six million Jewish Holocaust victims. This gold was smelted, restamped, and then sold through Germany's Reichsbank. As Germany and the Axis powers were isolated during the height of war, the countries needed a neutral party to buy the gold in exchange for hard currency. Neighbouring neutral Switzerland, with its banking secrecy laws, was an obvious choice.

At the same time, many wealthy Jews anticipated being taken away to concentration camps and hid their wealth away from the Nazis in Swiss banks to be recovered during better times. They often used pseudonyms and intermediaries in opening accounts, in some cases even unknown to their immediate families. As we know, many of these Jews who put money into Swiss bank accounts did not survive the Holocaust.

In the years following the war, the Swiss banks (among them the Union Bank of Switzerland, or UBS) were asked to return the deposits and profits from trading with the Nazis to their rightful owners/the victims. The Swiss banks argued that it was impossible for them to trace where the gold actually came from and that they could not look into every single bank account that might have been opened by Holocaust victims. Individuals' claims on dormant Swiss accounts had repeatedly been met with legal requirements for bank documents as proof of ownership (most of which had been lost or destroyed during the Holocaust). Stories of strict insistence on Swiss bank confidentiality laws and lack of co-operation in identifying dormant accounts grew. In a number of negotiations, Switzerland and the Swiss banks later returned some money to individuals, but the international community remained suspicious about the full scope of these returns, arguing that this was only the tip of the iceberg.

In 1995, 50 years after the end of World War II, when many international archives were opened after the 50-year rule of disclosure, the issue of the Swiss Nazi gold appeared once again in the headlines of newspapers world-wide, turning the issue into a public relations nightmare for Switzerland and its banks. Historians found that the sums owed to Holocaust survivors and victims were many times higher than post-war estimates. UK Foreign Office documents estimated the figure to be US$500 million (which equates to US$4 billion today).[1]

In the wake of these new revelations, UBS was accused of having accepted, and of still possessing, Nazi gold and money from the Jews. UBS is one of the big three banks in Switzerland, the others being the Swiss Bank Corporation (SBC) (with which it decided to merge in 1998) and the Credit Swiss (CS). UBS has more than 400 branches world-wide and in 1996 the total assets of the bank were CHF 437.3 billion with operating profits of CHF 4.48 billion. The giant bank's image has suffered severely from this issue. Let us now use our company checklist and try to work out whether this could have been foreseen by the managers of the Swiss banks.

1. Are the arguments against the issue plausible?

The claims against the bank are plausible. There is proof from reliable sources that Swiss banks profited from trading gold with the Nazis, and that the Nazi wealth consisted partly of gold looted from conquered countries and Holocaust victims. There is also documented proof that many Jews tried to protect their fortunes from the Nazis by putting them into Swiss banks. If they died in concentration camps and left their heirs no information concerning the money, the accounts remained dormant.

2. Does the issue evoke emotion? Is it understandable – visual, touching – by the public?

The fact that gold was taken from Jewish jewellery, wedding rings and dental fillings is especially repulsive to most people. In the eyes of the public, the Swiss banks have grown rich on the misery and deaths of people in other countries. Although today there are no strong visuals to link to the issue, there are still many documents from the period that describe the atrocities in a manner that can be visualised by the broad public. In recent years there has been a resurgence of public anguish over the Holocaust issue – the popularity of Stephen Spielberg's film *Schindler's List* is a good example of this mood.

The Holocaust itself still is an emotional issue, and not just for victims and their families – it was one of the worst atrocities in the history of mankind. As investigations with the newly revealed documents probe deeper, the behaviour of the Swiss during the war comes more and more into question. There are accusations that Switzerland was not really neutral, but secretly co-operating with Germany. So yes, the issue is a highly emotionally charged one.

Many people thus can reason easily that if the Swiss banks did indeed profit from the Holocaust, they should be made to pay financial reparations to the victims.

3. Is the issue media-friendly?

When the issue of the Nazi gold arose again in the years after 1995, there was much media speculation. What might have been a

boring review of historical documents turned into a media specta-
cle. It was new and extraordinary. This time, the focus of the
blame was not on the Germans, but the normally highly regarded
Swiss. The media had found yet another interesting Holocaust
story to tell, and yet another "dirty little secret" to uncover in
idyllic Switzerland, the country that many people were delighted
to point out as not as perfect as it seemed. The media were able to
provoke and accuse a nation that was spoilt by its own economic
success, and it was extremely pleasing for them to help uncover
what CNN called "the biggest theft by a government in history".

Since many people were interested in voicing their opinions,
accessibility was no problem for the media. New characters
became involved in the issue, attracting broad international attention and media interest; even US Senator Alfonso D'Amato
found it to be a very good topic for his re-election campaign.

4. Are there connections to other issues of the company or other companies?

This issue involves connections to the Swiss banking industry and
to Switzerland as a neutral country.

First, there is a connection to the confidentiality rules (e.g.
private numbered accounts) of the Swiss banks, which allow
everyone and anyone to deposit money "safely" and anony-
mously in Switzerland. This possibility attracts not only people
who want to avoid higher taxes in their home countries, but also
international dictators such as Imelda Marcos, Saddam Hussein,
Mobuto, and many other undemocratic leaders, as well as drug
lords, Russian Mafia bosses and other criminals who are alleged
to have secret Swiss bank accounts. The Swiss banks have been
berated regularly by international law-enforcement officials, who
claim that the privacy afforded by Swiss banking law attracts ill-
gotten gains from criminal and corrupt elements. By harbouring
"blood money", Switzerland makes it easier for these undesirable
personalities to continue their criminal activities – and gets rich
from it.

Secondly, Switzerland, in general, is discovering that neutrality
can easily lead to isolation. Quite recently, the Swiss rejected their
government's wish to join the European Union. They are not a

member of the United Nations either. Because of this isolation, the world is beginning to perceive a certain egotism and lack of solidarity on the part of the Swiss, with connections between this and Switzerland's situation during the Third Reich. The resulting domino effect continues through to a number of Swiss companies who traded ball bearings for gold and who assumed shops vacated by Jews. For example Bally, a Swiss shoe retailer, has already come under fire for the pre-war purchase of German shops that may have been confiscated from Jews.

5. How strong is the key activist group?

In this case, a number of potential activist groups with different interests exist, e.g. the Holocaust victims and their relatives, seeking reimbursement of family wealth and restitution of confiscated money and gold. Their power is indirect and comes from the sympathy and broad-based support of many people in the world. But they are also using the legal system. One individual Holocaust survivor and Jewish claimant, Bert Linder, filed a lawsuit against the Swiss banks, which then encouraged others to do the same, so that now altogether 12 000 Jews have filed a US$20 billion class-action case against the four largest Swiss banks.

Many of the Jews are represented by the World Jewish Congress (WJC), which aims to examine Switzerland's war-time role, and restore the assets of Holocaust victims. The WJC has good relations with the Clinton administration. It is experienced in dealing with the media and public opinion, and can therefore be considered a powerful adversary for the Swiss banks. To increase and centralise its power in special regard to the Swiss banks, the WJC created in 1992 the World Jewish Restitution Organisation with only two objectives (a kind of decentralisation): to further investigate the assets deposited by the Nazi victims in the Swiss banks and to investigate Switzerland's role in World War II.

Other activists play an important role in the issue without being central to it. These are, for example, US Senator D'Amato and the Clinton administration, who have used the debate for their own public relations purposes. Senator D'Amato is pressuring the Swiss banks with the loss of their banking licences in the state of New York if they do not allow investigations on the lost Nazi gold. In the extreme, this could lead to an international boycott similar to the one against South African banks during the apartheid era. Overall, the Swiss banks face a number of powerful adversaries.

6. How isolated is the company?

There are a number of groups who have to defend themselves against the accusation of conspiracy with the Nazis: Swiss banks in general, the Swiss Bank Association (SBA), the Swiss National Bank, the Swiss government, Swiss industry and commerce, the Swiss population, and other governments, both neutral and from the former Allied Forces. Also some insurance companies in Switzerland and Germany are accused of hiding Holocaust victims' money.

However, one episode following the newly opened discussions might put UBS by itself in the hot seat. In January 1997, a UBS security guard found documents concerning the UBS's dealings with Nazi Germany shredded and waiting to be destroyed in Zurich. In breach of the bank's confidentiality rules, he picked up the shredded documents and took them to a Jewish group who then took them to the police. UBS was found in violation of a law forbidding destruction of any documentation that might help clarify Switzerland's role in wartime Germany. This heightened public suspicions that the Swiss banks were covering up to hang on to the wealth. The guard was investigated by the private security firm that employed him for breach of bank secrecy laws and has subsequently emigrated to the United States following repeated threats from angry Swiss. In this case, the UBS is definitely isolated and its image has suffered severely.

On the side of the activist groups, the clear key players are the Holocaust victims and their heirs represented through lobbying organisations.

7. How far have the dynamics of the crisis already evolved?

The dynamics of the issue of Swiss Nazi gold have been developing over more than 50 years. After a first appearance of the issue at the end of the war, it lost public interest and has resurfaced only 50 years later. The following events were key:

1944:	During the war, the Allies made efforts to stop trading between Germany and Switzerland and other neutral nations (Safehaven programme).
March, 1946:	At the Allied Swiss Negotiations, the Swiss rejected the Allied claims to monetary gold sold by Germany to Switzerland during the war that was estimated to be worth US$289 million. After several failed attempts, the Allies and Switzerland finally agreed in spring 1951 on revised terms for the 1946 accord. The onset of the Cold War and the US need to contain the Soviet Union made Switzerland an important neutral country.
May, 1946:	The Tripartite Gold Commission (TGC) was established with the task of reviewing and adjudicating the claims from governments (not individuals) for the restitution of looted monetary gold recovered in Germany or acquired from the neutrals in their negotiation with the Allies. The Commission agreed to receive from Switzerland US$60 million as a refund of looted gold from occupied countries.

In the following years, the Nazi gold issue came up again from time to time, but did not really make any impact in public discussion. Only 50 years after the end of World War II and with the Cold War over as well, the issue has taken on new proportions. New documents became available and created public interest in reopening the history books. The World Jewish Restitution Organisation had as its mission to determine the whereabouts of assets deposited by Holocaust victims in Swiss banks. As many Holocaust survivors are now coming to the natural end of their lives, they have an urgent desire to ensure that long-suppressed facts come to light:

September, 1995:	Representatives of the WJC meet with the SBA to request an investigation of dormant

accounts of Holocaust victims. The SBA orders all Swiss banks to identify accounts that had been dormant for 10 years. Only US$32 million are found in 774 accounts and only 26 out of a total of 500 banks respond. The SBA nevertheless concludes its study.

April, 1996: US Senator Alfonso D'Amato, who is chairman of the Senate Banking Committee begins US Congressional Hearings to reopen negotiations. In the hearings, New York lawmakers propose removing Swiss banks from the state if they fail to open their banks to local auditors searching for Jewish accounts. The Nazi gold affair offers D'Amato the perfect opportunity to raise his profile. Then he approaches Governor Clinton, who, with the Presidential election ahead, agrees to launch a US enquiry.

May, 1996: An enquiry headed by Paul Volcker, the former chairman of the Federal Reserve, (Volcker Commission) commences with a mandate to audit all searches made by Swiss banks with regard to dormant accounts.

September, 1996: The UK Foreign Office publishes a report entitled *Nazi Gold*. It reveals that Switzerland bought Nazi gold and other assets then worth US$500 million that belonged to Jews killed in the Holocaust. Swiss bankers deny the claims, arguing that even if Jews decided to hide their wealth abroad, they probably would have favoured Britain or the United States as a safe haven rather than Switzerland, which was more vulnerable to being overrun by the Nazis.

October, 1996: The Poland Treaty is rediscovered, an agreement that gives inheritance rights to assets located in Switzerland and belonging to Polish subjects as of 1 September, 1939.

November, 1996: The Swiss government passes legislation lifting banks' and professional secrecy laws and

	opening government records for a period of five years.
December, 1996:	The Swiss parliament passes a law authorising a Swiss International Committee of experts to investigate all Swiss financial transactions with the Third Reich.
January, 1997:	A security guard finds documents concerning the UBS's dealings with Nazi Germany waiting to be destroyed in Zurich and takes them to a Jewish group.
January, 1997:	After the publication of a leaked memo urging his government to "wage war" against the allegations that the Swiss banks had failed to account for the missing funds, Switzerland's Ambassador in the United States, Carl Jagmetti, resigns.
February, 1997:	The major Swiss banks announce that they would create a US$70 million humanitarian fund for the remaining survivors of the Holocaust and families of victims.
March, 1997:	Switzerland proposes a US$5 billion fund for Nazi victims using the country's gold reserves. The fund would entail selling gold over a 10-year period. The plan has to be approved by a vote of the Swiss citizenry.
May, 1997:	The Eizenstat Report (which gets its name through Stuart Eizenstat, the responsible Under-Secretary of State for International Commerce) is published on the basis of President Clinton's mandate. It describes how each of the neutral states co-operated with Nazi Germany for their own economic benefit, stating that these tradings prolonged World War II. The report states that Germany transferred US$400 million worth of looted gold to the Swiss National Bank; however, there is no evidence that Switzerland knew where the gold had originated. Switzerland rejects the accusation of the US report on the Nazi gold as one-sided.

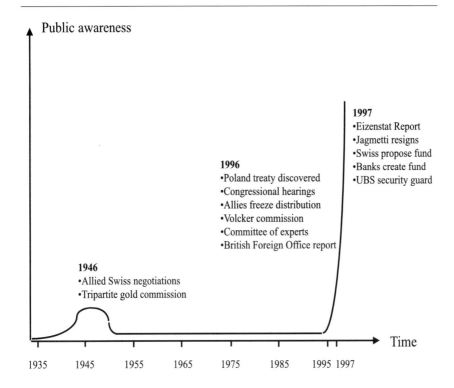

Figure 7.1 Diffusion curve for the Nazi gold issue

The diffusion curve for the Nazi gold issue is as in Figure 7.1.

Looking at this pattern, it becomes obvious that the escalation of the issue is based on multiple facts after 1996: availability of new historical documents; new interest due to 50-year end-of-war celebrations; support of the American public, i.e. the Clinton administration. UBS could have recognised in early 1996 that this constellation could cause the issue to "take off". A proactive approach to the problem would have been a good decision, rather than waiting as long as possible with the revelation of more facts.

In attempting a scenario analysis, the Swiss banks could have started by identifying the primary "driving forces" at work. These might have included the following:

Political and legal dynamics

- Actions of other neutral governments (e.g. Sweden and Portugal) who accepted and traded Nazi gold, and their ability to handle and communicate the issue.
- Requests of governments of countries formally under Nazi occupation.
- Attempts to change Switzerland's secrecy laws.
- Pursuit and outcome of the class action suit.
- The outcome of the Swiss referendum on the creation of the US$5 billion solidarity fund.

Economic dynamics

- Threats of a possible loss of the operating licences of Swiss banks in New York.
- Boycott of Swiss banks and industry.
- Loss of trust in the Swiss bank secrecy law.
- Reactions of shareholders to the issue.

Social dynamics

- Anti-Semitic tendencies of the world's societies.
- Opposite tendencies (anti-fascism, anti-racism).

Technical dynamics

- The "logistical" possibilities of tracing Nazi gold in dormant Swiss bank accounts.

Among the above, there are two key uncertainties. One is the approval of the solidarity fund of US$5 billion, which is designed to re-establish Switzerland's humanitarian reputation. The fund requires the agreement of the Swiss citizens through a referendum in 1998 and a majority of cantons. It is far from certain that this referendum will pass, as it is already getting strong opposition from

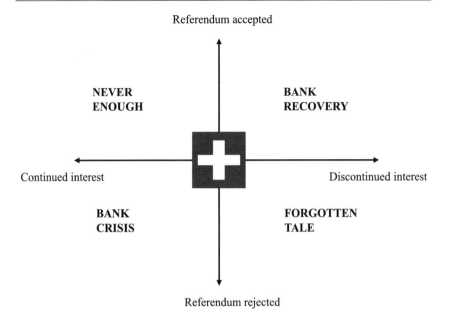

Figure 7.2 Scenario analysis for the Nazi gold issue

right-wing nationalists. This outcome will be interpreted by the international community as indicating the willingness or non-willingness of the Swiss people to accept their historical role and to apologise to the victims. It will, in turn, influence future events such as the class-action suit and media coverage.

The second uncertainty is the pressure of the international public on the Swiss banks. People may continue to put pressure on the Swiss banks or may eventually give up and turn their interest and efforts to other issues. On the basis of these two key uncertainties, we get a two-dimensional matrix as shown in Figure 7.2:

The events in these scenarios are as follows:

Bank crisis

The referendum is rejected and more facts are found. This scenario will probably imply the loss of the class-action suit filed against the Swiss banks. US pension funds will withdraw their investments in Swiss banks and other shareholders may follow, implying falling stock prices. A boycott of Swiss banks will gain momentum and Switzerland may lose credibility and trust as a banking centre. Public attention will continue to focus on Switzerland, while the role of other neutral countries will not be fully investigated.

Bank recovery

External stakeholders see the positive referendum as a sign that Switzerland is not only accepting its historical guilt, but is also ready to pay reparation to the victims. The class-action suit against the Swiss banks will be dropped. Swiss banking credibility will be restored. The Jewish interest organisations will accept the solidarity fund as an adequate recompense and drop their requests for further inquires.

Never enough

The referendum is accepted by the Swiss public. However, the activist groups argue that such a general fund is still insufficient to compensate the material loss. They increase the pressure and want each individual case to be examined.

Forgotten tale

The referendum is rejected. The public gives up and loses interest in the Swiss banks as well. It may happen that the pressure shifts to other companies that profited from the Nazi regime, such as German insurance companies.

On the basis of these scenarios, the Swiss banks can plan for further action. One measure that is good in any of the four scenarios might be to pursue a clear and open communication strategy. Furthermore, the Swiss banks should try to help to avoid the fuelling of anti-Semitic tendencies, because this would increase tensions further.

8. How easy is the solution?

As the Nazi victims want justice for their wartime financial losses, the Swiss banks and Switzerland as a whole could solve the issue through compensation. This would solve at least the financial part of the problem (but not the moral part). However, to assess the amount required to compensate the victims fairly is difficult because most documents are missing. The Swiss banks are facing a logistical nightmare in trying to trace the gold and other assets transferred by third parties into the country. It is clear that they cannot accept a complete change in the confidentiality rules, because this could provoke the loss of important clients. Still, many people believe that the Swiss banks could do a better job than they have in finding the lost accounts.

Table 7.2 Visualised company checklist for the Nazi gold issue

Assessment criteria	Rating					Comments
	++	+	0	−	−−	
Plausibility	●					Swiss banks received gold and other assets from the Nazis and their victims.
Potential for emotions		●				Biggest cruelty in the history of mankind.
Media-friendliness		●				New and extraordinary story; however, few visuals
Connections with other issues		●				Other demands against Swiss banks (confidentiality rules) and Switzerland as a country
Strength of the key activist group		●				WJC founded World Jewish Restitution Organisations aiming only at Swiss banks.
Degree of company isolation		●				No Swiss bank isolated, except UBS, with regard to security guard issue. Switzerland as a whole is isolated.
Dynamics			●			Proposed funds may slow down diffusion process.
Ease of solution			●			Fund does not solve individual cases.
Overall assessment		●				

Another solution for the Swiss banks is to pay a general amount of compensation, because this has already been decided upon: the Swiss banks have set up a humanitarian fund of US$70 million that will benefit Jewish charities. The disadvantage of such a fund is that the issue of specific accounts will not disappear. No matter how high the level of compensation, people will believe that the banks are hiding much more.

Another part of the solution can come from the Swiss government. In 1997 it proposed to set up a US$5 billion fund for Holocaust victims, to be approved through referendum. Furthermore, the government has lifted bank confidentiality laws and launched an independent commission to investigate the issue.

Table 7.2 shows the company checklist for this issue.

The Results

UBS could have foreseen in early 1996 that a constellation of factors was evolving that could cause a "take off" of the Nazi gold issue. A more pro-active stance in the search for Jewish assets in its bank accounts would have been very wise and could have helped to avoid the negative headlines.

The public relations nightmare has not yet reached its climax, because more information is likely to reveal itself over the coming years. The Swiss banks should, therefore, be prepared to discuss the topic of Nazi gold whenever it comes up. A goal in the current state of debate should be to compensate the Holocaust victims and their families generously now, so that any new findings that may come up are more acceptable to public opinion. Additionally, they should try to oppose anti-Semitic tendencies in Switzerland.

Now let us use the activist checklist to look at the issue from the adversaries' point of view.

In the Swiss Nazi gold issue, the Swiss banks face several adversaries, the most important among them being the WJC, which has been the representative of Jewish communities since 1936, advocating Jewish concerns to governments and international organisations. We now analyse why the WJC singled out Swiss banks when it created in 1992 the World Jewish Restitution Organisation, which focuses much less on banks in other neutral states such as Portugal, Sweden or Argentina.[2]

1. The campaign should have a clear aim or goal

The WJC has clear goals both for the short and long term. The immediate goal is to make the public and the politicians aware of the events during the war with special reference to the role of Switzerland. The long-term goal is to get the Swiss to ensure that the looted gold and the dormant bank accounts are used to compensate individual victims of Nazism. This long-term goal is probably difficult to reach because of problems in finding the beneficiaries of the gold. Alternatively, the WJC seeks a general compensation fund without regarding individual claims.

2. The issue is easily understood by the general public

Though half a century has passed since the Holocaust, the issue is still widely known and understandable. Debates about it involve the entire world. People can identify with the issue of ethnic persecution and moral indifference by third parties who were passive accomplices. Of course, it is difficult for them to review the precise historic details of the issue, but the allegation fits well with many peoples' suspicions about Switzerland and its banks.

3. The issue has a high symbolic value

The claims against the Swiss banks have a high symbolic value from various perspectives. First, the object of debate – gold – has a high symbolic value. The idea that some of the gold was picked from the bodies of innocent Jewish victims by their Nazi murderers heightens the symbolism.

Then, the Swiss banks as an industry have a high symbolic value as they stand for confidentiality laws, being a safe haven for all kinds of money – and appear to be the most wealthy and profitable banks in the world. Many people point to a "moral bankruptcy" in the well-fed, "business-as-usual" attitude in the Swiss banking system.

The WJC and its supporters actively tried to construct images. One example is the now wealthy Holocaust survivor, Bert Linder, who hired a lawyer and put his case to the banks. The image of one lone man against the might of the Swiss banks was taken up by the press as a David and Goliath story. The banks' technical solutions, voiced by lawyers, did not take into account the symbolic value of his act. If individual claimants like him, as first-hand witnesses to Nazi genocide, can prove wrong-doing by Swiss banks, Switzerland and Swiss banks may experience intense international scorn.

4. The issue has the potential to damage the image of the company

Independently of the Nazi gold claims, the banks had already been seen as the keepers of dirty money. With specific reference to UBS, at the time when the WJC started its campaign, the organisation did not know that UBS would make things even worse for itself by trying to shred documents. The security guard's discovery during the campaign, and UBS's reprisals against him, caused serious damage to UBS itself.

The issue is damaging the image of not only Swiss banks, but of the entire country, pushing it into uncomfortable soul-searching. Its image as a proud neutral country – founder of the Red Cross, defender of democratic values – has been profoundly challenged.

5. The opponent is strong enough (no "underdog" effect)

Both at home and abroad, Swiss banks have been seen as pillars of the Swiss economy and of the global financial market. Also, Switzerland as a whole makes a good target: it is rich, small and suggests the stereotype of a nation of greedy bankers.

6. The issue can be "packaged" in a campaign in which the public can get involved

It will probably be difficult to get the world population involved besides informing them about the incidents. The only chance would be to encourage people to write letters to Swiss banks or to boycott them. Most customers of Swiss banks outside of Switzerland are not really members of the general public, and many of those customers probably have an interest in maintaining the status quo – it is therefore not probable that this will succeed.

7. There are solutions that are confrontational, not gradual

The solutions of the WJC coincide in this case with the goals of the campaign: draw attention to Switzerland's role in war and get compensation for Jewish victims on both an individual and general basis. In this issue, the populations in the various countries are probably going to support the WJC, because the solution would not lead to any disadvantages for them (with the exception of the Swiss population, which might consider the compensation claims as unacceptable).

8. There could be a dramatic element to the campaign to engage the media

The revelations of Nazi gold still held by Swiss banks, and, in particular, by UBS, have all the ingredients for an excellent and sustained media campaign: new events and discoveries that retain media and public interest; a mix of influential and interesting people, power and money; a search for hidden "truth"; and, for some people, a moral crusade against the most powerful image of evil this century. So the WJC had good chances to make a successful campaign out of it, consisting of allegations, investigations, threats of boycotts, etc. The story turned into the most sensational since the Hitler diaries.

The activist analysis may look like Table 7.3.

The Results

Using the activist checklist, it becomes clear that the WJC had good reasons to push the Swiss banks. Among the neutral states in World War II, Switzerland was mostly forced to co-operate with the Nazis, as the country was surrounded by Axis powers.

Table 7.3 Visualised activist checklist for the Nazi gold issue

Assessment criteria	Rating					Comments
	++	+	0	–	– –	
Clear aim or goal		•				Awareness and compensation.
Understandable by public	•					Holocaust easily understandable.
Symbolic		•				Blood gold and Swiss banks.
Image can be damaged		•				Lots of suspicions against Swiss banks.
Strong opponent	•					Swiss banks are profitable and wealthy.
Public can get involved			•			Boycott difficult for public outside Switzerland.
Confrontational solution			•			Solution could be awareness and compensation.
Dramatic elements		•				Allegations, investigations, threats.

Overall assessment	⬚ ⬚ ● ⬚ ⬚	Good object for outside pressure campaign.

Also there is probably more money to be found in Switzerland than any of the other countries. The Swiss banks were a good opponent and the gold made a good symbolic issue. The WJC knew probably that the interest and drama could be maintained and magnified, as through the opening of historical documents more revelations could be made and other parties drawn in.

CASE 2: NESTLÉ AND THE USE OF GENETICALLY ENGINEERED SOYA

In this case, we put ourselves in the shoes of managers of the Swiss food giant Nestlé, who plan to use genetically engineered (GE) raw material in the manufacturing of many of its food products. Low-cost GE soya is of special importance for Nestlé, as more than 60% of all processed supermarket food including bread, chocolate, cakes, magarine, ice-cream and pasta contains soya in some form.

In 1996, Greenpeace and other critics like the Union of Concerned Scientists, the Environmental Defense Fund and Jeremy Rifkin's Foundation on Economic Trends began a campaign against the use of GE food in Europe, choosing GE soya as a symbolic product for their attack. Greenpeace argues that GE food increases antibiotic resistance in dangerous bacteria and could increase pesticide resistance in insects.

We begin with the company checklist.

1. Are the arguments against the issue plausible?

The claims regarding the issue can be considered plausible, since the long-term dangers of GE food are still unknown. Scientists, who can be considered reliable information sources, arc worried about risks to both human health and to the environment. Risks to human health are generally considered low, because few of the micro-organisms used in research or industry are pathogenic to humans. However, there is a larger risk that undesirable environmental effects could be caused by novel organisms released into the environment. Some of these effects may be difficult to predict accurately or may only be apparent in the longer term. These risks include, according to the European Union (EU):

1. excessive increase in the numbers of GE organisms released into the environment, and their establishment;
2. direct but unanticipated effects on non-target species – infectivity, pathogenicity, predation on other micro-organisms, plants and animals, or shifts in host range;
3. negative influence on the interactions among species – predators, prey, hosts, symbiots;
4. unanticipated involvement in biogeochemical cycles – nitrogen-fixation, mineral cycling, etc.;
5. transfer of undesired characteristics to other organisms.

Some scientists of the University of California argue that even if only 1% of all GE products turn out to be hazardous, this will lead in ten years to a large-scale ecological and economic catastrophe. On the other hand, Monsanto (the main manufacturer of GE soya) claims that the new beans are even environmentally beneficial because they will reduce the overall need for herbicide spraying. In the United States, GE foods have been successfully reviewed by the Food and Drug Administration (FDA) and the Environmental Protection Agency (EPA).

**2. Does the issue evoke emotion? Is it understandable –
visual, touching – by the public?**

Food is always an emotional issue. In addition, the environmental
aspect affects society as a whole. However, it is clear, after long
and intensive research on GE food, that producing and eating
these products will have no immediate negative effect on human
health or the environment. Possible disadvantages may be found
only in the long term, so that the immediate emotional impact
cannot be considered important. Also, the visual aspect of the
problem is limited.

3. Is the issue media-friendly?

This campaign will most probably not be one of the most media-
friendly ones ever run by Greenpeace; there is just too little to
show in the media to make it extraordinary. Stopping ships and
occupying headquarters does not really excite people any more.
The issue of voluntarily "optimising" food through genetical engineering is, however, new and therefore some reports on it will
appear, especially in the "higher-class" television programmes.
The media will have no problem of accessibility in this case,
because Nestlé's administration and production sites are easily
reached and scientists from both sides are willing to communicate
their opinions.

**4. Are there connections to other issues of the
company or other companies?**

There are a number of connections between GE food, Nestlé and
other issues. First, Greenpeace argues that there are similarities
between GE food and the recent European mad cow disease
scandal in the United Kingdom, where researchers had been tell-
ing the public for years that there was no danger to humans. Of
course, there are also connections to other genetic engineering
issues, like animal testing.

Secondly, there is a perceived company connection between
Nestlé and non-ethical business behaviour, because in the 1970s

Nestlé came under strong criticism for selling infant formula in Third World countries. And there is a second company connection with the supplier of GE soya, Monsanto, because the EU decided in 1995 to take a moratorium on Monsanto's Bovine Somatotropin (used to boost milk yield in cows) because of health concerns.

5. How strong is the key activist group?

The strength of Greenpeace can be assessed as high, because the organisation has almost three million supporters. Greenpeace is highly centralised, can react quickly and is known for surprise manoeuvres. It is additionally supported by a number of other activist groups with more scientific credentials like the Union of Concerned Scientists. However, GE food is an atypical Greenpeace topic, so the organisation is inexperienced at dealing with this issue.

The strength of Greenpeace might also be reduced because Nestlé is still in a strong coalition with the chemical and biotechnical industries that have invested billions in the new technologies and will, therefore, use all their power to ensure that this investment pays out in the future.

6. How isolated is the company?

For a long time, the major food chains in Europe like Nestlé, Unilever and Danone had a common position on GE food. However, since Unilever is decentralised, some of its country organisations agreed voluntarily to not sell GE food. The German and Austrian subsidiaries of Nestlé said that they would not use GE soybeans in their main products. Some of the main food producers even gave in completely: Kraft Jakobs–Suchard and Ferrero guaranteed their European customers GE-free soya products. Nestlé headquarters, on the other hand, does not want to give in for all of Europe. With reference to a labelling of GE food, the company declared on 20 November, 1996: "Although we see no safety or scientific justification for such labelling, we recognise the consumer interest in this information and will, therefore, in addition to any legal requirements, indicate the use of ingredients produced with the aid of gene technology on the label *wherever reasonable and practicable.*" So Nestlé can be considered somehow isolated.

Some European retailers argue that they do not want to sell food containing GE soya without labelling. In Sweden, the two largest food retailers ICA and KF are on the list of those demanding separation and labelling. In Norway, it is the Daglivarhandelns Environmental and Packaging Forum, which includes almost all Norwegian food retailers. In the UK, Safeway, and in Switzerland, the two biggest retailers Migros and Coop, are making the same demands. And in Austria, Germany, Belgium and the Netherlands some supermarket chains have called for labelling. In the United States, some 1500 top chefs have joined the Pure Food Campaign, with the slogan, "We do not serve genetically engineered foods."

On the other hand, there are big industries behind Nestlé that support the company with arguments, investigations, etc. in its fight against Greenpeace; for example, pesticide producers and biotechnical companies. They have a vested interest in keeping the food producers in line. A loss of the symbolic fight for GE soya would have a tremendous negative effect on the whole biotechnical industry. Additional support for this coalition comes from the European Commission (EC) Scientific Committees on Food; the Scientific Committee on Animal Nutrition and the Scientific Committee for Pesticides, who approved GE corn.

7. How far have the dynamics of the crisis already evolved?

A diffusion curve for genetic engineering discussion would show a long period of time in which the issue was interesting only to researchers and scientists, beginning in the 1970s. The technique promised to have an enormous impact on many sectors of the economy and became in the mid-1980s a topic for legislation. Broader discussion began much later, in March 1996, when a team of researchers published an article in the New England Journal of Medicine about allergenic components of brazil nuts that were genetically transferred to soybeans.

Greenpeace started the current campaign against GE food in September 1996, and has already succeeded in raising awareness of the issue with a broad public. Some surveys found that 85% to 90% of European consumers support clear labelling of bio-engineered products. To translate this opinion into action, Greenpeace would need more scientists to certify the danger of GE food, and, at the same time, convince retail companies not to accept GE food even if it is properly labelled.

Parallel to Greenpeace, the Foundation on Economic Trends in Washington, DC has called for a boycott of corporations that use GE soy or corn in their products. In October 1996 they led a coalition of 300 agricultural, health and trade groups from 48 countries, which has now launched a boycott against products containing GE corn and soybeans.[3] Their protest began with farmers and consumers marching in front of the Chicago Board of Trade, the country's largest commodity exchange.

Also, on the legal side, 13 European countries have objected to GE maize being brought into Europe, despite the fact that the maize was approved by the EC for cultivation and sale in Europe. In December 1996, Austria's health minister imposed an import ban on GE corn. He argued that the ban was consistent with an EU provision that allows a member state to challenge EU decisions that pose a health or environmental risk. On 15 May the EU Regulation 258/97/EC on Novel Food labelling took effect. However, critics argue that the planned labelling cannot be understood by the consumer. The dynamics so far point to immediate danger for Nestlé.

8. How easy is the solution?

The easiest solution for Nestlé would be not to use any GE soya. This is, however, not acceptable for the company because it would imply competitive disadvantages against other food processors. A second option for Nestlé would be to accept complete and transparent labelling of GE food. This would probably have negative impacts on sales of many of its products. Another solution would be to label food only in those countries where the pressure is highest and where it is legally required. However, in the long run,

Table 7.4   Visualised company checklist for the GE soya issue

Assessment criteria	Rating					Comments
	++	+	0	–	––	
Plausibility		●				Some plausible concerns.
Potential for emotions		●				Food is involved; however few visuals.
Media-friendliness			●			Topic is new and extraordinary.
Connections with other issues		●				Interconnections for Nestlé and to other food issues.
Strength of the key activist group		●				There are several strong activist groups involved.
Degree of company isolation		●				Nestlé might become isolated.
Dynamics	●					"Take-off" of broad diffusion may be close.
Ease of solution		●				Labelling would be possible at least in the near future.
Overall assessment		●				Nestlé has to avoid becoming further isolated.

this would be difficult to maintain, as the EC is aiming at a common product certification policy. Besides the positive labelling, there could be also negative labelling enforced by governments. This would mean to introduce labels for all food that does not include changed genetic material.

Even if Nestlé wanted to label GE food, they would in the mid- and long term probably have a separation problem, because the mutated seed gets mixed with non-mutated seed. A third (and probably the most preferred) solution for Nestlé would be to ignore Greenpeace and hope that the industry will hold together and break the resistance among their own peers. For this strategy to succeed it would be necessary for consumers not to get even more heavily involved in the discussions and for the entire food industry to stay in line.

The company checklist for Nestlé may look like Table 7.4.

Now we use the Activist Checklist in order to identify why Greenpeace is running this campaign, even though the topic falls outside their normal concerns.

1. The campaign should have a clear aim or goal

The Greenpeace campaign has a clear goal for the short and long term. The immediate goal is to force consumer goods companies to label GE food in a much broader and transparent way than that proposed by the EU novel food regulation. While Greenpeace hopes that this will lead in the long term to strict laws banning the sale of GE food in Europe and world-wide, it knows, however, that such a goal is not very realistic.

2. The issue is easily understood by the general public

Society, as a whole, is becoming increasingly supportive of genetic engineering. One reason may be due to AIDS research. Many scientists, religious leaders and citizens applaud genetic experiments, as long as altered genes might cure human "diseases" or "improve the human lot".

However, people are more choosy about food issues, especially when they are told that they are eating something dangerous or unnatural. To make the campaign understood by a large public, Greenpeace decided not to attack genetic engineering in general, but specifically in food. Nevertheless, it is difficult for the general public to understand this issue. The relationships between cause and effect are uncertain and long term, and expert opinions are sometimes contradictory.

3. The issue has a high symbolic value

Greenpeace focuses on a single symbolic product as a representative for all GE products: soya beans. This product was chosen because of its broad usage and because GE soya technology is already highly developed. Labelling legislation would provoke major impacts, because many food companies are heavily dependent on soya. Greenpeace has not focused on the fact that genetically modified enzymes are already present in all cheese, yoghurt and yeast products.

In general, it is difficult for Greenpeace to use many symbols in the GE food campaign in ways as dramatic and highly-visible as those they have used in other campaigns. The debate is driven by different scientists' opinions, from which it is fairly difficult to derive any meaningful symbolism. The low symbolic value is, therefore, a problem for Greenpeace. However, because of its broad usage in the food industry and consumption among individuals, soya is the best target to choose in this case.

4. The issue has the potential to damage the image of the company

Damaging the image of the company will be difficult, because Greenpeace is fighting against a large number of companies in this case. The value chain in the food business is long and includes farmers, the biotechnology industry, pesticide producers, traders, food companies and retailers. Mainly affected would be Monsanto, an American chemical and biotechnology company that developed new GE soybeans. The company's beans are engineered to be resistant to Roundup (also sold by Monsanto), a herbicide that kills normal soybeans.[4] Besides Monsanto[5] there are also Novartis, Du Pont, Dow Chemical, Zeneca and Hoechst who have invested in genetically engineered crops.[6] Since all of them are involved in GE food, it is difficult for Greenpeace to single out one opponent for attack.

Greenpeace, nevertheless, will try to focus on one opponent. It will therefore choose a company that is in direct contact with, and known to, consumers. Here, a food processing company is ideal (e.g. Unilever, Danone, Nestlé), because its name appears on the packaging, as opposed to, for example, the pesticide producer who is generally unknown to the end consumer. If Greenpeace is able to force some of the big food companies to give in and accept labelling, it may be possible to damage the image of other food companies (e.g. Nestlé) who remain in their old positions.

5. The opponent is strong enough (no "underdog" effect)

Without a doubt, Nestlé, as the world's largest food company, with sales of around CHF 50 billion in 1996, is a strong opponent for Greenpeace.

6. The issue can be "packaged" in a campaign in which the public can get involved

There are few high-profile actions that can be staged in this campaign. Among their arsenal of actions may be stopping ships, occupying supermarkets and office buildings, as they did in November 1996, when Greenpeace activists unrolled a huge banner across the front of Nestlé headquarters in Vevey that said, "Gene Food: Force Fed by Nestle". Greenpeace occupied beanfields in the United States, and at the November 1996 World Food Summit in Rome three female activists stripped naked in front of United States agricultural Secretary Dan Glickman as part of the protest.

Since Nestlé is a consumer brand, a boycott might be possible; however, the campaign will probably not be among the most exciting to be undertaken by Greenpeace.

7. There are solutions that are confrontational, not gradual

As product labelling is already extremely complicated and few consumers can understand it, achieving this goal can be only an interim solution for Greenpeace.[7] The preferred solution for Greenpeace would be a complete ban on GE food.

Finding confrontational solutions will become more difficult as time passes, because separating GE from non-GE soya will eventually become next to impossible. Soya is a commodity crop, which means that the harvest from thousands of farms is normally mixed together in huge bins before shipping. Greenpeace therefore accuses American and European multinational companies of stalling for time to be able to eventually present consumers with a "fait accompli". In the United States, the demands for separation have been met with flat refusal by Monsanto, the American Soya Association and the major traders, Cargill and Archer Daniels Midland.

8. There could be a dramatic element to the campaign to engage the media

To date, there has been no such element, because discussion has been led by scientists arguing about the pros and cons of genetic

Table 7.5 Visualised activist checklist for the GE soya issue

Assessment criteria	Rating					Comments
	++	+	0	–	––	
Clear aim or goal	●					Labelling and banning of GE food.
Understandable by public			●			Difficult to understand details, but general suspicion.
Symbolic		●				Soya as symbolic product; however, few symbolic campaign elements.
Image can be damaged		●				Many companies involved in the value chain.
Strong opponent	●					Nestlé is biggest food company in the world.
Public can get involved		●				Difficult, but boycott is possible.
Confrontational solution	●					Labelling and banning of GE food.
Dramatic elements				●		Difficult to create because of scientific discussion.
Overall assessment			●			Difficult campaign for Greenpeace, but it is an important topic for them.

engineering. Greenpeace has to create its own drama to stir things up and single out the "bad" food companies. However, this drama will be difficult to realise, getting back again to the lack of meaningful symbols.

Table 7.5 shows the activist checklist for this issue.

Results

It is obvious that Nestlé is facing severe criticism for its use of GE products. However, it may be possible to hold its ground against Greenpeace by:

- keeping the food processing industry in line and lobbying retailers;
- maintaining legislators' positive attitude toward GE food;
- trying to keep consumers out of the discussion;
- playing for time in order for a real separation problem to begin, making it impossible to stop GE food.

CASE 3: BRITISH FARMERS AND BSE

Bovine Spongiform Encephalopathy (BSE) or mad cow disease, a fatal brain disease of cattle, is believed to have emerged from the introduction of the "Carver–Greenfield" meat-and-bone cattle feed manufacturing process from the United States. Many countries adopted the new manufacturing process, which uses carcasses of scrapie-infected sheep but includes a sterilisation period for the animals. However, the United Kingdom adopted the new manufacturing method without any sterilisation period.

The origin of BSE is believed to be a self-replicating, rogue form of the naturally occurring prion protein finding its way into meat and bone meal made from carcasses of scrapie-infected sheep, and cattle infected with BSE. BSE is a highly stable agent, resisting heating to normal cooking temperatures and even higher temperatures such as those used for non-sophisticated forms of sterilisation, as well as freezing and drying. Even small amounts of contaminated meat and bone meal can introduce BSE, and the disease can be transmitted from species to species (cross-contamination).

Since 1986, in the United Kingdom more than 166 000 cases of BSE in cattle have been identified. The epidemic peaked in 1992–1993 at almost 1000 cases per week. Currently, fewer than 300 cases are occurring per week. By May 1995, BSE had been reported also from 10 countries and areas outside the United Kingdom, but in low quantities. In one group of countries – France, Portugal, the Republic of Ireland and Switzerland – the disease occurred in native cattle, and this was thought to be in part related to the importation of cattle feed from the United Kingdom. In another group – the Falkland Islands, Oman, Germany, Canada, Italy and Denmark – cases were identified only in cattle imported from the United Kingdom.

Creutzfeldt–Jakob Disease (CJD) is a prion disease related to BSE, and is found in humans. In the late 1980s, some scientists began to argue that BSE could be transmitted to other species or to humans. However for a long time the UK government's health agencies denied this possibility. Only in 1989 was a ban imposed by the UK government on the use of the brain, spinal cord and tonsil, thymus, spleen and intestine of cattle origin in foods for human consumption.

In 1994 and 1995 there occurred in the United Kingdom 10 strange cases resembling typical CJD, which highlighted scientific concerns about the possible transmission of the BSE prion to humans. Some features of the disease were different from those of classic CJD. The cases occurred in people under the age of 42 years (the classic CJD average age is 63, while the new CJD cases averaged 27.5) and the duration of the illness of the new form of CJD was about 13 months as opposed to six months for classical CJD. Despite the relatively few cases, the scientific community was alarmed. People feared that because of the lengthy incubation period of CJD in humans of 5–15 years, a large number of CJD cases caused by eating beef before 1989 would emerge soon.

The real public debate took off in 1996, when the British Spongiform Encephalopathy Advisory Committee (SEAC) concluded that the most likely explanation at present was that the new CJD cases were linked to exposure to BSE before the introduction of the specified bovine offal (SBO) ban in 1989. The government stressed that there was still no proof of a definite link but accepted that the new evidence was cause for concern. As a consequence of these publications and the resulting European-wide outcry in 1996, the European Commission imposed an all-embracing ban on UK exports of bovine meat and related products. Across Europe, consumers reduced their red meat consumption. The financial consequences for the British beef industry were tough, even if part of the loss was shouldered by the British government: beef sales (in volume and price) in the United Kingdom dropped by more than 20% after the announcement; a shift in consumer demand from beef to pork, lamb and poultry occurred, with a corresponding increase in prices of the preferred meats; some of Britain's leading meat producers went out of business; shares in food companies fell (Kerry, Cavaghan & Grey, Hillsdown) and EU beef consumption fell from 2.5 to 1.7 million tons in 1996. The biggest decrease was reported in Portugal (–31%), Greece (–25%) and Italy (–21%).

Obviously, the issue had severe consequences for British farmers. However, as in many health issues, there has been no single key activist group. A number of groups were involved, including consumer associations, animals right activists, vegetarian organisations, non-British farmers in the EU and families of CJD victims. The issue was also strongly driven by EU legislators. However, these groups had different interests. Therefore, we use the activist checklist in this case in a more general way, analysing the interests of the different activist groups rather than applying it only for one group. But first we apply our company checklist to find the reasons for the huge outcry in this case, despite the small number of human victims to date.

1. Are the arguments against the issue plausible?

There is no scientific dispute that the human food chain has become contaminated with the BSE agent. Most people in the United Kingdom who ate beef before government measures were assumed to have been exposed to the agent through the many thousands of cattle infected by BSE before the ban in 1989. Some microbiologists suggested that average British consumers have eaten about 80 meals containing meat from infected animals since the disease was first identified in the mid-1980s.

Many scientists are also convinced that the new cases of CJD were caused by eating meat products contaminated by BSE in the 1980s, before the UK government banned human consumption of specified bovine offal (brain, spinal cord and other glands). However, so far, no statistical link has been proven between mad cow disease and CJD. Identified cases of CJD were less than 55 per year in the United Kingdom in the period 1991–1995, an incidence in line with the international average. A recent World Health Organisation study showed that the age distribution and duration of illness prior to death was similar to other European countries as well. The 10 strange new cases of CJD are therefore still largely unexplained. Still the concerns about human effects are very understandable.

So, overall, the issue can be considered plausible, even if the worst fears – a high number of affected humans – have not yet come true and hopefully never will. We will have to wait a number of years to be able to make any definitive statements on this, however, as CJD has a long incubation period.

2. Does the issue evoke emotion? Is it understandable – visual, touching – by the public?

The issue creates strong emotion. Speculation about a link between the two diseases had been going on since the late 1980s, but as long as the government denied the link, many people disregarded the reports as they ate the traditional Sunday roast. In 1996, however, beef sales plummeted by as much as 70%, cattle markets were deserted and the EU imposed a ban on beef exports world-wide. The then British Prime Minister, John Major, blamed "hysteria", which he said had been whipped up by the Press and Opposition politicians.

Food involves trust. When consumers buy it, they trust manufacturers and government regulators to have done their jobs and put a safe product on the grocery store shelves. When the government admitted that they had misinformed people for many years about the BSE–CJD link, people felt their trust had been violated. Attempts by government officials and scientists to allay public fears – for which they were mostly responsible – were futile. Consumers angrily accused the British Ministry of Agriculture of putting food producers' interests above the health and safety of consumers, and of failing to act sufficiently quickly when presented with evidence of a threat to public health.

The issue can be understood by the broad public, even if it is complicated from a scientific point of view. People know that what they eat affects their health. Mad cow disease is visual – filmed footage of the cows' bizarre behaviour on the nightly television news programmes makes most people think twice before eating a steak. It is also alarming to imagine that everyone who has ever eaten beef has potentially been exposed to the disease, including our children, who had been told to eat their meat to make them strong. One young man who gave up beef explained his decision this way: "They say the risk of getting the disease is one in a million or about the same as winning the lottery. And that may be true. But every week I play the lottery".

And in continental Europe another factor that played on people's emotions is the fact that after a number of cases of negligence, trust in the British government was already at point zero. John Major and his colleagues were considered in Europe to be totally insensitive to the harm caused to health and the environment by big industry (as could be seen, for example, in the Brent Spar case).

3. Is the issue media-friendly?

Although the issue was not new in 1996, media coverage of it exploded and played a significant role in the escalation of public emotions. Again, the powerful pictures of the terrible effects of the disease on cattle whose brains had turned to sponge made for a very good story, almost guaranteed to keep audiences glued to their television screens. The media could argue that it actually helped to prevent more people being infected by the disease. The media loved the issue, because it was the perfect opportunity to expose the faults, lies and mistakes of the British government and specifically to damage the personal image of John Major, who had already lost his media popularity some time before. Additionally, public protests and hysteria could be covered easily by the media. For example, schools across the country that had been advised to take beef products, including hamburgers, off their lunch menus provided excellent media fodder in the form of interviews with students and teachers about how they felt about the issue.

4. Are there connections to other issues of the company or other companies?

There are a number of connections between the mad cow scandal and other issues, which explains why the outrage was so strong. First, there is a general connection to the debate over the health effects of meat. Many people have turned away from beef because of research findings linking red meat to cancer and heart diseases. Then there is a perceived connection between BSE and other kinds of brain diseases, including scrapie and similar neurological diseases in animals such as the mink, mule deer and elk; and, recently, neurological disease in household cats.

In Continental Europe there were also general connections to a number of other failings of the British government, such as its failure promptly to inform the EC of the probable link between BSE and CJD, and its refusal to send its main BSE experts to share information with Brussels until the imposition of the ban.

Later, in 1997, although not directly related to mad cow disease, a coincidental connection came up with the subject of cloning. In

March, front pages of newspapers carried photographs of two identical sheep, clones produced from a laboratory-grown cell. Much discussion ensued about the abominations that man is perpetrating upon nature, making people more highly suspicious of what they eat: hormones, chemicals, genetically engineered food, etc.

5. How strong is the key activist group?

In this issue there was no single strong activist group. Instead, the range included consumer associations, vegetarian organisations, animals right activists, non-British farmers in the EU, families of CJD victims, and EU legislators. Despite the fact that a single strong group was missing, because of the high level of concern, the issue had a significant impact on British farmers. Once the media interest caught up, politicians "jumped" on the issue as well.

6. How isolated is the company?

The issue affected all players in the beef production chain, including beef producers (farmers and cattlers), abattoirs (slaughterhouses), butchers, etc.

However, British beef farmers in general were isolated from their European counterparts. When the other EU countries adopted the "Carver–Greenfield" meat and bone manufacturing system from the United States in 1980, they supplemented the new process with a sterilisation stage, which the United Kingdom decided not to adopt. So the European beef producers could argue with some reason that their beef was much safer than UK beef.

However, for consumers it is difficult to identify the origin of the meat that they buy. In most cases, beef is not sold with a brand name, but as a kind of commodity. Therefore, isolating British meat from continental European meat was easier said than done. As a result, the entire European beef industry was severely affected. To protect its own interests, the EU decided in 1996 to ban imports of British meat. This is what finally isolated the British farmers.

7. How far have the dynamics of the crisis already evolved?

A diffusion curve for the BSE case shows the following events:

1976:	Carleton Gajdusek wins the Nobel Prize for classifying scrapie and CJD as the same kind of disease.
1980:	The process of preparing cattle feed is changed by the introduction of "Carver–Greenfield" meat-and-bone-meal manufacturing system from the United States. The system uses the carcasses of dead cattle in the feed. The process lowers the temperature for meat-and-bone sterilisation from 140°C to 100°C. Scientists warn the UK industry of the risks, because the United Kingdom is the only European nation to adopt the new process without a sterilisation stage.
April, 1985:	The first case of BSE is identified by a veterinary surgeon on a small farm in the South of England, who assumes it to be a severe case of scrapie.
November, 1986:	BSE first comes to the attention of the scientific community with the appearance of a newly recognised form of neurological disease.
July, 1987:	The UK government is aware of the existence of BSE and of the fact that scientists could not determine whether it could or could not be transmitted to other species or to humans. However no public announcement is made.
June, 1988:	The UK government enforced compulsory declaration of all BSE cases to health authorities.
July, 1988:	With increased cases of BSE, the UK government decides to ban the use of cattle carcasses in the preparation of cattle feed. This ban excludes existing stocks.
December, 1988:	The use of milk from suspect cattle is banned for any purpose other than that of suckling calves.

July, 1989:	A ban is imposed on the use of brain, spinal cord and tonsil, thymus, spleen and intestine of cattle origin – known as Specified Bovine Offals in foods for human consumption. By this stage, neighbouring countries are getting increasingly worried about BSE and cattle are monitored continuously in these countries.
August, 1989:	Public awareness of the issue intensifies and the government decides to ban the feeding of meat-based meal to ruminants.
June, 1990:	Scientific findings show that infection could cross the barrier between two species. There is evidence that the disease could be transmitted to cats and pigs. France and Germany sought to introduce trade restrictions on British beef. Emotions run high within the United Kingdom as the media emphasises the danger of consuming British beef and the fact that the government had known about the danger for nearly 10 years. The Minister for Agriculture, John Gummer, stolidly reassures the public by sharing a Big Mac with his six-year-old daughter.
May, 1995:	BSE is reported in 10 countries and areas outside the United Kingdom. In one group of countries, disease occurred in native cattle that had been fed with cattle feed imported from the United Kingdom. In another group, cases are identified only in cattle imported from the United Kingdom.
March, 1996:	The UK government admits for the first time that human CJD is linked to BSE in cattle. The EU imposes a ban on British beef.
June, 1996:	Partial lift of the EU ban on UK beef exports is announced after protest by the British government.
July, 1996:	The European Parliament (EP) decides to set up a temporary committee to inquire into BSE.

October, 1996:   The strongest evidence yet of a human link to BSE is declared and the EP recommends that the British Parliament undertakes a selective culling programme. The programme is not approved by the British Parliament.

December, 1996:   The United Kingdom agrees to a selective culling programme.

January, 1997:   Consumer confidence plummets and a political row erupts over BSE, which results in the Agriculture Minister's order for the destruction of 5200 cattle imported from Britain.

February, 1997:   The results of the EU inquiry and the recommendations for the future are submitted.

This diffusion curve is shown in Figure 7.3.

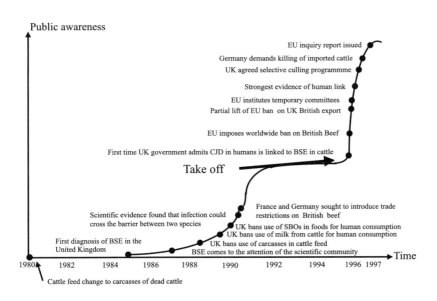

Figure 7.3 Diffusion curve for the BSE issue

What we can see from the diffusion curve is the clear take-off point. In 1996, suspicions that had been building up for six years suddenly reached a critical mass and the result was a spontaneous boycott and the EU ban of British meat. For some days, even hamburger chains stopped serving British beef because people refused to eat it. The "hysteria" in the United Kingdom and other EU countries lasted throughout 1996. Only later in 1997 was the confidence of consumers partially restored and the sales of beef (in volume and price) beginning to return to pre-crisis levels.

Possible scenarios

To forecast how future dynamics of the issue might play out for the British farmers, we develop some scenarios for the issue. As key uncertainties for this question we may identify:

- the success of the complete eradication of BSE from existing cattle through incinerating all infected animals;
- the number of new CJD cases in humans that are linked with the consumption of BSE-contaminated beef.

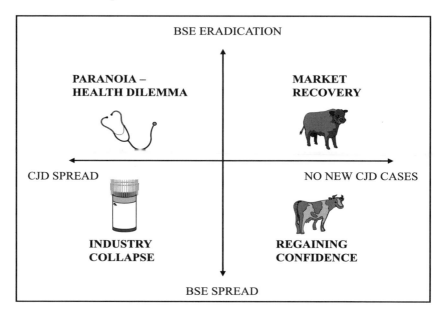

Figure 7.4   Scenario analysis for the BSE issue

Combining these two uncertainties, we get a four-field matrix, which can be seen in Figure 7.4.

The four resulting scenarios can be described as follows.

Market recovery

The situation comes back to a normal level. The United Kingdom has completed its massive killing programme and carcasses have been destroyed. BSE and CJD are no longer making the headlines. The beef industry is working toward a normalisation of the situation. However, consumer associations insist that some preventive measure be enforced in order to avoid a new crisis. The British farmers, UK government and other EU States must implement and enforce some new regulations and ensure the future safety of the breeding industry.

Paranoia

The UK culling program has been completed successfully. No new cases of BSE have been diagnosed among British cattle or any others. However, CJD incidences among the population rise. Every new case is examined and reported on in detail by the media. Rumours and beliefs about the possibility of large-scale contamination and an epidemic make their way around. The government and the scientific community are under severe pressure from the public. The EU is not willing to lift the ban on UK beef. Prices and consumption are declining again. Consumer associations and public opinion call for clear and reliable diagnostic tools at animal and human level.

Industry collapse

A limited culling programme has been conducted. Only cattle with declared BSE are being killed and incinerated. After a low in the number of cases, BSE makes a come back within British herds and numerous cases are diagnosed. At the same time, the number of patients infected by CJD continues to increase, in spite of the domestic bans on cattle bone-meals, implementation of new in-activation methods in the beef derivatives industry and the ban on the distribution of offal. The media publish these stories in the headlines and the general public avoids beef and beef products like the plague. Prices and volumes reach a historical low. The industry is devastated and cattle farmers are switching to poultry or pork farming *en masse.*

Regaining confidence

The public "forgets" its concerns over the BSE issue and beef consumption enjoys a moderate but steady increase. The media and scientific community assume that the preventive measures taken since 1988 have finally proven efficient in preventing further human contamination. However, the industry still suffers from the EU ban and urges the government to allocate extra subsidies to farmers and other players in the beef chain. The situation evolves chronically, as UK domestic markets recover and British beef gradually comes back to its previous market shares. Still, no chances of a lifting of the EU ban are envisioned. The public is reassured by the current media campaign orchestrated by the beef industry. Consumers have no more interest in BSE and believe that British beef is now as safe as that of any other origin, but suspicion remains and any new incident might provoke a new crisis.

8. How easy is the solution?

In 1996, when the issue exploded, a large part of the damage had already been done and, for British farmers, solutions were not so easy to find.

In order to regain public trust in UK beef, one proposed solution was the selective culling of animals that could potentially develop the disease (all cows over 30 months of age) – to incinerate them. However, objections to incineration as a method of disposal of the culled cattle were being raised by some environmental associations because of the risk of dispersal of the BSE agent into the sky. Additionally, the UK currently had only nine incinerators specially licensed for this purpose, thus creating a serious capacity problem.

There are also a number of preventive measures that can be taken by British farmers and the government. This includes neutralising the BSE or scrapie agent in feed, putting in place a system for cattle identification and making use of better veterinary controls. Some of these measures have already been taken. Meat producers have started to join their sector's quality assurance scheme. Launched in 1992, Farm Assured British Beef and Lamb (FABBL) sought to assure buyers and consumers not only of the high quality of the meat, but also of the origins, feeding, welfare and management of the animals concerned. The total membership of this organisation has jumped from 500 UK beef producers in 1993 to 9300 in 1996, ensuring that an estimated 25% of UK beef producers have been inspected thoroughly and accepted into the scheme and can market their animals with quality assurance.

Table 7.6 Visualised company checklist for the BSE issue

Assessment criteria	Rating					Comments
	++	+	0	–	– –	
Plausibility		•				Contamination of food chain certain; CJD cases still largely unexplained.
Potential for emotions	•					Food is emotional; mad cows give visuals.
Media-friendliness	•					Good opportunity to upset British government.
Connections with other issues		•				Other diseases and other mistakes of British government.
Strength of the key activist group			•			No strong single activist group.
Degree of company isolation		•				UK as a whole isolated.
Dynamics		•				Discussion has reached preliminary peak; further diffusion depends on which scenario will unfold.
Ease of solution			•			Only selective culling, better quality and marketing efforts.
Overall assessment		•				

To rebuild the image of the industry, these measures must be accompanied by a good communications strategy. For this purpose, the industry has launched an advertising campaign titled "Meat Matters" against the negative publicity and misinformation about red meat, claiming that meat-eating is healthy.

The company checklist is shown in Table 7.6.

The Results

As we said, the impact of the BSE crisis on farmers was strong, hitting many points of the company checklist. The fact that the media were looking for a good scandal involving the British government was especially instrumental in getting the issue all the media attention it needed. A single farmer would have been unable to protect his own company from the crisis, because many of the critical decisions were not taken by the companies, but by the British government.

What the checklist shows as well, however, is that there is some hope for the future. For one thing, there is the "short memory" of consumers whose concern for the issue is expected to decrease as the media gradually lose interest in the subject. And secondly, a number of corrective measures have been taken, which could eventually help to rebuild trust in British farmers.

Now we use the activist checklist to find out the adversaries' points of view on the issue. As we mentioned, none of the activist groups involved in the BSE issue constituted a single key group. So, contrary to the other case studies, we have to analyse the interests of these *several* groups in the "campaign" against British farmers.

1. The campaign should have a clear aim or goal

As there was no single adversary, the issue did not involve a single campaign with a single goal. Rather, there were a number of different campaigns with different goals:

- *Consumer organisations*: ensure high quality of meat, ensure adequate labelling.
- *Animal rights activists*: ensure better treatment of cattle.
- *Vegetarian organisations*: reduce meat consumption in general.

- *Non-British farmers*: keep their industry's good image, ban the sales of beef from the United Kingdom and establish food and health policies.
- *Families of CJD victims*: compensate CJD casualties economically.
- *EU legislator*: ensure high food safety standard in Europe and protect national industries.

2. The issue is easily understood by the general public

In general, consumers are becoming increasingly wary of what they eat. They are always concerned about food issues, particularly when told they may be eating something dangerous or unnatural. People are paying more attention to the close relationship between human health and nutrition. So, despite some lack of clear conclusions and some contradictory data material in the BSE case, people could understand the issue. Also, the UK government's and beef producers' negligence is a story that the public have seen many times before. Therefore, each of the groups' campaigns and agendas were understood by the general public because the "bad" guys were easy to find.

3. The issue has a high symbolic value

The contamination of beef with BSE is somehow symbolic of the behaviour of the entire beef industry. It symbolises the frequent unhygienic circumstances in the industry. Additionally, the symbolic value increases because of the fact that in the United Kingdom, beef is deeply rooted in society's nutritional traditions (i.e. Sunday lunch). This suggested that there was another national institution in which the population had no confidence, changing the eating habits of a nation and of their European neighbours as well.

4. The issue has the potential to damage the image of the company

The activists' opponents were, in this case, both the British farmers and the UK government. The media and the various interest groups focused their critique on the farmers and less on other related industries (the biotechnology industry, traders, food companies and retailers). The image of the farmers was bad anyway because of animal welfare protests and concerns over the "fat" cheques that farmers were said to receive from Brussels. So it was quite easy to damage their image.

The second target was the UK government. People did not trust this government even before the BSE scandal. So the UK government, in particular, was vulnerable to any further image-damaging scandals. The contradictory information the government gave out about mad cow disease added fuel to the flames.

5. The opponent is strong enough (no "underdog" effect)

British farmers appeared strong in terms of turnover. Sales were worth approximately £4 billion in 1996. However, the industry was quite fragmented and there were only a few big players. So there was no single strong opponent and, additionally, the relatively high number of employees in the industry might trigger an underdog image effect. On the other hand, consumers claimed that the British farmers were being protected by a government that was putting the interests of farmers and beef producers before consumers. In addition to that, the public was displeased by the fact that agriculture had for many years received high subsidies.

Still, in an overall evaluation it seems there were no really strong opponents and the different activist groups were therefore a little bit more careful with their critique than they would probably have been in the case of one big company.

6. The issue can be "packaged" in a campaign in which the public can get involved

Since there were a number of key activist groups, none of them dominating, there was also no single campaign against British farmers. Still, the issue had a number of episodes that can be considered interesting and that helped to make the issue symbolic:

- Security was tightened to protect Douglas Hogg, UK Minister of Agriculture, after he faced heated protests about the handling of the beef crisis.
- In September 1996 French farmers drove a herd of cattle across the country, blocked roads, marched around the Eiffel Tower and harassed tourists to protest against falling beef prices.
- In November 1996 the French authorities shut down the Hard Rock Café in Paris after accusing the restaurant of serving British beef. The beef was actually of Irish origin, but had been stored in a warehouse in London, thus leading to the legal proceedings. The same thing occurred in Madrid.
- In December 1996 French farmers mounted a blockade at the Swiss border on the grounds that Swiss cattle could infect their herds and that the import of beef from that country was undermining consumer confidence (Switzerland is the country with the largest number of BSE cases in continental Europe).
- In January 1997 a German farmer whose cow developed BSE was placed under police protection after having received death threats.

7. There are solutions that are confrontational, not gradual

The different activist groups had different interests and sought different solutions. However, basically, none of the activist groups could offer solutions beyond the selective killing of cattle and improvement of general hygienic conditions. This solution is, of course, leading to quite significant disadvantages for British farmers and taxpayers.

The families of the CJD victims have the compensation solution in mind.

8. There could be a dramatic element to the campaign to engage media

The BSE issue had a number of dramatic elements to keep the interest of the media: the pictures of the mad cows, then

Table 7.7   Visualised activist checklist for the BSE issue

Assessment criteria	++	+	0	−	−−	Comments
Clear aim or goal				•		Different adversaries with different goals.
Understandable by public		•				Issue can be built on general food concerns.
Symbolic		•				Symbolic for poor hygiene in British beef industry.
Image can be damaged		•				General bad image of British beef industry.
Strong opponent					•	No, because farmers are only small companies.
Public can get involved			•			No single campaign; boycott difficult.
Confrontational solution			•			Selective culling, more hygiene, compensation of victims.
Dramatic elements		•				Some drama through mistakes of British government.

| Overall assessment | | • | | | | Good object for outside pressure campaign. |

the erroneous steps made by the UK government. Activist groups also created some dramatic elements, like blocking meat transports, campaigning in supermarkets, occupying slaughter-houses, etc. So the potential for some dramatic elements was present, even if the strategies of the different groups were not coherent.

The activist checklist may look as it does in Table 7.7.

The Results

From the activist checklist we can see that the issue could have made a good campaign for the mentioned groups. However, none of them really took the lead, and British farmers were therefore more affected by the media than by any action campaign. This is, however, a typical pattern for health-related issues, where the media often push a topic directly into broad public awareness.

CASE 4: FASHION DESIGNERS USING FUR AND ANIMAL RIGHT ACTIVISTS

The wearing of animal fur to protect oneself from the elements and for personal convenience has long been an accepted practice in society. However, in the modern-day Western world, animal fur is sold mainly for purposes of fashion and vanity and there are many lower-cost and more convenient alternatives to fur in clothing.

Between 1980 and 1987, fur fashion experienced constant growth in the Western world, especially in the United States. It reached its all-time high in 1987 when retail sales of fur coats in the United States hit an estimated US$2.3 billion before beginning to decline, plagued by animal rights protests and a combination of other factors. In 1991, retail sales bottomed out at close to US$ 1 billion.

Animal rights groups attributed the drop in sales to the strong anti-fur campaigns that they had fought over the years. Indeed, several major department stores across the United States stopped stocking and selling fur (citing the reason for the decrease in demand as being due to a repressed economy rather than deterrence by animal rights groups). Many super models signed contracts with animal rights groups promising to abstain from wearing furs. On the government side, the United States, heading into the bottom of the recession and looking for extra income, introduced a tax of up to 20% on the sale of luxury goods, which included fur coats. The EU passed a ban on the importation of fur that had been made from animals caught in leg-hold traps. The animal rights organisations also received a dose of pure luck from Mother Nature: the winters in 1989–1991 were some of the warmest the United States had seen.

After 1991, fur sales began to climb again, and some industry analysts expected them to top the US$2 billion mark by the end of 1997. Major designers began to use fur again in their latest fashions and department stores that had once abandoned fur began to stock it again. Several supermodels renounced their original agreements with animal rights activists, the most publicised being Naomi Campbell. It seemed that there had been a resurgence in the social acceptability of wearing fur. And finally, the US government, pressured by fur lobbyists, managed to re-open discussions with the EU in order to negotiate a delay in the implementation of the leg-trap import ban. In countries like South Korea, Japan and Russia, imports of fur from the United States and other Western countries were increasing rapidly. The end result: full-length coats may not be as popular they were 10 years ago; however, fur used in trimming and other accessory type designs is definitely making a resurgence. Still, animal rights groups are fighting against fur fashions, arguing that innocent animals are being tortured for sheer human vanity.

We now use the company checklist to analyse the issue of fur and animal rights from the viewpoint of the fashion industry; in particular, fashion designers like Oscar de la Renta, Karl Lagerfeld, Valentino and Perry using fur for their collections. Even if managers in other industries do not identify immediately with fashion designers, the case study may help them to understand the impact of similar campaigns on an extremely image-conscious industry with very rapidly changing product cycles. Should these designers worry about pressure from the animal rights groups?

1. Are the arguments against the issue plausible?

First, people have questioned whether it is acceptable to kill animals for their pelts. Secondly, there are discussions on the humaneness of the methods currently being employed to raise and kill the animals.

Throughout the history of mankind, humans killed animals for food, protection, convenience and sometimes for sport. In modern times, technology has advanced to the point where it is theoretically possible to exist comfortably without having to kill animals (except for medicinal purposes). This technical progress has opened the way for ethical discussions on the purposes for which mankind has the right to kill animals. Even if there is, so far, no agreement on this question, more and more people argue that animals should be used only when necessary, and not abused. Fur is no longer vital to human beings for surviving winters, so fur use, by these standards, falls into the "abuse" category. Therefore, the issue can be considered plausible from this perspective.

There are two methods of obtaining animal fur: trapping and farm-breeding. About half of all furs sold in the United States come from wild animals (fox, mink, etc.) who were caught in traps. The other half are raised on fur farms. Animals rights groups argue that both techniques seriously violate animal rights. Trapped animals die slow and painful deaths. Some animals have been known to chew their legs off in order to free themselves from serrated leg-hold traps. Larger traps for wolves, foxes and lynx are especially cruel as they cannot be constructed in any quick-kill way. And, unfortunately, traps are indiscriminate and, like dolphins in tuna nets, other animals often end up dying in them (dogs, cats or birds). Even humans have been caught in traps. When it comes to breeding (mainly mink), many of the farms that supply the US market seem to violate basic animal rights by keeping the animals in cramped cages, using inappropriate killing methods or other unacceptable treatment. For example, in order to get quality fur (soft hair) animals are often forced to live in cages where they can barely move.

Even if the designers do not have a direct responsibility for killing these animals, it is clear that their use of fur encourages the fur industry to continue its practices. So the arguments against the use of fur are plausible.

2. Does the issue evoke emotion? Is it understandable – visual, touching – by the public?

The issue has a strong potential for emotion. It does not take any scientific knowledge to understand that animals suffer terribly when caught in traps or live out their short existences in cramped conditions on fur farms. The issue can be made visual. Animal rights activists use photographs and video clips cleverly to fuel their campaigns. Some groups use pictures and videos containing horrendous scenes such as beavers being drowned slowly in underwater traps, foxes being crudely electrocuted and mink having their necks snapped by furriers.

The human touch comes in especially when beautiful animals are killed – for example, wolves, who closely resemble dogs. Commonalties with Man's Best Friend are obvious and there are strong feelings for these animals.

3. Is the issue media-friendly?

The issue has been media-friendly in the past. Between 1987 and 1991, animal rights groups staged a number of attention-getting media stunts. There were pictures of animals trapped in steel bars, mink held in narrow cages and baby seals clubbed to death. Additionally, the animal rights groups started a multi-million dollar advertisement campaign featuring many supermodels posing nude and stating "I'd rather go naked than wear fur," which was obviously extraordinary and received a lot of media publicity.

However, today, the issue seems to have lost its novelty and the media are less interested. One of the best-known designers, Karl Lagerfeld, may have been right when he said: "People are tired of being politically correct". Still, there is always some media-friendliness because of the nature of the issue. Designers love the media spotlight and will always have an interest in saying why they choose to use or not use fur in their collections.

4. Are there connections to other issues of the company or other companies?

The fur issue is connected to animals rights in general, including the prevention of the extinction of endangered species, the ban on killing animals for laboratory research, cruel training methods in circuses, hunting and fishing for sport, etc. However, it seems that none of these animal right issues has, at the moment, a very high priority in the value system of society.

Secondly, there are connections to general trends in society, such as vegetarianism. Another is environmental protection – fur processing is a rather crude technology that releases poisonous materials like formaldehyde and chromium into the environment. In 1991, two US pelt-processing companies were fined US$1.6 million for "massive pollution".

5. How strong is the key activist group?

The groups fighting the fur industry cover the spectrum from mainstream groups, such as The Humane Society, and People for the Ethical Treatment of Animals (PETA) with almost 500 000 members, to more extreme groups such as the Coalition to Abolish the Fur Trade (CAFT) and militant groups like Animal Liberation Frontline, which advocates violent protests and destruction of property. Altogether, it is estimated that in the United States alone there are about 400 animal advocacy groups. However, these groups do not co-operate with each other on any significant scale as each has different objectives.

Among these groups, PETA is probably the one with the most power. PETA is a professional, internationally operating, non-profit organisation with offices in the United Kingdom, The Netherlands and Germany. It brings together members of the scientific, judicial and legislative communities. PETA has good media access, its managers can take fast decisions and its thorough investigations are so respected that they have, in the past, led to government involvement in the issues investigated.

The fragmentation of the animal rights groups has been a problem in recent years. The violent antics of the more radical fringe groups undermine the credibility of the mainstream groups in public opinion. At the same time, the fragmentation provides some strength, making it possible to cover wide ranges of issues related to animal rights.

6. How isolated is the company?

The fashion industry is fragmented, consisting mainly of small entities that do not represent a uniform body to the outside world. To stay in business, it is extremely important for designers to differentiate themselves from their competition to create an interest for their own collections, even if they have to stir up some controversy.

The designers who still use fur are isolated only to a certain degree. Their number has risen from around 40 to over 100 in the United States within a decade. Only a few fashion designers like Calvin Klein, Donna Karan and Georgio Armani have declared a no-fur policy for their clothes and accessories, while others like Karl Lagerfeld, Valentino and Perry took it in again. So there is no real danger of being isolated, and any attention this might attract is not necessarily a bad thing in this particular industry.

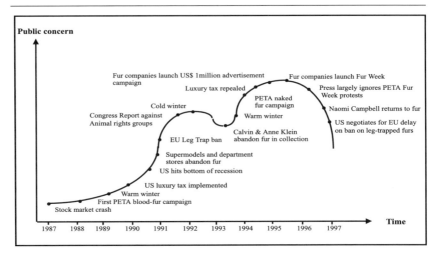

Figure 7.5 Diffusion curve for the fur issue

7. How far have the dynamics of the crisis already evolved?

In the early nineteenth century, the first animal rights groups formed to prevent the extinction of certain species. Later, they broadened their scope to protest at the use of animals for medical and scientific research. In the 1950s and 1960s, animal issues got more attention. The discussion focused at that time on whether animals really have rights. In the 1970s, groups first started to speak of oppression and liberation of animals. But the real anti-fur campaign took off only in 1987 and since then has had many ups and downs.

Figure 7.5 shows the diffusion curve of the fur issue.

Today, it seems that the interest in animal rights is on the decline, indicating that the dynamics of the issue will not accelerate further.

8. How easy is the solution?

If they wanted to, the fashion designers who are still using fur could use a number of options to avoid further confrontation with animal rights activists. They could simply design their clothes without fur. This would be not difficult, but they might lose a few customers and maybe even trademark parts of their identities. They could use artificial fur. Synthetic pelts look almost as natural as real ones and are much cheaper. Most fur-loving customers, however, only want the real thing and will simply switch to a competitor who can offer it to them. They could be more careful about the kind of fur they buy to encourage the fur industry to maintain certain animal treatment standards. One recent effort in the food sector in the United Kingdom shows a possible approach. The Royal Society for the Prevention of Cruelty to Animals is pioneering a "Freedom Food" labelling programme. Farms that meet the society's guidelines (for example, no battery eggs) can use the "Freedom Food" logo for their marketing. Something similar may be launched for the fur industry as well.

In general, the designers could solve the problem if they wanted to. They decide *de facto* what fashion will be in next year (supply drives demand).

The company checklist is shown in Table 7.8.

Table 7.8 Visualised company checklist for the fur issue

Assessment criteria	Rating					Comments
	++	+	0	–	––	
Plausibility		●				Fur is no longer vital for human beings; animals suffer.
Potential for emotions	●					People understand the issue, suffering can be made visual; humans are touched when beautiful animals are killed.
Media-friendliness			●			Issue not new and extraordinary.
Connections with other issues			●			Animal rights in general; environmental damages through pelt-processing.
Strength of the key activist group		●				Fragmented groups, only one strong adversary.
Degree of company isolation			●			No real danger for single designer.
Dynamics				●		Dynamics on decline.
Ease of solution		●				Designers could escape from pressure fast.
Overall assessment		●				Awareness: yes; immediate danger: no

The Results

It seems from our company checklist that although the fashion designers who use fur are aware of the dangers of activist pressure, the risks are outweighed by the advantages of the continued use of fur. To stay in the public spotlight, a slightly isolated position might even work to the designers' advantage. As fashion is a fast business, the designers can change their policies in the blink of an eye should the pressure start to cause some damage. So, at the moment, while fur sales are booming, there does not seem to be any reason for giving in to the activist groups.

We now use the activist checklist to analyse why animal rights groups such as PETA have a special interest in fighting against designers using fur in order to protect animal rights. If they want to protect animals they could also focus on food, which is the purpose for which most animals are killed. Even if they want to concentrate on clothes, they could protest against leather shoes and other leather items. Karl Lagerfeld argued for example: "Your shoes are made of leather, your Chanel bag is not plastic, and look, you have meat on your plate. So please, don't talk to me about fur." And we analyse why this activist group chooses designers who use fur as the main target of their protest and not the other companies in the fur value chain.

1. The campaign should have a clear aim or goal

PETA's overall mission is to prevent animals from being eaten, worn, experimented on, or used for entertainment. In its campaign against fur, PETA has more specific goals. In the short term, the activists are interested in getting the issue to come back into the public arena. They want to damage the image of those designers who are using fur, thus creating an anti-fur feeling in society.

In physical terms, one goal of PETA is to ensure a world-wide "humane" trapping standard by banning the use of leg-hold traps in the United States and Canada, because they are banned in Europe. Additionally, the group aims to eradicate fur farms, or at least improve breeding conditions. Their long-term goal is to ban all forms of killing for fur.

2. The issue is easily understood by the general public

The issue is easy to understand. Pictures of animal cruelty speak for themselves and people know that wearing furs is no longer a necessity, but done mainly out of vanity. The issue has been understood and strongly supported in the past. The animal rights groups themselves continue to educate the public to make the issue understandable. For example, they distribute pamphlets with pictures of bloody animals caught in traps, bearing the message: "Get a feel for fur – slam your fingers in a car door". The drop in attention to the fur issue should not be attributed to lack of understanding, but rather to waning interest in animal rights.

3. The issue has a high symbolic value

Fur is a symbolic product and basically stands for human vanity. The very image-conscious nature of the industry and use of symbolic images should be an advantage to an activist group if the campaign can be handled using professional public relations methods. The issue could be an ideal battleground for animal rights groups.

4. The issue has the potential to damage the image of the company

Activist groups nip at the heels of fur-using designers and may be able to sour their image with the general public. However, an important point to keep in mind is that these designers and their target customer segment are a rather atypical representation of the general public.

The designers live on their brand names, their most important assets, so their success depends on whether they are able to project a powerful and positive image. From this perspective they are vulnerable to activist criticism.

5. The opponent is strong enough (no "underdog" effect)

Designers such as Lagerfeld, Valentino, etc. are only the tip of the fur industry iceberg, which includes distributors, wholesalers and hunters, farmers, etc. Overall, the fashion industry seems to be a good opponent for animal rights activists. It has more of a spoiled dog than an underdog image. Still, it is generally accepted and even liked by the public since it represents the nice lifestyle that many people would like to enjoy.

Hunters and farmers, however, represent less powerful opponents. Statistics show that there are 80 000 trappers in Canada and in the event of a broad fur boycott, most of them would end up without a job. On the other hand, the animal rights activists argue that only a small part of the trappers' income is derived from trapping (it is usually a second job for extra cash). Certainly, the designers would not have to go hungry if they were to leave fur out of their designs. Therefore, it is quite understandable why animal rights activists go after the designers and target much less the other parties involved in the fur business.

6. The issue can be "packaged" in a campaign in which the public can get involved

Basically, the fur issue can be nicely packaged in an interesting campaign and animal activist groups have done this successfully in the past. The campaigns consisted of bloodying furs, lobbying designers, stoning and picketing stores selling fur products, and even throwing blood-red paint on anyone on the street wearing a fur coat. The main problem that animal rights activists face today is that the public are tired of the issue, and the public (mostly the American public) have simply forgotten how adamant they had once felt about fur.

Whilst at the beginning the campaigns were dramatic in order to give everyone a "wake-up" call, today lots of people turn away and do not want to see it any more. The various campaigns launched in the past two decades were heavily repetitive and attracted quite often the same audience. In this respect, the interest might have bottomed out somehow. Stunts like the latest one by PETA (smashing a pie on Oscar de la Renta's face during a fashion show while yelling, "Fur shame – Oscar kills") are not causing a commotion any more. Furthermore, fur is a seasonal product and it is difficult to maintain a campaign over a long enough period of time to raise a significant level of public interest. The fact that the campaign has to be re-launched every six months makes it difficult to keep momentum.

Still, compared to other possible animal rights campaigns, the issue is more symbolic and more interesting. People can participate in boycotts, criticise others who wear fur in public and protest actively.

7. There are solutions that are confrontational, not gradual

Basically, the solutions that PETA can offer coincide with their goals: not to use fur for fashion. This solution would imply less comfort for the people who wear fur coats, but they should be able to satisfy their vanity with other fashion items. Better trapping and farming techniques would be accepted by PETA as intermediate solutions.

8. There could be a dramatic element to the campaign to engage the media

As we have seen in the news, there are enough dramatic elements available to make the campaign interesting for the media. The problem for the animal rights groups at the moment is that they have already used everything in their bag of tricks at least once. Media interest will be difficult to regain. Table 7.9 summarises the activist checklist.

The Results

The activist checklist shows why fur is still a preferred target of animal right groups. Among all animal rights issues, it is certainly the one that has been able to stir up the most public attention. However, as the checklist shows, it is still difficult for these groups to keep up momentum, because the acceptance of wearing fur appears to be cyclical. The fashion designers can get away with using fur for a while longer at least.

Table 7.9 Visualised activist checklist for the fur issue

Assessment criteria	Rating					Comments
	++	+	0	–	––	
Clear aim or goal		●				Get issue back on agenda and ensure "humane" trapping.
Understandable by public			●			Animal killing is understandable and gives good visuals.
Symbolic		●				Fur stands for human vanity; fashion designers make heavy use of symbols themselves.
Image can be damaged			●			Designers exposed to criticism, even if broad population are not their customers.
Strong opponent			●			Designers are strongest opponent in the fur value chain.
Public can get involved			●			Possible, but issue is already drawn-out.
Confrontational solution			●			Do not use fur or at least use "humane" trapping methods.
Dramatic elements			●			A lot of possibilities, but all have been used before.

Overall assessment   [| ● | | |]   Still most promising issue for animal rights campaign.

CASE 5: MITSUBISHI AND ITS WORLD-WIDE LOGGING OPERATIONS

The Mitsubishi Corporation is the trading company of the Mitsubishi group, a *keiretsu* consisting of 190 interlinked companies, and hundreds of related firms. The total turnover of the Mitsubishi group is approximately US$166 billion and the gross trading profit is US$5 billion, making it one of the largest corporate economies in the world. The Mitsubishi Corporation fully or partially owns logging operations throughout the world and is also active in the timber trade. Mitsubishi's logging activities are spread across Brazil, Malaysia, Chile, Bolivia, Indonesia, Siberia, Philippines and Papua New Guinea.

Since 1989, Mitsubishi has been accused by environmentalists of destroying the rainforests. One activist group, the San Francisco-based Rainforest Action Network (RAN), is targeting the Mitsubishi Corporation as the world's worst corporate destroyer of rainforests. RAN is calling for an international boycott of Mitsubishi and all other companies in the *keiretsu*, including Mitsubishi Bank, Mitsubishi Heavy Industries, Mitsubishi Electronics, Mitsubishi Motors, Kirin Beer and Nippon Kogaku (the maker of Nikon camera equipment).

In the last years, this pressure has become quite intense for Mitsubishi and the company has had to take some uncomfortable decisions, like selling off a 40% share in the logging company, Daiya Malaysia Ltd, in 1996. We now use our company checklist to find out why Mitsubishi had to take these uncomfortable decisions and whether there might be more pressure ahead.

1. Are the arguments against the issue plausible?

Mitsubishi is involved in rainforest logging activities. Rainforests play a crucial role in the world's climate patterns and are an ecologically extremely important natural habitat because they contain about 50% of all living species. Current destruction of the rainforest is already taking its toll on the environment, and the future impact will undoubtedly be severe. While the rainforest used to cover 14% of the surface of the Earth, there is now only enough left to cover 6%. Yet deforestation has increased by 54% over the last 10 years. With the current rate of destruction it is estimated that the rainforest will be completely and permanently gone before the year 2050.

Rainforest destruction is caused partially by logging activities, but also by other activities such as conversion to farmland. Different (reliable) studies of the influence of logging on the rainforest suggest that logging is responsible for 10%–40% of the destruction. Even if many logging companies have programmes to replace the trees they cut down, these account only for a small portion of the magnitude of felled trees, and the replanted trees do not have the same ecological capabilities as the original trees. As Mitsubishi's Wood Products Division is involved in these logging activities, it is beyond doubt that the company plays a role in the destruction of the rainforest and even the company itself does not seriously put this in doubt. The contribution of the corporation is, however, unclear.

2. Does the issue evoke emotion? Is it understandable – visual, touching – by the public?

The issue evokes emotion to a certain degree, even if it is remote for most people in the developed Western economies. The issue can be understood by the general public. Environmental groups have worked over the last decade to raise awareness of the importance of the rainforests to the world's ecological balance in order to make the issue understandable. In the past two decades, society has become increasingly aware of: (i) the scale of rainforest devastation (not only with respect to the number of logging companies but also to their wide geographic action); (ii) the effects caused in the local environment (extinction of species and destruction of local community habitats); (iii) the potential damage to human life in the long run; and, maybe most important (iv) the negative impacts of past devastation on life today for a broader range of the world's population, notably with regard to changes in certain areas' climate. This growing level of awareness is, in turn, resulting in increasing public support for campaigns against rainforest devastation.

The issue is visual – it is relatively easy for activist groups to get pictures of large swathes of felled rainforest and associate it to timber-hungry Japanese companies. And activist groups have been quite successful in making the issue touching. Children around the globe have been learning about biodiversity in school, understanding the species of plants and animals at risk, while highlighting possible medical remedies that could be developed from rainforest-dwelling species. The use of loveable endangered rainforest animals as symbols keeps the issue touching.

So, in summary, the issue has some potential for emotion even if it is probably not the most emotional issue one can imagine. Besides the remoteness problem, another element that reduces the likelihood of emotional response is that the fight against logging is not concrete in terms of time and location. This makes it difficult to attract enough public attention in a short time to stir up a real emotional reaction.

3. Is the issue media-friendly?

The issue is, to a certain degree, media-friendly. Even if the debate over rainforest destruction is nothing new, the issue is extraordinary in the sense that for the first time the public are confronted by a well-known company that can be linked directly to rainforest destruction (not like McDonalds, which has been accused of indirectly destroying the rainforests). So there is a good playground on which to stage protests in the Western world without actually having to go to remote rainforest locations. This also reduces the media accessibility problem, making the issue easier to cover.

4. Are there connections to other issues of the company or other companies?

The issue is connected to a number of other issues, making it a dangerous battleground for Mitsubishi.

First, there are connections in that operations in rainforest areas are harmful not only because of deforestation. Environmental groups such as RAN are also worried about the plight of indigenous peoples and other social issues, such as the promotion of democracy. Mitsubishi is therefore, for example, accused of associating with political regimes like Myanmar/Burma that violate human rights, in order to maintain its logging operations in these countries. Other interconnected issues are bribes paid to politicians to get around local laws, and the transfer pricing policy of Japanese companies that engage in logging activities in developing countries.

Secondly, there are interconnections with other businesses where Mitsubishi is active. Mitsubishi Heavy Industries, for example, is providing the nuclear industry with plutonium, reactor cores, etc. It also manufactures aircraft, guided missiles and fighting vehicles. Additionally, Mitsubishi is active in mining and quarrying, which changes landscapes and dislocates populations. Furthermore, RAN alleges that some of Mitsubishi's operations are dramatic producers of waste, including the Canadian Chopstick Manufacturing Company, accused of wasting 85% of the trees they harvest because the wood is not white enough.

RAN points out that Mitsubishi's Alaska Pulp Company has been listed by the US Environmental Protection Agency (EPA) as one of the top ten worst polluters in the American West.

Thirdly, there are connections with the general behaviour of the company. At the moment, feminist groups, including the powerful National Organisation for Women (NOW) in the United States are protesting about allegations of sexual harassment at Mitsubishi Motors US facilities. And there are the often negative attitudes towards Japanese companies in general. RAN can rely on an element of the US population's anti-Japanese sentiment.

5. How strong is the key activist group?

RAN is not a strong opponent in comparison with groups such as Greenpeace with regard to its support basis (it only has 30 000 members). However, RAN has the advantage of forming a type of *keiretsu* with other action groups around the world such as Earth-Culture, Defenders of Wildlife, Rainforest Relief, Greenpeace, Japanese environmental groups like the Japanese Tropical Forest Action Network (JATAN) and smaller rainforest action groups. RAN is the co-ordinator of all these activist groups fighting against Mitsubishi. Through unifying its campaigns and forming an international coalition, RAN is able to take quick decisions and spring surprises on companies like Mitsubishi. So, overall, RAN can be assessed as a strong adversary for Mitsubishi.

6. How Isolated is the company?

Mitsubishi is quite isolated in this issue because it is one of the few logging companies that has a well-known consumer brand. There are two other corporations blamed for the logging of timber in the rainforests, called MacMillan Bloedel and Georgia Pacific. These companies are, however, less well known in the world and are thus less vulnerable to actions by environmental groups and consumers.

So, the players are clear: on the one side Mitsubishi as one of the world's biggest companies and on the other, the brave fighters of RAN.

7. How far have the dynamics of the crisis already evolved?

Looking at the diffusion of the topic, we can see that the dynamics of the issue have developed very well for RAN, while the situation seems to be getting uncomfortable for Mitsubishi. The following analysis of past events shows a discernible trend towards an escalation of the issue:

1980s: Growing awareness of rainforest destruction leads to international agreements of timber trade and the foundation of the International Timber Trade Organisation (ITTO).

1985: The Tropical Forestry Action Program (TFAP) is launched with the aim of slowing tropical deforestation and helping countries to formulate blueprints for environmentally sustainable forest management at the national, regional and global levels.

1989: "Ban Japan from the Rainforest" campaign. The World Rainforest Movement calls for the international boycott of Mitsubishi Corporation. An advertisement in the *New York Times* includes Mitsubishi along with seven other Japanese companies.

1990: "Ban Japan from the Rainforest" Day, with manifestations across the United States. Mitsubishi reacts with the foundation of an Environmental Affairs Department, which is in charge of co-ordinating all Mitsubishi communications activities regarding the environment. Also, a reforestation project in Malaysia is announced.

1991: "World Rainforest Week" brings heavy protests against Mitsubishi.

1992: Mitsubishi publishes a comic-book on deforestation which gets banned from further distribution.

1992: Earth Summit in Rio de Janeiro. Mitsubishi agrees on business principles on sustainable growth.

1993: RAN national advertising campaign against Mitsubishi. Full-page advertisement run in the *New York Times*.

1994: RAN takes over the responsibility of the entire campaign against Mitsubishi, co-ordinating the up-to-now isolated activities of Greenpeace, Friends of the Earth, Earth-First!, etc.

1995:   On 4 August, 1995 the Mitsubishi Corporation announces the sale of its 40% share in the logging giant Daiya Malaysia Ltd. The company indicates that it would reinvest profits from the sale in non-timber, value-added activities. It also states that the sale is part of its efforts to focus on core business areas and investments most closely aligned with the development of future business.

1995:   Eighteen American colleges sign a RAN-initiated resolution banning Mitsubishi products and recruiters from their campuses.

1996:   Circuit City, the largest personal electronics retail chain in the United States, announces that it is dropping Mitsubishi products because of low sales.

1996:   Fourteen more American colleges sign the resolution banning Mitsubishi products and recruiters from their campuses.

1996:   Three activists from Rainforest Action Network shut down the raw log export ship *Super Rubin* at the port of Longview, WA by chaining themselves to the ship.

1997:   San Francisco's Human Rights Commission (HRC) recommends against awarding Mitsubishi Heavy Industries of America a US$137 million contract to build a people-mover at San Francisco International Airport.

The diffusion curve for the different events is shown in Figure 7.6.

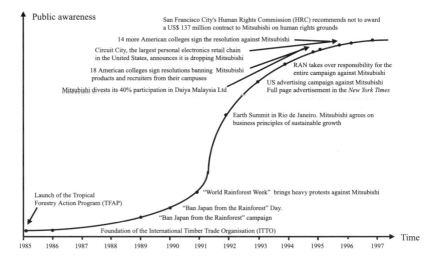

Figure 7.6   Diffusion curve for the Mitsubishi issue

8. How easy is the solution?

One partial solution for Mitsubishi could be to sell off its shares in the logging companies and give up trading timber. But this would mean a significant loss in business. Even RAN would like to avoid this solution, because the business would probably be taken over by small "pirates" who would be very likely to run irresponsible logging activities and would certainly be even more difficult to target. This situation is comparable with issues of nuclear weapons control where the public prefers these weapons to be in the hands of apparently responsible superpowers rather than in the hands of small and unpredictable countries.

Table 7.10 Visualised company checklist for the Mitsubishi issue

Assessment criteria	Rating					Comments
	++	+	0	–	– –	
Plausibility	●					Logging contributes to rainforest destruction.
Potential for emotions		●				People know about importance of rainforests; issue is visual.
Media-friendliness		●				To be able to catch one consumer goods company is extraordinary.
Connections with other issues	●					Mitsubishi companies are involved in a number of outside pressure issues.
Strength of the key activist group		●				RAN is small but highly co-ordinated to take fast decisions.
Degree of company isolation	●					Mitsubishi is the only renowned consumer brand involved in deforestation.
Dynamics		●				Pressure has not yet reached its peak.
Ease of solution		●				Mitsubishi could drop out of the business. This would still not save the rainforests.
Overall assessment		●				Mitsubishi has to fear more pressure to come.

So the solution would be rather that Mitsubishi implements a more sustainable form of logging, which takes care of environmental considerations as well.

The visualised company checklist for this issue may look as in Table 7.10.

The Results

The current situation seems to be risky for Mitsubishi. The analysis of actions directly aimed against Mitsubishi placed on the diffusion curve suggests that the momentum-gathering phase is not yet over, and the next evolution of campaigns is likely to be in favour of the activist groups rather than Mitsubishi, which has already been forced to give ground on a significant point.

Also significant is the current dark cloud over the brand name Mitsubishi as such, so that RAN can record as a personal success the sentence of the San Francisco Court against the concession of the SFO International Airport contract to Mitsubishi Heavy Industries, despite the fact that the reasons have nothing to do with the rainforest. By now, Mitsubishi's responses cannot be limited to rational point-by-point debate over RAN's arguments. To combat RAN, Mitsubishi will need to demonstrate that it is "environmentally friendly". Mitsubishi has tried this approach by advertising its contributions to the environment and changing its corporate literature through changing the mission statement. Mitsubishi has also responded directly to RAN in the media. These methods have, however, actually been more beneficial to RAN, because it has increased awareness even more.

We now use our activist checklist to try to work out what might have led RAN to decide to focus its "Save the Rainforest" campaign on Mitsubishi.

1. The campaign should have a clear aim or goal

By boycotting Mitsubishi, RAN hopes to stop what it believes to be Mitsubishi's "destructive activities in the world's tropical, temperate, and boreal forests". RAN wants Mitsubishi to stop its logging practices and implement environmentally conscious alternatives. This demand can be broken down into five specific points:

1. Allow an independent commission to investigate Mitsubishi's operations and those of its major timber suppliers, and implement the commission's recommendations.
2. Stop trading in any timber or timber products that are derived from natural forests, unless they are certified to be culturally, environmentally and socially benign.
3. Accelerate the research, development and implementation of alternative technologies and materials to reduce the demand for timber and other non-sustainable derived forest resources or products.
4. Make a written commitment that Mitsubishi and its affiliated companies will use their influence to convince other Japanese corporations to discontinue all operations that destroy natural forests or result in natural forest degradation.
5. Provide JATAN and RAN with a regular and complete report of its involvement in all logging operations, including partnership relations with other logging companies.

2. The issue is easily understood by the general public

The importance of the rainforests for world climate has been brought to the attention of a large public through the educative efforts of the activist groups. The issue can be framed in such a way that the public can distinguish the "good guys" from the "bad guys". And the issue is neither too technical nor too abstract – everybody can grasp the concept of destroyed rainforests and changing global climate.

3. The issue has a high symbolic value

Rainforests have a high symbolic value. They are one of the last symbols of the primitive, untouched earth, one of the favourite settings for adventure stories. Rainforest trees, such as the mahogany tree with its dark and beautifully grained wood, have symbolic value as well, to the point where they have become a lightning rod for environmental activists committed to saving the tropical forests of Latin America. However, as rainforests exist around the globe, environmental groups have to draw attention to the destructive activities of some companies through using symbols actively themselves.

RAN tries to create additional symbols in its campaign language with wording such as "The sun never sets on Mitsubishi's relentless global logging operation", or the assertion that the Malaysian rainforest is being demolished 24 hours a day by Mitsubishi's logging operations. RAN makes heavy use of symbols in its campaign, such as its weekly action consisting of placing a 35-ft inflatable chainsaw emblazoned with, "Mitsubishi, Stop the Chainsaw Massacre" at a Mitsubishi dealership or autoshow.

4. The issue has the potential to damage the image of the company

As we mentioned, people can easily understand that destroying rainforests for profit is something bad and such accusations can easily destroy the image of Mitsubishi. With its widely recognised brand name and product range, Mitsubishi is an ideal campaign target. By choosing Mitsubishi, RAN is able to put pressure on a specific company and hold it liable for the actions of many. Mitsubishi's image as a sound corporate citizen can easily be destroyed through this campaign and consumers can become involved by boycotting Mitsubishi cars and electronic goods, which are easily substituted by other brands.

The boycott is, however, unlikely to destroy the image of the trading group overall, because it is large and diverse. Many consumers are not aware of the linkages within the *keiretsu*, including Nippon Kogaku, Value Rent-a-Car and the Bank of California.

5. The opponent is strong enough (no "underdog" effect)

There is no doubt that the Mitsubishi group, consisting of 190 interlinked companies with total turnover of about US$166 billion, is a strong enough opponent.

Table 7.11 Mitsubishi campaign element

Consumer action	Media action	Research/education
• Boycott of all products or services from Mitsubishi companies. • Protests against Mitsubishi companies at their headquarters, auto shows, auto and electronics dealerships, and events. • Asked consumers to call a special number to send telegrams to the Prime Minister of Japan, President of Mitsubishi Corporation and Premier of Alberta.	• Hang giant banners over freeways, on high-rise office buildings and billboards. • Launch a national advertising campaign. • Promote the issue through a website. • Produce a documentation video. • Engage in an intensive national recruitment campaign to solicit additional environmental groups for the Mitsubishi campaign.	• Distribute material to high school and college students in the United States and Japan to inform them about Mitsubishi's destructive environmental record. • Assemble a team of top academic and industrial experts to provide Mitsubishi with feasible alternatives to forest destruction. • Reports on Mitsubishi's other operations.

6. The issue can be "packaged" in a campaign in which the public can get involved

The boycott against Mitsubishi could be packaged as an interesting campaign through maintaining constant and intense pressure on Mitsubishi. To get the population involved, RAN uses a broad range of non-violent direct actions. These actions can be split into three categories – consumer action, media action and research/education – and can be seen in Table 7.11.

RAN is also actively trying to attract children to the issue. In addition to the "kids' section" of its Internet Page, RAN has hosted various activities including the (now) annual Haiku project, which encourages teachers to ask their students to write a poem "concerned with the plights of the Earth and Mitsubishi's role in harming the environment." Teachers are reminded that students could "learn about the rainforest, Japanese culture and poetry, and express their knowledge creatively with a Haiku art project".

7. There are solutions that are confrontational, not gradual

To provide a confrontational solution, RAN has assembled academic and industrial experts and has provided Mitsubishi with guidelines for protecting the world's forests. Extracts of them are reproduced below:

What Mitsubishi can do

1. Take the position that the world's deforestation to date and its rate of increase have given rise to a state of global emergency and that an effective response to this problem will help us build a sustainable society.
2. Take the position that the underlying key ecological and human values or goals in this approach include:
   - a functioning biosphere (or healthy planet)
   - a network of large intact wild natural systems
   - migratory corridors and buffer zones around natural areas
   - an increase in primary forest cover throughout the world
   - helping foster viable populations of native species in natural patterns of balance, biodiversity and distribution
   - maintaining ecological and evolutionary processes such as hydrological processes and nutrient cycles
   - social equity between people and groups, now and in the future
   - a sustainable society with democratic self-governance
   - prosperous communities rooted in place, with meaningful work
   - accountability: transparency, access to information, effective public participation in decision making
   - economic models or systems that incorporate social and ecological costs
3. Implement an independently verifiable cap on investments (trapped capital) in ecologically harmful activities (such as logging in primary old growth forests or chlorine bleach pulp mills). Input on the types of investments that need to be capped should be sought from diverse interests including ecologists and citizen activists. All employees from entry level positions to the Board of Directors should be schooled systematically in the basic principles of ecology. This will help people identify problem areas and opportunities.
4. Take a systemic approach to global forest protection, certified logging fibre supply and demand-side reduction as a framework to halt deforestation and its consequences. This plan would encompass the following points:
   - Primary Forests
   - Secondary Forests
   - Commercial Restoration Zones
   - Alternative Fibres
   - Additional Demand-side Management
5. Mitsubishi Corporation could commit to a timetable and submit a transition plan for implementation and independent verification. Using its regular Kinyo-Kai meetings as a forum for a *keiretsu* task

force, Mitsubishi Corporation could additionally ensure that all re-lated companies, operations, or divisions integrate this systemic ap-proach into their business in order to become ecologically sustainable.

6. Mitsubishi Corporation could avoid working with other corporations which do not adhere to the above systemic approach and standards of ecological sustainability.

8. There could be a dramatic element to the campaign to engage the media

It is possible for RAN to include some dramatic elements in the campaign. In the past, they included climbing Mitsubishi buildings and hanging up banners, protesting with a giant inflatable chain saw, gathering in front of the headquarters in Tokyo, climbing and blocking transport ships. However, the fact that the campaign has been dragging on since the early 1990s shows that the dra-matic elements are not hitting the mark in this campaign.

Table 7.12 shows the activist checklist for the Mitsubishi issue.

Table 7.12   Visualised activist checklist for the Mitsubishi issue

Assessment criteria	Rating					Comments
	++	+	0	–	– –	
Clear aim or goal	●					RAN has a number of clear goals with regard to Mitsubishi.
Understandable by public	●					Issue is understandable and "good" and "bad" guys are obvious.
Symbolic		●				Rainforests are symbolic; RAN is designing anti-Mitsubishi symbols.
Image can be damaged		●				Mitsubishi is consumer brand; however, not all subsidiaries are known to the public.
Strong opponent	●					Mitsubishi is said to be the biggest *keiretsu* in the world.
Public can get involved	●					A lot of actions are possible.
Confrontational solution		●				RAN provides a number of solutions.
Dramatic elements			●			Difficult, because it is a long term issue.
Overall assessment		●				Mitsubishi is a good object for outside pressure campaign.

The Results

For RAN it is quite obvious that they have found a good adversary in Mitsubishi and it was natural for them to focus the general campaign to save the rainforests on Mitsubishi in order to spark public interest. Mitsubishi made the mistake of taking a reactive stance when the issue began to unfold. Only after five years of the campaign was Mitsubishi ready to meet activists from RAN, and even then it involved only rather junior management. But all is not lost for Mitsubishi, even now. The company would do well, however, to try to find a solution together with RAN because some of the demands of the activists may be fulfilled at a relatively low cost.

CASE 6: CELLULAR PHONE COMPANIES AND ELECTRO-SMOG

In recent years, cellular phones and other personal communications services (PCS) have become very popular. Today, there are about 80 million cellular phone users world-wide and their number is expected to more than double by the year 2000. In the future, wireless communication will have many new uses. Photocopier maintenance companies, for example, are installing mobile transmitters on copy machines, which can then automatically call headquarters for service or repair. The next generation of soda machines will be likely to live in the wireless world as well – they will call when they run out of Coke. Also the number of antennae transmitting the data of cellular phones and PCS has exploded in recent years: antennae for wireless communication can today be found on rooftops, towers, billboards and water tanks – and coming soon, perhaps, even on city lampposts.

Mobile phones, PCS and cell-site antennae emit radio frequency energy, operating at 860–900 MHz. The fields produced by these antennas are "microwaves", which belong to the non-ionising electromagnetic radiations.[8] In recent years, a number of scientists have warned that the radiation of the PCS might cause health threats such as allergies, brain tumours, pacemaker interference and cancerous growths. Basically, their criticism focuses on two related questions.

First, a number of researchers warn that if cellular phones are held too closely to the head, then the radiation could cause negative side effects to the person using the phone. Some early scientific evidence has suggested that mobile phone radiation can encourage and accelerate the growth of pre-cancerous and cancerous cells. Independent European scientists who conducted an initial programme concluded their studies with a reference to this subject: "There is no evidence of any health risk emerging from mobile phones but the results of present research are inadequate to draw firm conclusions on this issue. Further research is therefore required." Secondly, many people fear the cell-site antennae that distribute radiation. These antennae are usually mounted on the tops of towers and therefore are at some distance from the general public. The radiated power from each antenna is small. However, some antennae used at cell sites focus the energy in a fairly narrow range of specific directions, putting it into an intense beam. The highest power densities occur at distances of 30–300 m from the towers. Even though there are peaks in the power density, even the highest levels are approximately 100 000 times less than the limits established for human exposure to radio frequency energy.

A number of activist groups have organised protests against the placement of cellular towers, trying to stop the expansion of cellular phones and other PCS. The activist groups are rather scattered and consist often of parents worried about the health of their children. Usually, the groups are localised, small community activist groups that rally themselves around the "NIMBY" (Not In My Back Yard) battle cry, campaigning to protect the immediate environment in which they live and work. These groups have achieved some sporadic success. For example, in April 1997, the city of San Jose, in California's Silicon Valley, decided to delay the installation of 55 Personal Communications Service (PCS) antennae by Pacific Bell. If other US cities follow San Jose's example, it could affect seriously the roll-out of PCS services nation-wide and cost US PCS companies hundreds of millions of dollars in lost business.

We now analyse the issue from the perspective of a telephone company in the United States. The managers of this telephone company ask themselves whether the ongoing protest against radiation through PCS might cause problems for their profitable business. We begin our analysis with the company checklist.

1. Are the arguments against the issue plausible?

Within the scientific community, a number of researchers are concerned about human health effects from the hand-held cellular phones. These concerns exist because the antennae of these phones can deliver large amounts of radio frequency energy to small areas of the user's body, creating "hot spots". Animal tests have shown increased rates of cancer and damage to genetic material. So a certain plausibility of the issue of hand-held cellular phones exists.

On the other hand, the consensus of the scientific community, both in the United States and internationally, is that the power from base station antennae is far too low to produce health hazards as long as people are kept away from direct access to the antennae. Even if some scientists believe that it is possible that some groups in the general population might be more sensitive to the effects of radio waves, there is usually enough of a safety margin between antennae and public exposure. From this point of view, the issue can be considered only marginally plausible. Also, the groups that are pushing on the antenna issue are usually only local organisations, lacking resources for real scientific evaluation. So they are not necessarily a reliable information source.

2. Does the issue evoke emotion? Is it understandable – visual, touching – by the public?

The issue may evoke some emotions, even if they most probably will not become strong. The issue is only to a certain degree understandable to people because they cannot see the radiation coming from the towers or mobile phones. However, similar to the fears of radiation through nuclear power plants, people can imagine how radiation might cause health effects. The issue is not really visual, because, so far, no action has taken place in any of the campaigns. Up to now there have only been a handful of individuals appearing on television, arguing that their health has been damaged by radiation. Discussions are taking place on a more general level.

The issue is only to a limited degree touching. Probably the most touching event so far has been when in 1993 a Florida man named David Reynard appeared live on *The Larry King Show* and told a nation-wide audience that he was suing two cellular companies because his wife's pocket phone had caused the brain tumour that killed her.

3. Is the issue media-friendly?

Nobody can see the radio waves of cellular devices and their impacts. So from this point of view, the issue is not media-friendly. However, cellular phones are visible consumer items that have caught a lot of interest within the general public. The broad usage of cellular phones is new and the resulting general interest in cellular phones makes the issue somehow a little bit more media-friendly. Of course, witnesses in talk shows, promoting the issue, increase media-friendliness. Also, the media will have no problem of accessibility in this issue, because mobile phones and antennae can be found virtually anywhere.

4. Are there connections to other issues of the company or other companies?

There are some weak connections to other issues. First, there are a number of people arguing that cellular phones should not be allowed to be used in cars. Research findings have shown that talking on the phone and driving at the same time may substantially increase the probability of an accident. Other connections can be seen with the entire wireless telecommunications industry. In our information age, wireless communication grows in basically every business area and this might cause more people to think about the disadvantages that come with these technologies. For example, there is a new trend to build modern "wireless buildings" using high frequency radio systems. This might cause interferences, fear of data loss, a feeling of being observed, etc., which people might eventually relate to their health fears with respect to wireless communication. A third connection is the rising fear of people with respect to electrical power lines, which are increasingly suspected of causing cancer. The market-place provides some evidence that homes and properties in close proximity to electrical power lines have decreased in value by 30%–40%. In general, however, it seems that there are no strong connections.

5. How strong is the key activist group?

As we mentioned earlier, the protest in this issue is rather scattered and lacks one strong key activist group. The groups trying to stop the further growth of PCS-caused radiation are usually organised on an *ad hoc* basis and operate only locally. Some strength is added by landowners because towers can decrease property values. This loss of property values can result from a number of factors including the eyesore factor as well as the cancer fear issue.

6. How isolated is the company?

So far, no one telephone company has been isolated by the activist groups. The technology used by the different telephone companies is to a large extent similar and therefore it would be difficult for an activist group to single out one company nationwide.

However, when it comes to single grass-roots protests; for example, against one antenna to be built by one telephone company close to a school, the situation looks different. In such a case, the players are clear.

7. How far have the dynamics of the crisis already evolved?

The issue was "born" on 21 January 1993 when David Reynard appeared live on *The Larry King Show* and told a nation-wide audience that he was suing two cellular companies because his wife's pocket phone had caused the brain tumour that killed her. The enormous media attention given to the suit caused cellular stocks to tumble on Wall Street, even though this case was later dismissed because of insufficient evidence. In recent years, there have been some other documented legal cases concerning cancer and brain tumours that have allegedly been caused by the radiation generated from cellular phones. Following the television show, more scientists became interested in looking at the details of the issue. As we mentioned, so far, scientific research has not been able to show any clear results.

From a legal point of view, in 1996 the US Federal Communications Commission (FCC) adopted a set of guidelines for radio frequency microwave exposure that regulates cellular phone radiation levels to enforce compliance. The FCC and the Food and Drug Administration (FDA) said that, for the time being, they would not seek to regulate digital phones, but if studies showed that there were reasons for concern about the health effects of digital phones, new regulations might be imposed. Still, in a number of US cities, citizens have been successful in protesting against cellular phones and their antennae, at least for some time. Up to now, however, the growth of the cellular phone business shows no indication of slowing down. Single antenna-projects were not really given up, but usually relocated to places just around the corner from the original proposed sites.

8. How easy is the solution?

From a technical perspective, the technologies for mobile phones and other services are largely standardised. So an individual company cannot do too much about the issue. The only measure that can be taken is to reduce the power emitted from the PCS devices. However, this is usually not done by the telephone companies, but by the hardware providers such as Nokia, Motorola or Siemens. Such measures have already been taken in the last years, as a by-product of the miniaturisation of the telephone devices.

For the question of cell-site antennae, a possible solution is to build the antennae somewhere else, where there is less protest. This is largely done by telephone companies, and are often erected in poorer parts of a city where the likelihood of a protest is much lower.

The mobile phone user himself can also do a number of things to reduce the possible health dangers. For example, Medtronic, the largest manufacturer of pacemakers, has recommended that people with pacemakers use cellular phones on the side farthest

Table 7.13   Visualised company checklist for the electro-smog issue

Assessment criteria	++	+	0	–	––	Comments
Plausibility			•			Cellular phones to cause cancer is plausible; tower issue less plausible.
Potential for emotions		•				Understandable, but not visual and only to a certain degree touching.
Media-friendliness		•				Cellular phones are still a new product.
Connections with other issues			•			Only some weak interconnections exist.
Strength of the key activist group				•		Only scattered activist groups.
Degree of company isolation			•			Isolation may occur only with regard to towers.
Dynamics			•			Depending on future scientific findings.
Ease of solution			•			Issue difficult to solve in a general way.

| Overall assessment | | | | • | | At the moment no immediate danger for the telephone companies. |

from their pacemaker. Other consumers are buying devices that promise to minimise risk from electromagnetic radiation by forming a shield around the phone and antenna. However, many researchers argue that these devices cause an opposite effect, since a modern digital phone cranks up its power output if its signal is impeded.

Table 7.13 shows the company checklist for the Electro-Smog issue.

The Results

If there are no scientific findings that would really challenge the current status of research, the issue will not result in severe problems for the telephone companies. Cell-site antennae, where nobody can escape from the radiation, are unlikely to trigger any health effects. To use mobile phones, on the other hand, is a deliberate choice for many people. So far research shows no third person damage by using mobile phones. The main reason why telephone companies are not really worried at the moment is that, so far, no strong adversary has presented itself and none of the individual telephone companies can be isolated in a campaign. They are all in the same boat and will, therefore, do their best to help each other. With their combined financial power, they should be able to keep any challenges under control.

We now use the activist checklist to explain why, so far, only local groups are active on this issue and why no nation-wide group has taken action on it. We put ourselves in the shoes of a US nation-wide consumer organisation considering whether they want to launch a broad campaign on this issue.

1. The campaign should have a clear aim or goal

If the consumer organisation wants to attack the issue of telephone towers, its first clear goal will have to be to block the construction of towers anywhere in the United States and, secondly, to tear down every existing cell-site antennae. Activist groups fighting against the towers know that it is important to make their voices heard early on. It is much easier to block a proposed tower site than it is to bring down an existing tower. And it is easier to bring down a tower under construction than it is to bring down a tower that has existed for years. However, with the current status of scientific evidence about the health effects of cell-site antennae, these goals are nearly impossible to reach, especially as the critique cannot be focused on a single tower, but on all towers nation-wide.

The actual use of mobile phones, with any associated risks, is clearly an individual choice. The clear goal in a campaign aimed at the mobile phone users would be to convince people to refrain voluntarily from using mobile phones. They could try to force a labelling of cellular phones warning of the potential health hazards. Such a goal would be more within reach. It would, however, be challenged constantly by technical progress in telephone hardware and, with every new generation of telephones, manufacturers could argue that the new versions were not hazardous to health.

2. The issue is easily understood by the general public

It should be possible to make the issue understandable to a large public. People are aware of the many mobile phones that are sold and used at the moment and of the digital revolution in the air. They are also a little bit scared of invisible microwaves that could be damaging their brains. However, it will probably still be difficult to push the telephone companies into the role of the "bad guys".

3. The issue has a high symbolic value

The number of Americans using cellular phones increases rapidly, but they are still a small minority. Even in the United States, cellular phones are still considered to be a luxury product. They cannot be compared with public utilities, such as wired telephones and power lines for personal electricity, because almost every American enjoys both of these services. Additionally, cellular phones and other PCS do not provide a unique service because they merely expand wired telephone coverage. Given this situation, the issue could have some symbolic value in the sense that the cell-site antennae are causing health threats for all Americans, while only a minority can profit from them.

On the other hand, as we said, the phones themselves may carry a risk only for the individual user. So here it would be difficult to argue about a high symbolic value. As with other issues, e.g. drinking alcohol, the consumer is responsible himself.

4. The issue has the potential to damage the image of the company

The public perception of telephone companies is usually quite positive. They are sponsors of sport events, creators of many new jobs, and offer often monetary benefits to a popular community group in exchange for allowing the antenna placement. Often, companies will request placing an antenna on top of a school building in exchange for providing needed money or supplies to the school. Or they may negotiate an agreement with a church for the installation of the antenna in steeple facades in exchange for any number of things. Additionally, telephone companies usually argue that their services are inherently beneficial to a community; for example, with regard to public safety because drivers with cellular phones can call the police, family or friends to help them in an emergency situation. In the case of antennae, it would, therefore, be difficult to damage the image of the opponent.

As the technologies used by different telephone companies are similar, activist groups would also have a problem attacking the image of one company with regard to the hand-held PCS devices. The activist groups would have to go against all telephone companies.

5. The opponent is strong enough (no "underdog" effect)

Cellular phones are a profitable business. In 1996, the American mobile phone market was estimated to be US$23 billion (without hardware), growing by almost 30% per year. So the telephone companies could become good and strong opponents for the activist groups.

6. The issue can be "packaged" in a campaign in which the public can get involved

Campaigns usually consist of a combination of protests and lawsuits. An engineer for US manufacturer Motorola Inc., for example, won headlines in 1993 when he filed a lawsuit saying his work on a cellular telephone antenna gave him a brain tumour. So far, there have been street protests only against the towers and none against the hand-held devices. This is probably the biggest problem for an activist group in general. A good campaign can only be run with regard to the towers, because there "innocent" people are affected. However, scientists consider the risks of the towers as low and the towers are only of regional importance. There is probably more danger for the users of the phones themselves. But while using their phones, they are not endangering anybody else, so it would be difficult to run a campaign. The only option is to urge users to use their phones less or even stop the mobile phone service. This is apparently not the most interesting campaign.

7. There are solutions that are confrontational, not gradual

Activist groups can basically only offer the solution of not building antennae in their communities and not using PCS. Cellular communication technology is changing at a tremendously high speed, so that it is basically impossible for activist groups to work on a concept with which they may offer their own technical solutions. This impossibility to provide attractive alternatives is, of course, a major weakness in their campaign.

Table 7.14 Visualised activist checklist for the electro-smog issue

Assessment criteria	++	+	0	–	– –	Comments
Clear aim or goal			●			Stop tower construction; encourage people to give up their cellular phone.
Understandable by public			●			People are a little bit scared of mobile phone usage.
Symbolic			●			Mobile phones are still a luxury product and therefore a symbol.
Image can be damaged				●		Phone companies have positive image and a protest could not single out any of them.
Strong opponent		●				Cellular phone companies are profitable business.
Public can get involved				●		Difficult, because to use a cellular phone is a personal choice.
Confrontational solution				●		Technology progresses too fast; outside pressure groups cannot follow development.
Dramatic elements				●		Difficult, because no nation-wide campaign possible.
Overall assessment			●			At the moment no promising campaign object.

8. There could be a dramatic element to the campaign to engage the media

Dramatic elements would be difficult to include in the campaign, because, as we saw above, it would be difficult to organise a nation-wide campaign. Unless new research findings show real dangers, the media will not look on the issue with much interest.

The activist checklist is shown in Table 7.14.

The Results

At the moment it seems that the issue is not a good subject for any major nation-wide campaign. However, the industry has to be careful with new technologies coming up. For example, there are satellite-based phone services coming soon, like the Motorola-funded Iridium project or Globalstar, in which signals will shoot from pocket phones to satellites hundreds of miles up in space. With these systems, activist objections could increase again. Therefore, telephone companies have to monitor future research findings closely.

CASE 7: LANDOWNERS IN BRAZIL AND THE MOVIMENTO SEM TERRA ("LANDLESS MOVEMENT")

In 1997 Brazil had a population of about 165 million people. Among them, 1% owned almost 50% of the land. Estimates stated that some 42% of this privately-owned land lay idle, not even used as pasture. At the other end of the scale, there were 4 million poor competing for less than 3% of the land. They eked out miserable lives. Some of them were homeless city dwellers and others lived in roadside tents. Many of them earned less than a dollar a day. Politicians had been promising these people more equitable land distribution for half a century and the government even had the legal right to reallocate land that was not being farmed. But no regime to date has made use of this right to any meaningful extent.

Many of these poorest of the poor have organised themselves to form the "Landless Movement", MST – Movimento Sem

Terra. MST is a 17-year-old grass-roots movement that has about 220 000 members today, making it the largest popular movement in Brazil. The group's goal is to redistribute unused land on the biggest farms, so that it can be profitably farmed by millions of hungry peasant families.

Besides lobbying, MST organises active protests. The group is "occupying" (the land-owners would say "invading") ranches and resettling people on the occupied land. This practice is illegal, but the movement's leadership argues that it is merely speeding up the process of land reform. Once on the land, the peasants start farming, building houses and schools. After some time, they are, in most cases, officially "settled" through the approval of the legislative forces. In the past six years, MST has occupied more than 500 large ranches and resettled approximately 600 000 people. The landowners have hired a private army to protect their property from MST and, as a result, there have been a number of violent confrontations between MST and the landowners in which, so far, more than 30 people have been killed.

We now put ourselves in the shoes of the landowners and analyse the issue according to the company checklist. It probably holds true that many managers do not really see a connection between Brazilian landowners and their own businesses. We believe, however, that this case study may give some valuable insights into "industries" that get attacked because of historical possessions that may today be perceived as unjustified. We already know that MST poses a severe threat to the ranchers. But part of the question remains open: What is the danger that MST is able to escalate the issue ultimately to achieve their goal: large-scale land redistribution?

1. Are the arguments against the issue plausible?

Brazil is notorious for social injustice and it is a recognised fact that land is unequally distributed. Only Paraguay is worse in that regard. The land-tenure system in Brazil has hardly changed in 400 years, since the Portuguese crown distributed areas the size of modern countries to favoured families.

2. Does the issue evoke emotion? Is it understandable – visual, touching – by the public?

People in Brazil can understand the injustice that millions of their countrymen are hungry, while at the same time there are thousands of miles of unused land. MST has been able to make the protests visual. Whenever they occupy land, they invite television crews to film and report on it. To emphasise the visual aspect, in February 1997, MST organised a march to the capital Brasilia to demand justice from the president.

The issue became touching, thanks partly to a sympathetic television soap opera about the landless. More than 60 million people watched the show every night for a period of six months, making it one of the most successful productions ever aired by the Globo channel.

3. Is the issue media-friendly?

The issue is media-friendly because there is film footage of people invading land, trying to build their houses and farmers defending their properties. The pictures of common protests and social movements are rather new and extraordinary in a country where people are taught from childhood that they have to fight in order to survive. And certainly the soap opera made the issue even more media-friendly, because it made viewers want to find out what happened to their "heroes" in real life.

4. Are there connections to other issues of the company or other companies?

The issue is strongly connected to the general question of social justice in Brazil. The free-market and liberalisation policy of President Fernando Cardoso has helped the country out of an economic crisis. However, it has widened the gap between rich and poor. Some recent related issues were protests against the continued privatisation of state-owned companies, which forced many people into unemployment. Therefore, large parts of the population, even in cities, see interconnections between their own situation and that of the landless.

There is also an interconnection to the landless movement in the neighbouring country of Paraguay where the campaign has also gained momentum. The actors there are the Movimento Campesino Paraguayo (MCP) and Organizacion Nacional Campesina (ONC), who want a radical agrarian reform in Paraguay similar to what MST is demanding in Brazil.

5. How strong is the key activist group?

MST has 220 000 members and is the largest popular movement in Brazil. The group is highly organised. MST has, for example, training facilities for their managers and professional recruiting procedures for the future leaders that have to be screened in Brazil's slums. For them, MST published a booklet called: *How To Organise The Masses*. MST is made up of Brazil's dispossessed – the croppers, casual pickers, farm labourers and people thrown off the land by mechanisation and by land clearances. According to a poll in 1997, the group is enjoying the support of up to 90% of the Brazilian population. This makes it a powerful adversary for the landowners.

Additionally, the protesters have an ally in the churches. In August 1996, in São Paulo, the catholic church sponsored a "romaria da terra" (pilgrimage of the land), which attracted some 12 000 rural workers. At the closing act, São Paulo's Archbishop Paulo Evaristo Arns proclaimed that the agrarian reform was moving too slowly. The assembly approved a charter of rural workers' rights, which among other things said:

> All have the right to land, to fight for it, to occupy it, to resist and to produce for the sustenance of the family and for social justice. (. . .) All have the right to organise, to know their rights, to struggle, to resist, to protest, to strike, whenever they suffer injustice.

This is a strong statement for a church, and the Vatican later tried to moderate the situation. Some of the biggest sponsors of MST are the German churches with their help organisations, "Brot für die Welt" and "Misereor". Other supporters are: Christian Aid, Oxfam, the Catholic Institute for International

Relations, Human Rights Watch, Amnesty International and Anti-Slavery International.

MST can act swiftly through its centralised decision making for the surprise advantage. Often, it takes months to plan a land invasion, which is usually minutely organised. Once the moment is there, people are then trucked in, and they almost always catch the police and landowners off-guard.

6. How isolated is the company?

There is no one farmer that MST singles out. The target is all the rich land owners. However, the MST's demands are only on landowners and not on any other industries. So the players are in some way clearly defined: a few very rich landowners against the poor rural working masses.

7. How far have the dynamics of the crisis already evolved?

The issue of land redistribution has a long history in Brazil. Looking at the diffusion curve for this topic, MST has managed to push the land issue to broad public awareness in its 17-year history. One special achievement of the group was bringing the issue of land reform out of the countryside and into the cities. Sem Terra has forced what was a hidden issue – the landless – almost to the top of the political agenda.

Future dynamics may play out on the political side (especially with regard to the interconnection to the general privatisation issue), because with the broad awareness, the administration now has every reason to act on the issue and solve it, both for re-election and to avoid having large numbers of "outlaws" in its population.

8. How easy is the solution?

It may be easy for the rich farmers to give some land away. But how much is "some"? Brazil's population is growing rapidly and

Table 7.15 Visualised company checklist for the Landless Movement issue

Assessment criteria	Rating					Comments
	++	+	0	–	––	
Plausibility		●				Brazil's land is unequally distributed.
Potential for emotions		●				MST made the issue visual (occupation) and touching (soap opera).
Media-friendliness		●				Sympathy for MST in the general population is new and extraordinary.
Connections with other issues		●				Connections to general social justice in Brazil and landless movements in other countries.
Strength of the key activist group	●					MST has grown to a real force.
Degree of company isolation			●			No farmer has been singled out so far.
Dynamics		●				The "take off" point is passed: broad awareness.
Ease of solution				●		Difficult to define to what degree redistribution would be justified.
Overall assessment		●				Enormous problem for the landowners from an image point of view.

the need for more land will only grow with it. Once the farmers give in, the landless can come back and ask for more land because there are more hungry mouths to feed. The big landowners are afraid that the landless will also demand to have part of the land that is already being farmed once all the unused land has been distributed. In short, they are sure that if they give them an inch, the landless will take a mile. One solution would be for the government to offer adequate compensation for land taken for the poor.

The company checklist is shown in Table 7.15.

The Results

For the farmers, the MST is clearly a strong threat. Of course, we are now in the state of "late-awareness", because every farmer has realised this threat. However, looking at the checklist, they might have foreseen the danger long ago. Just considering the rapid population growth and the visual power of unused farm land could have convinced the farmers that they should find a solution for the budding problems as soon as possible.

We now go on to analyse the issue from the activists' point of view using the activist checklist. Our activist checklist analysis will be a bit different here from the other cases. For MST, there was no question as to why they should go for the issue of land redistribution, because this issue is the very purpose of the organisation. Their actions cannot really be considered a campaign – for the landless it is a fight for personal survival. The question is, how should they achieve their objective? So we will now use our activist checklist to try to find out why the landless use this occupation strategy and the march to Brasilia in their fight against the farmers. Could the farmers have predicted this development?

1. The campaign should have a clear aim or goal

In general, MST wants social justice for the poor. However, the precise goal of the group is the redistribution of the vast estates that lie idle, in order to be able to settle and give a fair chance to massive numbers of suffering people. Political lobbying for this goal has been largely unsuccessful over the last years, so MST had to go for a more aggressive type of campaign. The land occupation has a clear goal: to get people on the land in order to be able to present authorities with a fait accompli. The march to Brasilia's clear goal was to get politicians' attention.

2. The issue is easily understood by the general public

The issue is understandable to all Brazilians and the population is well aware of the general social injustice in the country. MST is making it even clearer by demanding a bit of land from the incredibly rich for the desperately poor.

3. The issue has a high symbolic value

Land has a high symbolic value. It stands for liberty, freedom and the basic needs of the human being. Land redistribution is a more attractive cause to rally behind than, say, the redistribution of money.

4. The issue has the potential to damage the image of the company

MST chooses carefully the land that it will occupy. The organisation prefers to occupy land that is disputed or that seems to be claimed illegally. They then have better arguments in their image campaigns and get more sympathy from the population. Since the television soap opera was aired, the landless have no longer been dismissed as vagabonds and trouble-makers by the general public.

On the other hand, the pictures of violent armies and thug squads protecting the farmers works against their image. Reports of violent tactics against the landless after areas were settled, like flying over and spraying pesticides from aeroplanes onto the new villages below, cause a major backlash of negative public feeling against the farmers.

So MST seems to be making a clear case by occupying the land directly, and is getting a lot more mileage than it did when its efforts were limited to political lobbying.

5. The opponent is strong enough (no "underdog" effect)

The landowners are rich and strong opponents for MST – and they are the only opponents. It is quite difficult to feel sorry for the rich and powerful losing land they never use.

6. The issue can be "packaged" in a campaign in which the public can get involved

MST formerly suffered from a negative image in the eyes of the average Brazilian. The group realised they had to work on this, so they learned how to improve their campaigns by playing to the media. Then they invited the media to the next escalation: the occupations and the much-publicised march to the country's capital. And they got a free "advertisement" out of the soap opera. However, the general population to date has not become actively involved in the issue. The only way in which they could change the chances for MST would be in elections where they could vote for left-wing politicians.

7. There are solutions that are confrontational, not gradual

The obvious solution for MST would be redistribution of some land. However, the landowners do not consider this solution in any way acceptable. One compromise would be for the government to reimburse the landowners financially. However, given the financial situation of the Brazilian state government, it is not likely that they will be able to offer an attractive price to the landowners. So there is little space for compromise.

8. There could be a dramatic element to the campaign to engage the media

MST was able to create some dramatic elements in their campaign. The occupations themselves were dramatic, especially when it came to conflict with the landowners. Secondly, the MST protest marches escalated the conflict and the government has come under higher pressure to allocate land. And the soap opera has increased the perception for drama, idolising the landless as real heroes. All these campaign elements were designed to engage the media. Table 7.16 shows the activist checklist.

The Results

Using the checklist, one can understand that the land occupations are a good strategy for MST. They are now able to go for more aggressive campaigns, especially since their image in the eyes of

Table 7.16 Visualised activist checklist for the Landless Movement issue

Assessment criteria	Rating					Comments
	++	+	0	–	– –	
Clear aim or goal	●					Land redistribution to the poor.
Understandable by public		●				Social injustice understandable.
Symbolic		●				Land is a symbolic object.
Image can be damaged		●				MST goes mainly for disputed land; owners often use violence.
Strong opponent	●					Land owners are very rich by Brazilian standards.
Public can get involved			●			Public can get aware, but not involved.
Confrontational solution			●			Little place for compromises.
Dramatic elements		●				Occupation and struggle somehow dramatic.
Overall assessment		●				Land occupation and image march are a promising strategy for MST.

the general public has improved dramatically in the last years. The ideal combination of strategies was, therefore, a powerful and peaceful political protest and running a fait accompli with the occupation. Only by using such a combination has MST had a reasonable chance to kick-start the issue that until then was going nowhere.

CASE 8: ABB AND THE BAKUN DAM

As with many other Southeast Asian nations, the Malaysian economy is expected to grow rapidly in the years to come. Along with this growth comes higher energy consumption. Currently, the major energy sources in Malaysia are fossil fuels; in order to be less dependent, the government has decided that it wants to diversify into other energy sources. One step in this diversification has been the decision to build a dam on the Balui River in the Bakun region, on Borneo Island, which could supply 15% of Malaysia's energy requirements.

The dam should have become the biggest dam in the region with a resulting total water surface of about 700 km². The project consisted of building the dam, a 2400 MW hydropower plant and power transmission to the Malaysian mainland via a 1300 km cable, half of it under water, and it was expected to be completed in the year 2003 at a total cost of approximately US$5 billion. After a bidding process in 1996, a consortium led by the Swedish–Swiss company ABB received the contract to construct the dam. The project was the largest project ever for ABB.

However, in September 1996, 205 NGOs/activist groups expressed disapproval of the Bakun project in a letter to ABB, warning the company that the project would tarnish its image as an environmentally advanced company. They argued that ABB was "dumping an outdated, inefficient, uneconomic, and environmentally and socially destructive technology" on Malaysia. One of their arguments was, for example, that the analysis of the Environmental Impact Assessment (EIA) neglected the social impact of the relocation of native people in the Bakun region, as well as certain ecological impacts. ABB refuted these arguments, but found itself, however, under strong pressure from activist groups and suffered a severe image loss. Still the company insisted that it wanted to do the project and went through one year of protests, accusations, contractual disputes and negotiations.

In September 1997, after the construction of the dam had already begun in May of that year, the Malaysian government decided to bring the project to a halt, because the financial risk had become unsustainable. The decision was taken for economic reasons; however, in a way, the activist protest had a certain influence on the final outcome. We now analyse, with the help of our company checklist, how this could have happened.

1. Are the arguments against the issue plausible?

Certainly, the Bakun Dam would have had some negative environmental and social effects. The construction of the dam was supposed to go hand-in-hand with the deforestation of ecologically, socially and financially valuable rainforests of about 70 000 ha. The flooding of these forests could have led to a substantial risk of the introduction and spread of waterborne diseases. Other environmental impacts would have been a loss of about 100 species of animals, plants and fish, possible effects on river life from the underwater high voltage cables and negative effects on agriculture, fisheries and water quality downstream.

In social terms, the project required the resettlement of the local population: 15 communities and 10 000 people had to be moved. Another social effect would have been that timber revenues from the inundated area were going to be lost. Additionally, opponents of the project pointed to a risk of flooding in the event that the dam should break.

Given all these impacts, there were some plausible concerns that ABB had to face with the project. However, the critical question for this issue was, Where does the Bakun project stand in relation to other technologies, primarily the use of fossil fuels? Here, the various groups involved had different opinions.

2. Does the issue evoke emotion? Is it understandable – visual, touching – by the public?

The issue evoked more emotion in Europe than in Asia, but even European protests probably would not have reached serious levels. It is difficult for the general public to understand all the problems and ramifications of the construction of a dam. On the contrary, the broad public typically regards hydroelectric energy as a clean energy source. The visual effect of the dam would have been delayed until completion of the construction in 2003; up until then, there would be no interesting pictures for the media to disseminate. Perhaps pictures of tractors tearing through the rainforest, native people being forced to leave their homes, rising water levels covering native huts and maybe children's toys left behind, etc. would have drawn some interest; but overall, the project would probably not have become visually touching, because there was only a small likelihood of real clashes between the dam builders and the indigenous people.

3. Is the issue media-friendly?

Although there were no riveting visuals around the project, it was still media-friendly. What made the issue new, extraordinary and

therefore interesting for the media, was the fact that Percy Barnevik, the Managing Director and Chairman of the Board of
ABB, was a leading figure and one of the strongest advocates in
the world-wide movement of industry toward sustainability. Thus,
it was quite interesting for the media that his company was arguing with 205 activist groups at the same time. There were even
some rumours that another leader of companies trying to become
more environmentally sensitive, Stephan Schmidheiny, retired
from the ABB board because of the dam issue. This made the
discussion quite extraordinary because eventually the media
could report that even ABB and Barnevik only gave lip service to
the environment.

4. Are there connections to other issues of the company or other companies?

There were a number of connections that made the issue more
dangerous for ABB's image. There were rumours about an
improper connection between the local construction company
Ekran Berhad and the Chief Minister of Sarawak, who is one of
the top 20 shareholders of the company. Also, the Malaysian
government's handling of the project and the manner in which
Kuala Lumpur tried to get the massive plan approved were seen
as shoddy and secretive, infuriating activists.

A connection could also have been found in the hydropower
industry: discussions and controversy over the construction of
another dam – the largest hydroelectric project in the history of
the world, on China's Yangtze River. This "Three Gorges Dam"
project will result in the forced resettlement of 1.5 million people.
Because of social and environmental concerns, the US government has denied any aid for Three Gorges and activist groups are
fighting against this dam project; however, the Chinese government is unlikely to consider, much less give in to, the demands of
any of these activist groups. So the Bakun Dam in Malaysia,
which affected fewer people in its social implications, was also
taking a lot of heat because of the Three Gorges project.

There were further interconnections to rainforest issues in general and logging practices in particular. According to studies
undertaken between 1988 and 1993, some 40 000 ha of forest

have been logged in Malaysia alone each year, creating a number of environmental problems (see Case Study 5).

5. How strong is the key activist group?

There was no one key activist group for this issue, but rather 205 groups that were acting in concert, agreeing on the issues and formulating them in a single letter to ABB, urging the company not to get involved in the project. This broad opposition also attracted media attention. However, as there was no leading adversary, future protests would most probably have lacked the co-ordination necessary to carry a strong and to-the-point message.

Among the 205 activist groups, the local opposition was un-likely to have any significant effect on the proposal as they did not have a strong support basis. Environmental protection does not enjoy high importance in Asia, and the Malaysian government has strong control over the political system and the media. Key government members were closely associated with the project. Still, ABB had to face the fact that activist groups in Europe might have generated some interesting debate, as they managed to do with their jointly-signed letter to ABB.

6. How isolated is the company?

ABB, as the main contractor in the Bakun project, was isolated. The company was singled out by activist groups as the soft spot in this project, although the key decisions were made by the Malaysian government. The activist groups mainly went after ABB because of its well-known name and because the company had a corporate image to worry about. It would have made little sense for the activist groups to pick on the smaller construction and engineering companies involved in this project, as they would, quite naturally, have hidden behind ABB and claimed to be by-standers. Trying to pressure the Malaysian government itself would also pretty much have amounted to pouring water on a duck's back.

7. How far have the dynamics of the crisis already evolved?

The Bakun Dam project has a long history. Studies relating to the hydropower potential of such a dam date back to the 1960s. A total of 26 separate studies encompassing technical, economic and environmental aspects have been undertaken, mainly in the 1980s. However, in 1986, the Malaysian government decided to shelve the plans for economic reasons. A 1992 review of the project concluded that it was economically viable and should be implemented, for commissioning by the year 2005. On the basis of this review, the Malaysian government agreed in September 1993 that the project be implemented. The necessary EIA was executed in 1995 by the University of Malaysia in Sarawak with the help of 30 international experts.

ABB has a long involvement in the project. The company began to make feasibility studies for the project in the mid-1980s and has thus invested more than 15 years in the project investigation. Here is a look at the events as of 1996 when the contract was signed:

19 June, 1996:   A court rules that the EIA breaches legislation. However, work does not have to be stopped.

27 September, 1996: 205 NGOs in 30 countries and 35 members of the European Parliament sign a letter to ABB to postpone the project.

2 October, 1996:   The contract is signed by ABB.

4 September, 1997: The contract is cancelled by the Malaysian government and the project delayed indefinitely.

As of 1996, the dynamics with regard to activist protest were already very negative for ABB, mainly because of the long planning period, which gave the activist groups a chance to build a common opposition. The company was not able to convince the NGOs that the dam was a socially and environmentally responsible project, and public interest in this stakeholder issue had already risen to serious levels.

8. How easy is the solution?

Before the contract was signed, one possible solution for ABB was, of course, to not participate in the project. Once the contract

Table 7.17 Visualised company checklist for the Bakun Dam issue

Assessment criteria	Rating					Comments
	++	+	0	–	––	
Plausibility			•			Bakun dam project has some negative environmental and social effects; however, also some positive effects.
Potential for emotions				•		Issue is remote from strong European pressure groups; no real clashes.
Media-friendliness				•		Nothing could be shown; common approach of NGOs was, however, new.
Connections with other issues		•				Mainly with the Three Georges Dam in China.
Strength of the key activist group				•		No single key activist group.
Degree of company isolation		•				ABB was isolated and the only possible target.
Dynamics		•				Due to its long planning period the protest was already very strong when ABB signed the contract.
Ease of solution		•				Only government could solve the issue.
Overall assessment			•			ABB had a quite risky project running.

had been signed, however, there was no way for ABB to pull out of Bakun unless the Malaysian government itself halted the project. Even the technology to be used could not easily be changed. Between October 1996 and September 1997, the only option ABB had was to keep the environmental and social impacts of the project as low as possible. They had already launched plans to do so; for example, by requiring every supplier of the project to work with a certified environmental management system according to ISO 14001.

The company checklist is shown in Table 7.17.

The Results

Looking at the checklist points, it is clear that ABB could have foreseen that its image would suffer for a time from its involvement in the dam project. However, the checklist also shows that the project would not have any lasting severe impacts on ABB. Hydro-electric power is one of the core competencies of ABB, and it is in the company's interest to promote this energy source. ABB's strategy of keeping an open dialogue with all interested NGOs to counter criticism was a wise one, as is evident from our checklist.

We now use the activist checklist to look at the issue from the adversaries' point of view.

As mentioned, ABB's adversaries were a coalition of no fewer than 205 NGOs urging the company to reconsider its decision, including Friends of the Earth, the International Rivers Network (IRN), Greenpeace, Berne Declaration, Rainforest Action Network and other like-minded groups. Why did so many NGOs consider it worth their while to put ABB under pressure for the Bakun project?

1. The campaign should have a clear aim or goal

The NGOs /activist groups had a clear goal in their campaign: to prevent the Bakun Dam from being built. At the same time, the activist groups knew that it was unlikely that this goal would be realised because of environmental or social concerns, but rather through economic reasons.

They knew they could not be too optimistic about achieving their main goal; therefore, they had their eye on a set of related goals that were more within reach. One goal was to at least delay the project until another EIA could be made which would have taken into account options such as solar power and demand-side management. In broader terms, the NGOs wanted to use the Bakun Dam issue to create a central body better to monitor and control the EIAs of major energy projects for the future. The goal of the campaign was also to spark a general discussion on large-scale hydropower projects.

2. The issue is easily understood by the general public

The broad public considers hydropower to be a clean energy source. The negative environmental and social impacts of larger water projects are usually known only to experts, because they differ broadly from project to project. The average "man in the street" is generally unable to come to any clear conclusions on the issue. So, from this point of view, the activist groups had a difficult stand.

But there was something in the issue that most people could recognise. It was the manner in which the dam project was pushed through by the interested parties. The Malaysian government made use of the support of Western industry aggressively to push through its prestige project, ignoring pleas for more careful consideration and warnings of environmental and social consequences from the NGOs. It looked like the typical behaviour of another big business and political machine bulldozing right over ecological and human rights concerns.

3. The issue has a high symbolic value

At the time of the protests there were no strong symbols to excite the public. The dam existed only on the drawing boards and was therefore not visible. Scientific discussions were not yet concluded, and it was not easy confidently to point the finger at any "good" or "bad" guys (except perhaps the Minister of Sarakaw, who would have profited greatly from the project he was pushing so hard).

4. The issue has the potential to damage the image of the company

It is difficult for an activist group to damage the image of a government domestically, even in this case where there were suspicions of personal interests. Therefore, criticism was focused on ABB, which is considered an environmentally best-practice company. It was clear that ABB's image, one of its assets, could be turned into a liability. Activist groups hoped to use this as leverage to pressure ABB to at least listen to their arguments.

5. The opponent is strong enough (no "underdog" effect)

ABB is the world's leading electrical engineering company with annual revenues of approximately US$33 billion and earnings of

US\$3 billion. The company employs 210 000 people world-wide. Clearly, ABB was considered a strong opponent for the activist groups.

6. The issue can be "packaged" in a campaign in which the public can get involved

It was difficult for the activist groups to stage a high-profile, exciting campaign around this issue. The images were rather static, and the project moved slowly. The fact that the project took place in Asia, far away from the powerful European activists, added a geographic disadvantage, making it difficult to get a large number of people involved. As a whole, the activist groups knew that this campaign would be mainly between them and ABB, and that there would not be a lot of public involvement.

7. There are solutions which are confrontational, not gradual

Of course, the most desirable solution for the activist groups was to stop the dam from being built. At the same time, they did not want Malaysian fossil fuel consumption to increase, nor did they want to see nuclear energy introduced. Some argued, therefore, that if all costs (including those borne by society and the environment) were included in the Bakun Dam project calculation, other technologies such as solar power would have been more attractive. ABB argued, on the other hand, that companies cannot possibly include all environmental and social costs in a project calculation, and still expect to survive in the current economic system.

An alternative solution that the activist groups suggested was demand-side management, a campaign to reduce Malaysian energy consumption. Such measures were certainly a possible solution for the expected energy shortage. However, it was not up to ABB to provide this solution, but to the Malaysian government and to the people in Malaysia who had to become convinced of the necessity. The only solution that the activist groups could demand from ABB was to refrain from the project.

Table 7.18 Visualised activist checklist for the Bakun Dam issue

Assessment criteria	++	+	0	–	– –	Comments
Clear aim or goal		●				Stop construction of Bakun Dam.
Understandable by public			●			Difficult as hydro power is still considered clean technology.
Symbolic			●			Dam existed only on drawing board.
Image can be damaged	●					ABB may lose its environmentally sound image.
Strong opponent	●					ABB is large and profitable.
Public can get involved			●			Difficult because remote and no consumer brand.
Confrontational solution	●					Gets ABB to refrain from the project, stop dam and use other energy sources
Dramatic elements			●			Not available.
Overall assessment			●			Medium potential for a successful campaign.

8. There could be a dramatic element to the campaign to engage the media

It was difficult for the activist groups to find a dramatic element to throw into the campaign against ABB. As the project existed only on the drawing board at the time of the protests, this reduced the possibility for staging dramatic elements in a sequential "strip-tease". Furthermore, the general Asian population seems comparatively uninterested in environmental issues, so any public support for the issue would have to come from Europe or North America, which is about as far away from the actual dam site as you can possibly get. However, there was one element of drama to the issue that provoked some media interest: the fact that for the first time 205 NGOs agreed unanimously and joined forces to act together on a common issue.

The activist checklist is shown in Table 7.18.

The Results

We see that it was difficult for any activist group to run a powerful campaign against ABB. However, the NGOs considered the issue to be still worthwhile and co-operated in their protest against ABB. They made a case through their common policy and showed companies that they will be measured against their environmental statements. At the end of the day, luck was on their side, and their most desired outcome was fulfilled. The deciding factor was the economic reasoning of the Malaysian government. Without this, ABB would most certainly have gone through with the construction of the Bakun Dam.

CASE 9: DOW CHEMICAL, SHELL CHEMICAL AND OCCIDENTAL CHEMICAL AND THE PESTICIDE DBCP

The global agrochemical market (the producing and selling of pesticides) is a moderately, but constantly, growing market. Sales are currently estimated at US$28 billion annually. It is a dangerous market to be in, because of ever more detailed product liability legislation and ongoing consumer activism. Di-bromo-chloro-propane (DBCP) is a good example of a profitable product gone sour and producers now facing high-stake lawsuits.

DBCP is a pesticide that was developed in the 1950s to kill nematodes, a type of worm that lives in the soil. After obtaining the US governmental official registration (necessary to sell legally), the product was brought on to the market by Shell Chemical, Dow Chemical and Occidental Chemical in the early 1960s under the commercial names of Fumazone and Nemagon. It was an instant success, because it was cheaper than other similar products.

First studies in 1961 showed, however, that rodents exposed to DBCP showed a reduction of testicular weight. For some years, nobody reacted to these findings. Until the mid-1970s, approximately 11 000 tons of DBCP were produced annually in the United States. In 1977, 35 Occidental Chemical workers in California were found to be sterile because of exposure to DBCP. Following the incident, the Environmental Protection Agency (EPA) provisionally banned the use of DBCP.

A pesticide banned in the United States can, according to the Federal Insecticide, Fungicide and Rodenticide Act, still be produced and sold to other countries where the pesticide is not (yet) illegal. So DBCP continued to be sold to Third World countries, where there was not enough technical expertise to establish the toxicity of the substance. Because of cost advantages, sales of the chemical continued until 1989.

In 1984, the chemical companies were facing their first lawsuits in the United States. Later, even the workers in the banana plantations in the countries where DBCP was applied began suing the producers. And they did this not only in their home countries, but increasingly in the United States. Lawyers managed to transfer the cases from the Third World countries to US courts in 1994 because there the chances for receiving adequate compensation are higher.

Also, from an environmental point of view, the pesticide has, in recent years, come under strong criticism for contaminating the ecosystem surrounding the production factories and plantations. In Costa Rica, for example, the pesticide is accused of having destroyed Costa Rica's coastline. In the United States, different states and cities are suing the manufacturers of the chemicals for polluting groundwater around their production sites. Dow Chemical and Occidental Chemical have so far agreed to pay a US$21 million settlement to the city of Fresno, California and US$25 million to the city of Sanger, California. But this would be only a minor sum compared with the US$5.6 billion environmental compensation bill demanded by California's Senator Charles Calderon because of water contamination.

Today, the chemical companies are worried about the financial implications of lawsuits that are still open. The outcome of these lawsuits will largely determine the financial impact of the DBCP issue on the companies. For them, this is much more important than the public debate. However, despite the "minor" importance, we now analyse whether this issue could – besides its legal implications – lead to strong activist involvement. We start with the company checklist.

1. Are the arguments against the issue plausible?

The arguments against the issue are plausible. The negative effects of the chemical are recognised by governmental agencies as well as the companies themselves. Scientific study has determined that DBCP reduces the number of sperm-producing cells in tests on human males. The level of sterility and its degree of permanence is dependent on the level and frequency of exposure. Those exposed over many years are often permanently sterile or capable of producing female offspring only.

Also, the pollution of groundwater is plausible. In the countries where DBCP was used, about 25% of pesticides applied by aerial spraying never reached its target and ended up in the water surrounding plantations. US drinking water was also polluted. Formerly, it has been assumed that drinking water is clean because it is protected by layers of soil and rock. However, recently scientists have discovered traces of pesticides in this water.

2. Does the issue evoke emotion? Is it understandable – visual, touching – by the public?

In the banana-producing countries, male reproductive capacity is viewed as a reinforcement of a "macho" image. Those who were affected by the product are seen by their society as less manly and many of their wives have divorced them. So, at least in the countries where the chemical was used, the issue has a high potential for emotion, regardless of the fact that in many circumstances the workers already had numerous children. Of the Costa Rican workers affected in 1988, 27% reported being divorced because of their sterility. Many encounter difficulties in being accepted in society. However, the issue is not visual, as nobody can see sterility. There are no indications that DBCP itself results in birth defects and so the highly emotive images of deformed and handicapped children are absent. People can only say in front of the cameras that they are unable to have children, but it cannot be seen. In other countries besides their home countries, this would, however, probably not evoke a very high level of sympathy.

3. Is the issue media-friendly?

In the United States, the cases found relatively little interest within American public opinion and the media. DBCP is a typical pesticide issue and also the lawsuits are not new or extraordinary. As most of the people who were damaged by the chemical live in the Third World, the issue is not as easily accessible by the media. Also, the span of time since the events actually occurred, and the lack of transparency, keep media interest in the events at a low level.

4. Are there connections to other issues of the company or other companies?

The first connection is to questionable export policies in the developed world in general. Many activist groups are unhappy with trade policies in the United States, especially when companies are allowed to export products that are not permitted in the home country. For example, the DBCP issue has opened discussions involving the ethics of the Federal Insecticide, Fungicide and Rodenticide Act, which allows chemical manufacturers to export pesticides banned at home.

Then there are some general connections to the companies producing these chemicals, because they are involved in a number of other controversies. Shell is, as we have seen at the beginning of our book, under pressure for various reasons, Dow Chemical's subsidiary Dow Corning is facing lawsuits because of faulty breast implants and Occidental Chemical was responsible for the waste dumping at the Love Canal.

Also, on the customer side, there are some interconnections. The banana industry is known for using a number of pesticides that are considered extremely hazardous and the industry is considered one of the main agents of deforestation.

5. How strong is the key activist group?

There are several activist groups involved in this issue that have to be considered, none of them being a key activist group. They include environmental organisations, governments of the adversely affected countries and the victims of DBCP. As the issue is a typical case where victims can get compensation through lawsuits, there is, in this case, no environmental organisation that makes itself the key adversary of the chemical companies. The environmental groups can rely on the fact that the victims themselves will do the best they can to get adequate compensation. The governments of the "banana republics" may be able to ban the use of chemicals by the companies concerned in the plantations. However, in general, they have an interest in keeping a positive relationship with the countries to which they export their product. As banana production is one of the most important industries in these countries, the governments tend to "minimise" the issue, because high levels of public awareness might decrease banana consumption in the Western world. The victims of DBCP pose a serious threat to the chemical companies as they have filed lawsuits against the manufacturers (for health as well as for environmental damage). Among them, the foreign plantation workers are rather weak and their chances of succeeding in court are low, while the US cities can be considered powerful and dangerous. Even if there are still a lot of sterile workers from Central America and Africa that have not yet tried to get compensation for their injuries, the law may come to the rescue of the companies, because it has become difficult since 1994 for foreign plaintiffs to file suits in the United States. This is not the case with the Californian cities, though. Given the success of Sanger and Fresno, other cities will (and some already have) filed suits against Dow, Occidental and Shell if their water systems are found to be contaminated by DBCP. So, in summary, there is no classical strong activist group involved in this issue. The threat for the companies comes rather from the lawsuits.

6. How isolated is the company?

The three manufacturers are somehow isolated from other chemical companies because they were the only ones producing DBCP. On the adversary side are mainly the individual victims of DBCP, who do not make up a uniform body. In a general sense, the issue tends to go further and affect all producers of pesticides – probably the most criticised chemicals of all – thus reducing the isolation of Shell, Dow and Occidental.

7. How far have the dynamics of the crisis already evolved?

The overall dynamics of the issue can be traced from the 1940s until today, although production is terminated. We can split the diffusion into three major phases:

1. Discovery (1940–1950)
2. Production (1960–1970)
3. Legal debate and protests (1980–today)

Discovery:
1950s: DBCP is developed.
1961:   Studies on DBCP by the University of California show that it is highly toxic and that it reduces the sperm and testicle size of rabbits and chimpanzees.

Production:
1960s: US-based banana companies such as Del Monte, Standard Fruit (Dole) and Chiquita started using DBCP to protect their crops, mainly in Central America.
1977:   Thirty-five workers of Occidental Chemical in California are found to be sterile due to exposure to DBCP. The EPA bans the use of DBCP in the United States, except in Hawaii.
1978:   Internal memo at Occidental Petroleum that as long as the product still shows adequate profit despite the estimated compensation costs, "the project should be considered further".
1979:   Complete ban in the United States.
1979·   Standard Fruit indemnifies Dow regarding potential damages but pressures for further produce and supply.
1979:   Costa Rican government bans the import and use of DBCP. Standard Fruit exports the remaining DBCP to Honduras, where no such legislation exists.
1981:   "Official" supply stops to the Third World.

Legal debate and protests:
1983:   First US lawsuit.
1985:   The "Pesticide Action Network" starts a campaign called the "Dirty Dozen List", one of the attacked pesticides being DBCP.

1986: Last use in the Philippines.
1988: Greenpeace publishes reports on the US export of unregistered pesticides and lobbies for legislation to prohibit
the export of unregistered pesticides.
1989: Last use in Costa Rica.
1990: Settlement of the Fresno city lawsuit: Occidental and
Dow are paying for monitoring and filtering the groundwater over a 40-year period.
1990: Texas Supreme Court rules a trial to be possible if the
courts in the different countries reject the cases back to
the United States.
1992: Standard Fruit settlement with 12 000 Costa Rican
workers for an alleged US$20 million.
1993: Dow settles with 800 workers at US$20 million.
1993: The city council of Sanger settles out of court in 1993 for
US$25 million.
1994: Texas law was changed so that it would be much harder
for a foreign plaintiff to file a suit.
1994: 4000 cases are filed in Louisiana and Mississippi.
1995: Standard Fruit, Dole and Chiquita face trials involving
30 000 workers.
1995: Lawsuits against chemical companies spread over 11
countries world-wide involving 16 000 workers.
1995: University of California finds that DBCP is responsible
for contaminating more California wells than any other
pesticide.
1996: Costa Rican government declares the remaining cases out
of their jurisdiction and sends them back to the United
States.
1997: Hearings of 2000 cases to be trialed in Texas are
postponed "indefinitely" over "technical" legal issues.

Looking at these dynamics we can see that it has taken a long
time for the issue to get noticed by the public and the governments involved. There is a gap of 16 years between 1961, when the
chemical companies knew that DBCP was a health hazard, and
the banning of the product by the United States in 1977. It is even
fair to say that the pressure on the chemical companies did not
really start mounting until the first lawsuit in 1984. Now, they face
numerous lawsuits that might very well diminish the profits (or

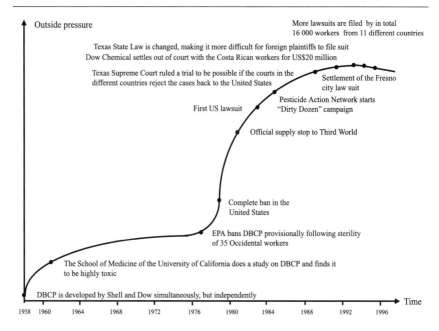

Figure 7.7 Diffusion curve for the DBCP issue

maybe worse) they have made with DBCP. The dynamics of the issue show that now that the issue is over, there will be no pressure other than the outstanding lawsuits.

The diffusion curve (non-time proportional) for this issue looks as in Figure 7.7.

With regard to possible future dynamics to make matters worse for the companies, there is pressure in the United States to tighten the DBCP acceptable level in drinking water from the current 0.2 parts per billion to 2 parts per trillion. It has been estimated that this would lead to multi-billion dollar costs and today it is unlikely to be carried because the level is unmeasurable. However, even the cities who have settled already with the chemical companies in the lawsuits reserve the right to litigate further if the recommended public health goal for DBCP becomes more stringent. The EPA estimates that besides California there are at least 23 other states that may have the pesticide in the ground. The companies cannot afford to take this case to court, either with the Californian municipalities or the plantation workers. A verdict in favour of the plaintiffs would mean two things:

1. A plaintiff verdict would probably also include punitive damages, something the companies have been able to avoid so far, by settling out of court. Once the companies' liability is established in a condemning verdict, it will be easy for other victims of DBCP to sue and get paid much more, either through a verdict or a settlement, than the companies are paying now.
2. It would set a precedent in product liability that could even have far-reaching consequences for other products. Once the precedent is set that a chemical company can be held responsible for injuries caused by its pesticide, because it knew or should have known the health hazards of the product, it will be easier to apply the same legal reasoning for other pesticides as well.

8. How easy is the solution?

The companies' primary concern focuses on minimising the damages from pending lawsuits. Within the lawsuits the companies have various possibilities. One possibility for the manufacturers would be to try to postpone all lawsuits by playing for time, or to try to keep the lawsuits out of the United States and moved to the native countries of the farm workers. If there is a possibility in those countries to sue for damages at all, awards will obviously be much less than a US verdict or settlement would bring. Another option would be to take the trial and try to win; for example, by referring to the warnings that were put on the product after 1979. As a third option, the manufacturers could try to settle with the victims out of court. However, the danger is that a settlement might be interpreted as a technical confession, which could damage the credibility of the producers, not to mention being quite expensive. Table 7.19 shows the company checklist.

The Results

With more than 16 000 unresolved cases of sterilised men and the threat of an environmental lawsuit in the United States, the issue

Table 7.19 Visualised company checklist for the DBCP issue

Assessment criteria	++	+	0	−	−−	Comments
Plausibility	•					Negative effects are proven.
Potential for emotions		•				Understandable and emotional, but no visuals.
Media-friendliness				•		Not new or extraordinary.
Connections with other issues		•				Interconnection to US export policy and to other issues of the concerned companies.
Strength of the key activist group			•			No strong activist group; lawsuits decide outcome of the issue.
Degree of company isolation			•			The concerned chemical companies and their customers are isolated.
Dynamics			•			Further "take-off" might only be caused by lawsuit.
Ease of solution			•			Solutions refer only to lawsuit.
Overall assessment			•			Outside pressure is coming only from lawsuits.

is still lingering in the US judicial system. However, up to now defence lawyers have been able to move the issue around the bureaucratic system, reducing the expectation that the cases will be either tried or resolved. Also, the fact that the pesticide has been off the market for more than 10 years makes it quite weak. Still, the chemical companies should keep looking over their shoulders. Therefore, they will most probably do the following:

- Let more time pass, gridlocking the lawsuits into the legal system.
- Reach agreements with the plaintiffs as quietly as possible.
- Avoid "surges" in other chemical products.

We now use the activist checklist to analyse whether the activist groups have a chance to make their campaign into a "strong" issue.

As we have already seen, there are several adversaries involved in this issue. First, there are the victims who worked on the farms. They can be found primarily in Africa, the Caribbean and the

Philippines. Then there is the US population, which is affected though polluted drinking water. And there are some activist groups pushing the companies. These include the Association of Atlantic Zone Victims (ANEZA), US-based action groups like the Pesticides Action Network, and the World Wildlife Fund (WWF), together with local groups in developing countries.

1. The campaign should have a clear aim or goal

The activist groups may attack the companies from different angles with potential goals including:

- Pushing for adequate compensation for all developing country victims who were poisoned when using DBCP on banana plantations. Even those workers who have already settled may have been pushed into unfair agreements by both the banana plantations and chemical companies. Addressing the issues should not be difficult, because around 95% of banana production in Costa Rica is controlled by three US-based transnational corporations and 90% of DBCP production was undertaken in the United States by three companies (Dow, Shell and Occidental). It is alleged that less than 5% of the affected men have ever been compensated.
- Pushing for the clean-up of Central American eco-systems that have been destroyed by the use of pesticides, including DBCP.
- Ensuring a much stricter control on the trade in toxic substances, especially when they have been banned as too dangerous for domestic use.
- Promoting countries to develop "greener" bananas through plantation certification and getting manufacturers to pay for constant patient monitoring after poisoning has occurred.
- Pushing for a broad clean-up of the US deep well water supplies, across all states affected, by US environmental lobby groups.

2. The issue is easily understood by the general public

The cause of the health issues is likely to be widely understood – the spraying of humans and environments with toxic chemicals in developing countries. It is especially understandable that it was irresponsible to use in developing countries chemicals that had already been prohibited in the United States. It is an example of the double standard that has been much criticised by environmental organisations. Also, the fact that pesticide contamination has destroyed Costa Rica's coastline can be easily understood. The whole issue is even easier to read by the general public because DBCP is one of the top "dirty dozen" pesticides in the United States.

3. The issue has a high symbolic value

Issues associated with sex and reproduction have always had a high symbolic value for society. In the affected developing countries, many local victims not only became sterilised but also impotent – a crushing stigma in rural Latin American culture that prizes family, virility and machismo. Five or more children in a family are the norm. Many men have been left by their wives and avoid their friends in embarrassment. Whilst sterility is an extremely important problem in the developing world it is viewed as less so in the developed Western world where often operations are performed to achieve the same effect. Also, as we have argued, there are no uncontroversial visuals to increase the symbolic value. However, what is symbolic about DBCP is that the chemical companies were shipping inventory from one country where it was banned to other countries where there were no regulations.

4. The issue has the potential to damage the image of the company

The unethical business practices of the chemical companies can certainly ruin their images. Internal reports at both Shell and Dow in the 1960s showed that DBCP was extremely toxic and could provoke male sterility. Guidelines were developed at this time on the use of face masks and protective clothing. However, these reports were not taken seriously enough by the organisations and for many years no warnings or guidelines were issued to the field. This is such a serious weakness in the defendants' case that they are doing everything legally possible to have the cases heard outside the United States where damages awarded will be significantly less.

Also, the documents in the hands of the defendants that show that Dow had discovered the effects of DBCP in 1978 and still decided to continue selling the product, may destroy Dow's image. Even if Shell Chemical, Dow Chemical and Occidental Chemical are not consumer goods companies (only in the oil business is Shell a known consumer brand through its service stations), their names are still well known. However, the issue is in the past and people tend to forget. Therefore, the image effects cannot be as severe as they might be in a current case.

5. The opponent is strong enough (no "underdog" effect)

There is no doubt that the three companies, subsidiaries of multi-national oil and chemical companies, are strong opponents. There is no danger of these corporations being considered underdogs, particularly when compared with the poor individuals from underdeveloped countries who are the plaintiffs. So far, the chemical companies have been able to use their financial power for an out-of-court settlement.

6. The issue can be "packaged" in a campaign in which the public can get involved

The current campaign is not interesting for the population, since it is embroiled in technical and legal arguments. This holds true for the infertility victims as well as for the drinking water issue. Also, an involvement through a boycott is almost impossible, because chemicals are not really direct consumer goods, and bananas are not labelled as to whether or not toxic pesticides have been used to produce them.

7. There are solutions that are confrontational, not gradual

The solutions that the activist groups are presenting coincide with their goals. The solutions would not lead to any severe disadvantages

Table 7.20 Visualised activist checklist for the DBCP issue

Assessment criteria	Rating					Comments
	++	+	0	–	––	
Clear aim or goal		●				Goals aim at compensation and policy change.
Understandable by public		●				Effects can be understood; also the apparent double-standards.
Symbolic			●			Sterility is more symbolic in third world than in first world.
Image can be damaged		●				Clear mistakes of companies; however, it is a past issue.
Strong opponent	●					All involved companies are large and profitable.
Public can get involved					●	At the moment only legal discussions.
Confrontational solution				●		Compensation and policy change.
Dramatic elements					●	Past issue with few remaining visuals.

Overall assessment		Issue could come back on the companies' agendas if lawsuits reveal new facts.

for the American population at large, but, of course, would imply significant costs for the concerned companies.

8. There could be a dramatic element to the campaign to engage the media

As the main incidents took place some time ago and the effects are not visible, the campaign does not appear suited to drama. Also, the court actions will not create a drama such as, for example, in the "O.J. Simpson" case, because the positions are clear. The activist checklist is shown in Table 7.20.

The Results

There are two main angles for attack by activist groups:

1. Sterile victims of DBCP in developing countries (a court case for 16 000 victims is still outstanding).
2. Drinking water quality around the sites of manufacturing plants in the United States, particularly in Central Valley, California.

However, in both of these cases much time has passed and neither is a "hot" issue or shows signs of becoming one in the short term. For these reasons, the DBCP issue is likely to be supported in the wider context of a campaign on pesticides in general or at a low level on DBCP specifically.

Notes

1. This figure was restated in May 1997 by the Eizenstat report from the United States, which reports US$580 million or US$5.6 billion today (using a different conversion factor).
2. Our analysis includes facts that came to light after 1992. Although they had no knowledge of these facts at the time, the WJC could at least have guessed that there might be something.
3. Explicitly, the group refers to Similac infant formula, Kraft salad dressings, Nestlé Crunch candy bars, Karo corn syrup, Fritos corn chips, Fleischmann's magarine, Quaker Oats corn meal, Green Giant harvest burgers, McDonald's french fries and Coca-Cola.
4. By this Monsanto benefits twice, from the sales of the beans and the increased sales of Roundup. In order to protect their business, the company has forced farmers who grow Roundup ready (RR) beans to agree not to save part of their harvest for sowing next year. To do so would violate Monsanto's patent on any plants containing RR genes. Monsanto's contract says that the company can send "field monitors" to the farm to check compliance with these rules.
5. Ironically, Monsanto was, until this discussion, supposed to be an environmental best-practice company. In 1990, CEO Richard Mahoney created the Monsanto pledge – a pledge to be environmentally responsible by reducing emissions, eliminating waste, working for sustainable agriculture and managing corporate land to benefit nature. However, Monsanto apparently has changed sides already several times. In the past the company has produced toxic chemicals like Agent Orange (chemical used in the Vietnam War) and PCBs.
6. Merryl Lynch reckons that the global market for genetically engineered seeds is likely to grow from around US$450 million in 1995 to US$6.6 billion in 2005, provided that European consumers do not "overreact".
7. The impacts of labelling on sales are not yet clear. A successful example of labelling in Europe is a genetically engineered tomato invented by Zeneca, a British firm. This tomato, which went on sale in February 1996, has, despite its special labelling, captured 60% of tomato-paste sales in big

British supermarket chains. This was reached through an intensive campaign to make the consumers aware of its safety and benefits.

8. An example for ionising radiation are X-rays which have frequencies above one million megahertz (MHz).

8
Conclusions

All the case studies in the previous chapter illustrate application of the checklists using publicly available sources. Certainly, behind the scenes of each company there is much more to say under each checklist item. However, we think that these examples show how the developed tools can give managers real-life conclusions for their own strategies. Using the checklists, managers can better understand situations in which they think the company is doing the right thing, but where activists are not of the same opinion.

At the beginning of this book we said that we would focus only on the identification of issues. However, now that we have accomplished this, we have a few words to say about what managers can do once an issue is analysed and they have assessed the danger resulting from it. Basically, there are two options:

1. Drop the project/action.
2. Stick with the project/action.

Companies do not really have this choice in the case of an accident. In that case, the company has, albeit involuntarily, chosen option 2, and management's task by default is damage control, taking appropriate actions after the accident.

DROP THE PROJECT/ACTION

If a company decides to drop a certain project, change its processes or its behaviour, the solution is easy. The activist group
claims victory and the company lives with the "damage". In this
case, the company has realised that the potential damage from
holding its ground would be higher than the gains. So even if the
company still thinks it would have been the right thing to do and
the project/action would be in the best interest of society as well,
it might turn out that this project invites activist groups to run a
ruinous campaign against the company.

Refraining from a certain action does not necessarily mean
giving up. The company can drop the project temporarily and
come back later with a modified version that is more acceptable
because it holds different issue characteristics. A good way to
gauge this would be to apply the checklist again.

STICK WITH THE PROJECT/ACTION

A company may decide that it is better to run the project as planned
for either of two reasons: (1) Managers may have identified the issue
as *weak*, and they do not consider the pressure a serious threat; (2)
Even if the issue might be considered *strong*, they may decide that
the interests of the company are so important that they are willing to
run the gauntlet. In both cases, we do not want to encourage companies to carry out a project/action that is against the interests of
society as a whole. If managers are, however, sure that they can
morally justify the project, then they have to act differently depending on whether the issue in question is *weak* or *strong*.

If a company assesses correctly that an issue is *weak*, then the risk
of crisis is low. However, even in this case, the company's management should not forget periodically to review the issue in question,
and check whether the assumptions and premises of the first analysis
are still valid. This means that managers have to use a kind of
strategic control, and check assumptions and premises at regular
intervals in order to avoid missing a change in the parameters.

Even if a company sees a potentially strong issue, it might still
decide to continue with the project as it was planned from the
beginning. The corporate interests in this project might be so high

that a way out does not exist. In this case, it is absolutely vital that the company communicates well with the activist groups, public, media and legislators, taking a proactive approach. If this works well, it might at least minimise the damage.

At the early stage of an issue, the first communications step is to engage in an open stakeholder dialogue, focusing especially on the key activist group. The company can and should choose this proactive way of communicating, because the checklist analysis has shown that the issue will come up anyway. Such a dialogue can be fruitful and sometimes both activist group and company may find mutually beneficial solutions. The dialogue should not appear as an attempt to convince the stakeholders of the company's position. It should, rather, aim at creating some understanding of the issue in question and initiate a move beyond the traditional adversarial stance.

For example, after Shell had suffered from a high number of clashes with activist groups in recent years, it decided in 1997 to consult with activist groups on a regular basis. The company would start to invite human rights and environmental groups to planning meetings for some of its more sensitive projects in the developing world, especially in Africa and Latin America. This would help the company to listen better, according to John Jennings, the chairman of Shell Transport and Trading UK. So even if Shell would most probably not agree with the activist groups on many issues, it could learn something about the way these groups think. Or as Jennings put it: "We should use the increased scrutiny of NGOs as a tool to strengthen our performance." (*Financial Times*, 17 March, 1997).

Secondly, in the case of a strong issue, the company can begin working with the media at an early stage. While pressure is still in its formative stages and relatively weak, companies may use their PR departments to influence opinion with a certain expectation of a positive outcome. One of the key rules in a crisis is, therefore: do not let your adversary be the source of information. From an image standpoint, this cannot be over-emphasised. For example, the consumer backlash against Exxon over the 1989 oil spill in Alaska was probably increased by chairman Lawrence Rawls' delayed appearance on the screens.

In the case of major accidents or strong issues, the CEO should appear on the scene immediately, even if he/she does not know all the facts. It shows that he cares: at least one answer that is always possible is to describe the steps the company is taking to find out the facts. And even if legal considerations prevent managers from speaking, they should not cut off reporters with "no comment". A company that says nothing will certainly not get fair coverage.

To improve their communication situation, companies can also use our checklists in order to "redesign" the issue in question. On the basis of the identified weaknesses, they can work on making the company's point of view more plausible to a large public through:

- finding a supportive and believable information source
- using visuals, symbols (e.g. in their wording) and emotions to support their own point of view
- making the issue new, extraordinary and accessible for the media who take the company's position so that it is worth them reporting on it
- designing their own campaign, using positive interconnections to support the position, isolate and maybe even damage the image of the adversary and, of course,
- try to solve the problem.

Skilled PR work can imply that the company moves the society's perception or tries to find ways to harmonise a company's goals with the needs of society. At that early time, opinions are not yet formed and in getting a first crack at structuring and diffusing topics, rather than letting the activist group set the agenda, a lot of damage can be avoided. Companies who understand issues explicitly negotiate on important ones and seek agreements in time. They use a marketing approach to serve their stakeholders and try to influence the stakeholder environment. If, however, pressure against the company is already in the developed stages, the chances are slim for a successful transformation of public opinion by the company. By that time, the activist group has "infiltrated" the media for its own purposes and public opinion has already built up against the company. Companies are able only rarely to overcome these set opinions.

To work with media, businesses have to co-operate and overcome the lack of credibility that reporters assume. Companies tend to report only good news, while media representatives feel that they should talk openly about the other side of the coin.

Therefore, it could be useful for companies to provide balanced information on certain issues instead of making only positive projections. What the media wants is a good story, so rather than just providing good information, companies should try to "tell the story". They should think about the question and which pieces of information matter to the media. The story should be, for example, that the company is working hard to improve its environmental performance, and not that the concentration of toxic substances in parts per billion has declined.

In summary, we believe that these tools can be valuable for managers struggling to analyse activist demands and decide how to handle them. Our survey at the International Institute for Management Development (IMD) in Lausanne, showed that, in the opinion of managers, the importance of pressure coming from the contextual environment of an organisation is bound to grow. We hope that the methodology, recommendations and case studies in this book can help managers to deal with these developments. We hope that the countervailing power of citizen activism will have positive effects on our society as a whole, helping to determine the social and environmental directions in which we move.

As the idea of this type of analysis is new, and the checklists we have included in our book are the first of their kind, we hope that this book will spark discussion on the subject. As the relationship between activists and companies intensifies and becomes more sophisticated, so new management techniques will be born, and we hope that our tools will be refined and improved upon by others.

References

Ansoff, H.I. (1975). Managing strategic surprise by response to weak signals. *California Management Review*, **18**(2), 21–33.

Boulton, L. (1997). Business "Paying more heed" to activists. *Financial Times*, **14 January**, 8.

Carson, R. (1962). *Silent Spring*. Houghton Miffin, Boston, MA.

Cohen, B.C. (1963). *The Press and Foreign Policy*. Princeton University Press, Princeton, NJ.

Conservation Foundation (ed.) (1985). *Risk Assessment and Risk Control*. The Conservation Foundation, Washington, DC.

Covello, V.T. (1991). Informing people about radiation risks: a review of obstacles to public understanding and effective risk communication. In *Nuclear Energy: Communicating with the Public*. Nuclear Energy Agency (NEA), Paris, pp. 29–38.

Deal, T.E. and A.A. Kennedy (1982). *Corporate Cultures, The Rites and Rituals of Corporate Life*. Addison-Wesley, Reading, MA.

De George, R.T. (1990). Biomethical ethics. In L.R. Graham (ed.), *Science and the Soviet Social Order*, Harvard University Press, Cambridge, MA, pp. 195–224.

Drucker, P.F. (1990). *Managing the Non-Profit Organization*. Butterworth–Heinemann, Oxford.

Emery, F.E. and E.L. Trist (1965). The causal texture of organisational environments. *Human Relations*, **18**, 21–32.

Fisher, H. (1995). Philanthropy is not business: advice to new nonprofit board members. *Nonprofit World*, **13**(5), 16–18.

Freeman, R.E. (1984). *Strategic Management: A Stakeholder Approach*. Pitman, Boston, MA.

Friedman, M. (1962). *Capitalism and Freedom*. Chicago University Press, Chicago, Il.

Galbraith, J.K. (1952). *American Capitalism: The Concept of Countervailing Power*. Houghton Mifflin Company, Boston, MA.

Garrett, D. (1987). The effectiveness of marketing policy boycotts: environmental opposition to marketing. *Journal of Marketing*, **April**, 46–57.

Gelb, B.D. (1995). More boycotts ahead? Some implication. *Business Horizons*, **March–April**, 70–76.

Greenpeace means business: Greenpeace's success as a multinational organization. *Economist*, **336** (7928) (1995) 59.

Grube, L. (1995). Litigation: cost of litigation to US businesses. *Chief Executive*, **19**, 56.

Haour, G. and J. Miller (1995). *Ciba: Attempting to Live Up to a Vision in a Crisis Situation (A) and (B)*, IMD Case Study GM 607. International Institute for Management Development, Lausanne.

Harrison, J.S. and C.H. St. John (1996). Managing and partnering with external stakeholders. *Academy of Management Executive*, **10**(2), 46.

van der Heijden, K. (1996). *Scenarios: The Art of Strategic Conversation*. John Wiley, Chichester.

Hilts, P.J. (1994). Cigarette manufacturers debated the risks they denied. *New York Times*, **16 June**, 1.

Hirschmann, A. (1970). *Exit, Voice and Loyalty*. Harvard University Press, Cambridge, MA.

Jurkowitz, M. (1995). A kinder gentler press? *Boston Globe*, **1 May**, 15.

Kund, A., C. Gale and G. Taucher (1979). *Nestlé and the Infant Food Controversy*, IMD Case Study OIE050. International Institute for Managment Development, Lausanne.

Lindblom, C.E. (1959). The "science" of muddling through. *Public Administration Review*, **14**, 319–340.

Lipset, S.M. (1986). Labor unions in the public mind. In S.M. Lipset (ed.), *Unions in Transition: Entering the Second Century*. Institute for Contemporary Studies, San Francisco.

Meadows, D.H., D.L. Meadows, J. Randers and W.W. Behrens (1972). *The Limits to Growth*. Dennis L. Meadows, New York.

Post, J.E. (1978). *Corporate Behavior and Social Change*. Reston, Reston, VA.

Pruitt, S.W. and M. Friedman (1986). Determining the effectiveness of consumer boycotts: a stock price analysis of their impact on corporate targets. *Journal of Consumer Policy*, **December**, 375–387.

Rappaport, A. (1986). *Creating Shareholder Value: The New Standard for Business Performance*. The Free Press, New York.

Reichheld, F. (1996). *The Loyalty Effect*. Harvard Business School Press, Boston, MA.

Savage, G.T., T.W. Nix, C.J. Whitehead and J.D. Blair (1991). Strategies for assessing and managing organizational stakeholders. *Academy of Management Executive*, **5**(2), pp. 61–75.

Senge, P. (1990) *The Fifth Discipline*. Doubleday, New York.

Shell to consult pressure groups. *Financial Times*, **17 March 1997**, 19.

Steger, U., P. Killing, M. Winter and M. Schweinsberg (1996). *The Brent Spar Platform Controversy (A), (B) and (C)*, IMD Case Study OIE 070 – 072. International Institute for Management Development, Lausanne.

Susskind, L. and P. Field (1996). *Dealing with an Angry Public: The Mutual Gains Approach to Resolving Disputes*. The Free Press, New York.

The Tylenol rescue. *Newsweek*, **3 March 1986**, 52–53.

Tzu, Sun (1991). *The Art of War*. Shambhala, Boston, MA.

Vogel, D. (1978). *Lobbying the Corporation: Citizen Challenges to Business Authority*. Basic Books, New York.

Wagstyl, S. and R. Corzine (1997). Rights and wrongs. *Financial Times*, **18 March**, 18.

Weinberger, M.G. (1986). Products as target of negative information: some recent findings. *European Journal of Marketing*, **3**, 110–128.

Index